Intelligent Embedded Systems

Intelligent Embedded Systems

Louis L. Odette

Addison-Wesley Publishing Company, Inc.

Reading, Massachusetts   Menlo Park, California   New York   Don Mills, Canada
Wokingham, England   Amsterdam   Bonn   Sydney   Singapore   Tokyo   Madrid   San Juan

Many of the designations used by manufacturers and sellers to distinguish their products are claimed as trademarks. Where those designations appear in this book and Addison-Wesley was aware of a trademark claim, the designations have been printed in initial caps.

The programs and applications presented in this book have been included for their instructional value. They have been tested with care, but are not guaranteed for any particular purpose. The publisher does not offer any warranties or representations, nor does it accept any liabilities with respect to the programs or applications.

The publisher offers discounts on this book when ordered in quantity for special sales. For more information please contact:

Corporate & Professional Publishing Group
Addison-Wesley Publishing Company
Route 128
Reading, Massachusetts 01867

Library of Congress Cataloging-in-Publication Data

Odette, Louis L.
    Intelligent embedded systems / Louis L. Odette.
        p.   cm.
    Includes bibliographical references and index.
    ISBN 0-201-51753-1 (alk. paper)
    1. Embedded computer systems—Programming.   2. C (Computer program
language)   I. Title.
QA76.6.034   1991
005.1—dc20   90-40888
                                                                        CIP

Sponsoring Editor, Ted Buswick
Production Coordinator, Peggy McMahon
Cover design by Virginia J. Mason
Text design by Webster Design
Set in 11 point Times by Camden Type 'n Graphics, Camden, ME

005.1
023i
1991

Book/disk package ISBN 0-201-51753-1
Book only 0-201-56319-3

Printed on recycled and acid-free paper
ABCDEFGHIJ-MA-9543210
First Printing, December 1990

To my family

Contents

Chapter 4 **Logic Systems**

Chapter 5 **Virtual Machines in Hardware**

Chapter 6 **Examples and Future Directions**

Acknowledgments

I am grateful to Norton Greenfield, Elizabeth Chelowsky, and Walter Wilkinson for their many useful comments on the original outline and on subsequent drafts, and to Ellen Gaffney for her constant support and tolerance. Permission to reprint parts of the source code for CFORTH83 and CLIPS is also gratefully acknowledged to Bradley Forthware and COSMIC respectively.

More information on CFORTH83 may be obtained by contacting Bradley Forthware, P.O. Box 4444, Mountain View, CA 94040.

Information on CLIPS may be obtained from COSMIC, The University of Georgia, 382 East Broad Street, Athens, GA 30602.

Intelligent Embedded Systems

Chapter 1 **Technologies of Representation and Reasoning**

Goals and Objectives

The purpose of this book is to endow any developer who is responsible for embedded system development with a thorough understanding of basic expert system technology. By *basic* I mean that the developer should understand in depth the most fundamental functionality of inference and representation as used in the construction of expert system applications. The developer also should understand how to implement these basic elements of the technology. Familiarity with such implementation techniques is important since embedded systems do not often come in off-the-shelf packages, nor can they always be built with standard building blocks, so the standard technology components do not necessarily fit together exactly. Furthermore, understanding how expert system technology can add value to embedded system applications goes hand in hand with an understanding of the fundamentals.

One of this book's target audiences is electrical engineers (EEs), who increasingly must design for a significant software component in the systems they build, whether instrumentation or controllers, electrical or mechanical or a hybrid. The large number of engineers who are concerned with software and integration issues is evident by the recent appearance of magazines like *Embedded Systems Programming*.

Over the last decade, the software written by EEs has grown in complexity well beyond the bit manipulation routines of the early days of the microcomputer. More sophisticated hardware and software development tools, widespread use of higher level languages—at levels way above the machine code assemblers—and the increasing sophistication of the embedded system design and development process have all had an impact on the requirements for embedded system software. These factors have also clearly had an impact on the embedded system software developer. Though primarily electrical engineers by training, they are becoming software engineers by necessity, recognizing that the techniques that were good enough for designing hundreds of bytes of code do not necessarily scale up for application programs like expert systems programs that are likely to require millions of bytes of code. Similarly, much more sophisticated applications are enabled (and demanded by end users) as processor performance increases, processor architectures become more sophisticated and targeted at application niches, and resource constraints such as chip count and power consumption become easier to meet through design and manufacturing advances.

Many software and systems engineers are faced with the task of embedding certain functionalities in larger systems. An intelligent assistant for credit authorization is one well known example. In this example, the mechanization of the credit authorization expertise is embedded in a much larger system that includes mainframe database and transaction systems, wide area networks, and human organizations. Here, too, processor performance increases have combined with advances in other technologies such as image processing and voice recognition to enable important value-added applications. By the same token, such resource constraints as RAM and disk storage and the limitations of the development tools themselves have made the technologies in this book attractive.

The task of this book is to provide software-savvy engineers—be they electrical engineers responsible for instrumentation and control or system architects responsible for the information systems infrastructure of a large organization—with a head start in identifying good expert system applications and planning for their inclusion in an embedded system. Identifying good applications involves at a minimum a solid understanding of the technology fundamentals and familiarity with some case histories.

Understanding the technology fundamentals from an implementation perspective is important for two major reasons. First, the engineering problems that need to be solved to deliver an embedded system are always unique to the application and may not have been anticipated by a tool developer. Ultimately, understanding why something works the way it does is the key to understanding how to make it work the way you want it to work. Second, the bulk of the literature on expert system technology does not always distinguish between the practical and the possible. A firm foundation in some implementation approach usually facilitates those back-of-the-envelope calculations that serve as essential reality checks.

With expert system technology about to enter its second decade, there is no lack of case histories of expert system successes and failures. Therefore, good application areas are usually more readily agreed on by users and developers than the technological composition of the applications themselves. This is true even though commercial expert system tools, too, are in their second generation, having migrated from the LISP machines and dedicated workstations to the PC and mainframes. So, given the years of experience with the technology that has accumulated in the engineering community, and acknowledging the existence of a large and diverse group of commercial technology suppliers, why should the embedded system developer worry about implementation techniques for an application technology? After all, most software or system developers do not worry about their compiler or other development tool technology.

The answer is that a developer cares about implementation techniques for expert system technology for the same reason that there has always been a need to be familiar with the implementation details of floating-point numbers, digital signal processing, and numerous other common software building blocks. The embedded system more often than not reflects tradeoffs and balancing of multiple constraints, and the ability to be flexible in choosing either hardware or software components may make the difference between meeting the design specification or not. Understanding how to implement the basic components of a design—be it a floating-point routine, a multitasking executive, or an inference engine—is ultimately very important.

In understanding the implementation issues involved in building expert systems we need not get bogged down in all the interesting questions still open in the larger area of artificial intelligence (AI). There are many interesting questions and opportunities to push the technology forward. No doubt the next several years will bring successes with neural net applications, voice recognition, and image processing. Nevertheless, making something practical today demands tried and true technology. The good news is that there are expert system technology components that are well enough established to be considered tried and true.

It is never really cost effective trying to figure out how to use, modify, or remove all the bells and whistles you find in a commercial expert system development tool or language, in order to shoehorn code into an application. This book tries to get to the root of embedding expertise primarily by illustrating and discussing implementation techniques for the basic inference and representation components of the technology. Studying a specific design is an effective way to approach the theoretical issues that a technology might address, so this book examines one design from each of the two major lines of technical evolution, data directed reasoning and goal directed reasoning.

This book is not an introductory treatment of the broad array of expert system technologies, nor is it a collection of stories of wildly successful applications, mostly descriptive and very inspirational, but lacking in some details needed for emulation. On the contrary, there are chapters on only the most fundamental aspects of the technology, aspects appearing in some form or other in all expert systems, and the treatment of the implementation techniques is as extensive as possible. Since the best way to illustrate implementation techniques is to study the code that implements a segment of the technology, the chapters include ample and substantial examples of code, most in the C language because C is a common denominator for implementation from microcontrollers to mainframes. However, an early discussion of virtual machine design and implementation will pay dividends when we discuss the implementation techniques for the elements of expert system technology.

Although C is eminently qualified to be used as an implementation language for embedded systems, exactly because it is not the highest of high-level languages, it can fall short where more abstraction is useful. It can be tough to decipher the code even with copious comments and good coding practices. The use of a virtual machine can more often provide the desired level of abstraction in a very straightforward and simple way without imposing any performance penalties. Moreover, some special-purpose hardware, closely related to the virtual machine concept, may in some cases be necessary for performance reasons. Thus the material on expert system technology is bracketed first by a general discussion of machines in software and last by a discussion of machines in hardware.

The basic elements of the technology will be treated in some depth here and at a substantial level of sophistication, rather than at the survey level. In many situations, once the implementation issues are fully understood, it is easier to scale down than to scale up. Application case studies in the final chapter attempt to describe and discuss the engineering issues in depth.

Contents

Chapter 2 introduces a basic approach to programming embedded systems code. This approach forms the background for the remainder of the book. Topics in Chapter 2 include the use of virtual machine designs as the basis for embedded system development, and the use of threaded code as both an implementation and a development technique for virtual machines.

The basic observation behind the virtual machine approach is that every application in practice consists of several layers of machines, where *machine* in the most abstract sense means a set of objects and operations. Each object has a collection of attributes, or properties, which can be the subject of the members of some class of operations. Objects might be as disparate as numbers, memory locations, or accumulator registers. The fact that these may not be physical entities makes the machine a virtual machine. Keeping the same high level of abstraction, but shifting the context somewhat, a machine is described by a set of nouns (things), adjectives (attributes), and verbs (what you can do to the things).

One way to understand the need for layers of virtual machines in an application, particularly since each layer is not without some cost in terms of space and performance, is to put it in terms of impedance matching—a way of matching the power and expressiveness of one machine with the machine in which it is implemented. For example, a very high-level language written for the sake of performance entirely in the machine code of the hardware would take a lot of memory, be difficult to test and debug, and be impossible to port. Using a series of machines to do the same job is more clever, elegant, and robust.

But no matter how it is built, a high-level language needs to have the right set of elements for the problem-solving task in which it is to be used. So it, too, should be a virtual machine—a tool that matches the job.

Not all applications are entirely suited to or absolutely require a virtual machine design. However, since virtual machine design often makes very efficient use of computing resources and requires minimal operating system support for development, testing, or deployment—as measured by resources required for these functions—it tends to be an extremely useful design and implementation approach for embedded systems. Many expert system components are specified by virtual machines. Thus a natural and effective relationship exists between design and implementation using virtual machines.

Chapter 3 presents the basic design and implementation of data-directed reasoning systems. Data-directed reasoning is a time-tested processing strategy in which transfer of control in the program is determined by data that is made available to the program at run-time. For example, applications in which pattern recognition is a large and important component are often good candidates for implementation with data-directed reasoning components.

Another way to get a sense for this kind of reasoning process is to look at it in terms of initial state. Data-directed reasoning is useful when there are a large number of initial states that narrow to a few final states. Applications that fit this description include data analysis and fusion, some design problems such as experiment design in conjunction with sophisticated analytical devices, and condition/fault diagnosis.

Data-driven reasoning is also termed forward chaining, and it forms the underlying technology basis for many of the shells and language environments used by rule-based expert systems. Examples of these shells are Goldworks (Gold Hill Computers), Automated Reasoning Tool or ART (Inference Corporation), and Knowledge-Based Management Systems or KBMS (AICorp, Inc.). In Chapter 3, the code for CLIPS, a public domain forward-chaining system developed by NASA, is studied in detail.

Chapter 4 presents the basic design and implementation of goal-directed reasoning systems. Goal-directed reasoning is a problem-solving approach based on the divide-and-conquer strategy. According to this strategy, the procedure for solving a problem is to break it down into its component subproblems and then solve each subproblem. Proceeding recursively in this way, we eventually hit upon a subproblem that can be solved only by reference to some fact about the world, at which point the problem solver knows that the fact is true, knows that it is false, or knows neither but can perform some procedure—like asking, taking a sample, or performing a test—that will determine which is the case.

There are a number of variations on this approach, such as allowing the knowledge about the fact to have a value somewhere between absolute certainty of truth and absolutely certainty of falsehood. The appropriate calculus of uncertainty then has quite a significant role to play in determining the usefulness as well as the validity of the approach. The calculus of certainty forms the basis of various types of formal logic.

Goal-directed reasoning is also termed backward chaining, and the control strategy that this represents has been used to build problem solvers based on the principles of formal logic. Applications where reaching a goal or satisfying a set of constraints is important are good candidates for backward-chaining reasoning systems. Example systems include those used for diagnosis and planning. In Chapter 4, code for an implementation of Prolog is studied in detail. Prolog is a mechanized theorem prover based on the first-order predicate calculus.

Chapter 5 discusses some ways to accommodate the hardware and software tradeoffs that might be made in building an application as complex as an embedded expert system. Hardware tradeoffs are made along at least one dimension that expresses the specialization of the machine to the task, whether this is numerical processing or symbolic processing. Software tradeoffs are made along a similar dimension that expresses the language's degree of specialization to the programming task, where the main application characteristic is whether the reasoning is primarily numerical or symbolic, algorithmic or heuristic. This chapter may be of most immediate interest to those tasked with instrumentation or control systems.

Although the concept of a specialist expert system machine and specialist languages has a certain attraction, there is generally less development risk in sticking to the mainstream—the more conventional processors and languages. Thus the tradeoff made in moving from the mainstream is risk versus reward. A middle ground involves the implementation of virtual machines on special-purpose but commodity hardware like digital signal processors and bit-slice devices. New commercial microprocessors specifically designed for virtual machine implementation are also discussed in detail in Chapter 5. These virtual machine processors tend to enable more intelligent embedded applications by delivering performance with less development complexity than special AI language processors.

Introduction to Embedded Intelligence

The primary mission of the research program of computational intelligence, as it has existed from the mid 1960s, is to develop a model of human problem-solving behavior. The model is to be a computational mechanism that exhibits "intelligent" behavior. This constructive point of view nicely stickhandles by the question of the definition of intelligence and shifts the focus instead to accepted examples of "intelligent behavior" such as diagnosis, planning, synthesis, and analysis. This is not unreasonable. The nonconstructive point of view, which regards anything done by machine as a priori not intelligent, has difficulty in the face of the increasing problem-solving capabilities of machines. Engineering practice has overtaken the philosophical discussion, as system specifications, responding to what's needed and what's possible, more routinely call for the ability to manage complexity beyond what humans can do. This trend is as old as systems. Labeling this ability "intelligence" began a generation ago.

At the first formal conference on artificial intelligence in 1956, a theorem-proving program called the Logic Theorist was presented by Newell, Shaw, and Simon. This program could use its programmed expertise in logic to prove some theorems from principia mathematica, and it is one of the earliest examples of programming a computer to perform a task that had been thought to require human intelligence. It is clear from this example that research into computational (artificial) intelligence has been intimately connected with expertise and expert systems from the beginning.

From the development in the late 1970s of a number of computer programs that exhibited expert level performance at some task to the demonstration of commercial potential and viability of the technology at Digital Equipment Corporation in the early 1980s, the technology of expert systems rapidly emerged from the laboratories and was reduced to engineering practice. *Business Week* finally announced the arrival of commercial AI with a cover story in 1984.

The evolution of the technology during the 1980s has been dramatic. As the hype faded, the value of the technology was demonstrated, and it became a known quantity. Applications that once could only be built by Ph.D.'s in AI, using exotic programming languages for delivery on special-purpose hardware, are now built by DP staff or manufacturing engineers, in the C language for delivery on the IBM mainframe or PC. The way that expert systems are envisioned in use has changed dramatically as well. We've moved on from the paradigm of expert consultation, with its emphasis on user interrogatory and explanatory dialog with the machine. Now expert systems commonly work in the background, operating in a high-volume transaction environment, producing reports just like their counterparts made of sterner stuff. Or expert system technology is part and parcel of a central system, just another component.

As this trend broadens, the embedded expert system will become more commonplace. The natural extension of the trend would make the qualifier "embedded" redundant. The application areas for intelligent embedded systems are legion, and include

- Assembly and inspection control

- Avionic control systems

- Consumer electronics, including video and games

- Communications systems

- Heating, ventilation, and cooling systems

- Power systems control

- Process control

- Robotics

So, consistent with the general sense of the term and the evolution of the technology, we have achieved embedded intelligence when we have an embedded system that exhibits intelligent behavior, for example, problem-solving ability.

Remember, though, the distinction between expertise and intelligence, so you can keep the term "expert system" in the proper perspective. As often alluded to, the usual starting point in a discussion of embedded intelligence is to use *expertise* as a proxy for *intelligence*. This approach has the advantage of making some progress toward answering the questions: What is intelligence and what does it mean to put it in a box? But the progress is achieved in part by changing the question. A constructive definition of intelligence such as "performs like a human expert" is a good way to set the scope of the discussion, and it is a practical necessity when you are dealing with a loaded term like "intelligence." Similar considerations led to the articulation of the concept of procedural semantics—a clever engineering response in the face of questions about *meaning:* What is meaning and what does it mean to put it in a computer program?

It has always been understood that the success of the research program in computational intelligence is measured by the extent of the problem-solving capabilities that the proposed mechanisms exhibit. So, the highest stated goal has been the creation of computer systems that can solve problems in some problem area at the level of a human expert—thus the term "expert system." In the late 1970s and early 1980s, as the early prototypes were scaled up to produce some practical outcome, the AI research community realized that expertness is not a discrete attribute nor an entirely satisfactory classification. Most people can become an expert in some things in a very short time, and there are some things that only a few people can become experts in if they invest a very long time to do it. With this realization, *expert system* lost its meaning as a description of what systems built with the technology could do. Thus the majority of systems that incorporate expert system technology do not function at an expert level. Nevertheless, the techniques used to build the mostly early and truly expert systems have proven to be of considerable value in building systems to solve difficult problems. In other words they can exhibit intelligence via expertise without expert level performance.

In looking for commonality in the technology, it is apparent that in each example of a successful application program the key to success—defined in terms of problem-solving capability—is the use of some aspect of symbol manipulation. Computation with symbols is the thread that unifies the various technologies that have been used to build expert systems. Thus symbolic representation and the procedures of symbol manipulation are the basic elements of the architecture of the computational mechanism that exhibit intelligence.

These features, in more language-oriented form, are asserted as particularly important for expert system applications programming by Barr and Feigenbaum, in *The Handbook of Artificial Intelligence*. The features are

- The ability to define data structures that are both expressive and easy to handle.
- The existence of flexible control structures, in particular, nonhierarchical transfer of control.
- Pattern matching as a single mechanism for selecting procedures, passing parameters, and accessing the components of compound data structures.

In other words, the common architectural components of expert system technologies are the data structures that represent the objects being reasoned about and the mechanisms that pass control during the computation. This book is primarily concerned with the implementation of the second of these two components, with particular application to embedded systems.

There have been two basic schools of design with respect to representation and reasoning technology for intelligent systems. Broadly, they are the top-down and bottom-up schools. Each has its adherents. The top-down school is represented by goal-directed reasoning (logic), and as illustrated by the logic theorist program, the connection between logic and AI goes back to the earliest days. However, various difficulties with theorem provers and general problem solvers (notably the tendency of the search space to grow beyond reasonable space and time bounds) and redundancies that compounded the problem (backward chaining restricts the problem-solving process proposed to deal with the problem) led to a period in the 1970s when logic was out of favor and ad hoc reasoning and representation formalisms were very actively explored.

Ad hoc approaches were a reaction to the top-down designs that produced inherently sequential programs where control was subordinated to procedures and functions. These programs were in contrast to the apparent nondeterministic problem-solving processes that research in cognitive science provided evidence that humans used. The theory was that human experts reason via a process of correlation of previous solutions to problems, experience, and heuristics. Heuristics are the rules-of-thumb, strategies, tricks, or any device that limits the search space for solutions. Experts seemed to work from data to conclusions, thus reasoning bottom-up, or data-directed.

Both approaches have been used to build successful applications, and it seems clear now that each represents a major design school. The next section discusses each approach in more detail to provide background for the technology of implementation that is covered in later chapters.

Technologies of Representation and Reasoning: Lines of Evolution

The technologies of representation and reasoning have evolved over the last several decades and the current practice reflects many influences. The fundamentals of these technologies and their major lines of evolution are traced in the next two sections.

To a certain extent, the division of the technology into separate categories for representation and reasoning is artificial. The knowledge that needs to be incorporated in an application is both knowledge about objects and their interrelationships (facts) and knowledge about the sort of computations that take place in the manipulation of the objects (rules). Object-oriented languages do this within one implementation structure. The definition of an object type, called a class definition, defines the prototype object in terms of the possible operations on it (variously rules or methods) and encapsulates the data structures and initialization conditions that constitute a definition of object attributes and relations.

For our purposes, the term "representation" is used for the static aspects of the architecture, whereas the term "reasoning" refers to aspects of the inference engine's operation. This follows the tradition of separating the domain (static) knowledge from the control knowledge. Presumably, then, in formulating the domain knowledge, efficiency considerations other than the efficient use of storage may be set aside. However, efficiency in areas of static knowledge is always a consideration. Control knowledge concerns itself with the effectiveness of the reasoning process. The primary focus in its implementation is efficiency.

The nature of expert system computation is very different from numerical calculation. Procedures, like those that might be used in a digital signal processing routine, are algorithms that have properties like efficiency and correctness, which are important to the design decision and can be determined rigorously. By contrast, the expert system tends to be mainly concerned with empirical procedures. Design questions revolve around the tradeoffs between the memory requirements for knowledge storage and the time for knowledge processing and reasoning, while always weighing the expected utility of explicit knowledge and the physical limitations of the underlying hardware.

Representation

The function of any representation scheme is to capture the essential features of a problem and make that information accessible to the problem-solving apparatus. Preferably, the representation should also make the information accessible to the programmer. This is no insignificant attribute of a representation scheme since a representation loses much of its usefulness if it becomes opaque in its machine usable form. At the same time, a representation loses much of its usefulness if it cannot be tuned to be efficiently used by a machine.

The issues involved underlie any discussion of the relative merits of procedural versus declarative representations of knowledge. Procedural knowledge representation allows direct interaction between facts and heuristic information. However, the meaning of the knowledge that is represented is not always exactly clear because the characteristics of these interactions are known to the programmer who invariably uses them in the program by effectively "compiling" some knowledge. Once compiled, the knowledge is no longer accessible to another party. The procedural representation can only be understood in terms of its behavior, the actions that it performs, and the order in which they are performed.

On the other hand, declarative representation schemes offer cleaner semantics and greater clarity and conciseness. Thus they cater to the needs of the application, in many cases without any provision for tuning to account for the peculiarities of the hardware or the implementation language. Declarative representations, in the ideal, state true facts that can be understood without reference to the behavior of the inference mechanism. There are several declarative schemes, illustrated by the functional, logic-programming, and object-oriented languages.

At a minimum, the representation language needs to allow the programmer to express the knowledge that is either known or thought to be required for the problem-solving processes in the application domain. The more natural representation of that knowledge is preferred. Most schemes have some area of awkwardness. Some rule systems that express all knowledge with *if . . . then . . .* constructs allow no choices other than to shoehorn all procedures into this form. This can become awkward when the problem-solving process is most naturally expressed as a set of problem-solving phases. The *if . . . then . . .* form does not express very well how control is passed, and the solution is often to use conditions in each rule to test the phase. But the fact that a phased approach is central to the solution process cannot be directly expressed by the programmer.

Supporting the expression of the knowledge at the most natural possible level is a function of the development environment and the major application development features mentioned by Barr and Feigenbaum. Particularly in the case of the representation of objects and their relationships, graphs and diagrams are useful, both for implementation and design. Thus picture-based I/O devices or design conventions are quite common in development tools.

It is also important that the resulting representation be computationally efficient. By contrast with expressiveness, which determines the ability of the scheme to capture all the necessary knowledge, efficiency gives the ability to use the information embodied in the representation to solve a problem in a timely fashion. Expressiveness is a function of the language architecture, while efficiency in the use of the representation is a function of the implementation. Expressiveness and efficiency are the major attributes of a representation scheme.

The tradeoffs between expressiveness and efficiency are illustrated in a very simplified way by the representation of floating-point numbers in computer systems. Since real numbers generally require an infinite number of digits, they cannot be directly represented in any machine with finite resources. Thus there is a tradeoff between expressiveness and efficiency leading to the common representation of floating-point numbers in terms of two components—the significant digits and the decimal point position. Therefore, there can be a computer representation that captures the computationally important features of real numbers. Note that, in common with all representations, the implementation of the floating point number is a symbol that refers to an entity, and it is not the entity itself.

The floating-point example illustrates the tradeoffs between expressiveness and efficiency and the fact that such issues are not limited to expert systems. By contrast with the floating-point number system, expert systems tend to be more concerned with organizing and representing qualitative rather than quantitative knowledge. To fully support this, a representation should be able to

- Represent qualitative knowledge.

- Represent general principles and specific situations.

- Capture complex semantic meaning.

Approaches to representation and the representational capacity of existing tools and languages are examined throughout the text. Two of the more significant schools of representation are network-based and logic.

Network-Based Representation

A knowledge base is meant to be nothing more than an abstract statement of a mapping between the objects and relations between objects as they exist in a problem domain and the computational objects and relations in the machine. The computational objects, relations, and inferences available to programmers are a function of the knowledge representation that they choose. Thus if explicit knowledge is important in solving problems, the proper language and representation scheme may make the difference between the success and the failure of the system or between making the problem-solving task easy or difficult to accomplish.

Some early formalisms for knowledge representation that are based on the idea of networks were motivated by intuitive psychological considerations. The argument runs as follows. We think of the world in terms of concepts and internalize our experience in terms of new concepts or relationships between existing concepts. Thus our first impulse is to represent this knowledge in terms of graphs, where the nodes represent the concepts and the links (vertices) represent the relationships between the concepts. The term "concept" should be interpreted here as a more abstract version of the term "object." Such "semantic nets" were designed to facilitate certain kinds of inference such as inheritance of properties from concept to concept.

Another important network-based notation with psychological roots is the Conceptual Dependency network developed by Roger Schank (1972). Schank elaborated on earlier work by the philosophers Katz and Fodor (1963) to propose that there exists a set of primitive concepts out of which all meanings can be constructed. A Conceptual Dependency network is, by design, independent of any particular human language—a virtual meaning machine.

There are two major criticisms of the network representation schemes. First, they can be semantically ill defined and unable to capture some important distinctions such as the distinction between subset and membership relations. Second, they lack structure in that they are unable to represent groupings of concepts and relationships into higher level concepts.

Structured representation schemes are somewhat like networks, but they extend the implementation of networks by allowing each node to be a complex data structure that can store a variety of types of information about the objects that they represent. These complex nodes are commonly called frames, scripts, or objects. The script, for example, illustrates an expectation-based representation for events, where prototypical events are structured as sequences of expected actions.

Most of the important issues in knowledge representation have to do with the semantics of the representational formalism and the constraints that the semantics can impose on what can be known or inferred. For example, there is a large difference in the granularity of representation between the predicate calculus and the frame. The predicate calculus uses simple symbols with little or no internal structure—the frame can describe in detail multiple features and attributes of an object.

Logic Representation

There are several advantages to using logic as the main knowledge representation formalism in a system that is to have some expertise. First, logic comes with a formal semantics, unlike many other representation formalisms. Formal semantics assigns a precise meaning to the expressions in the formalism. A formal semantics also allows a comparison to be made between different logical languages, thereby making it possible to construct guidelines as to which logical formalism to use for particular domains and tasks.

Logics also have well-understood properties with respect to completeness, soundness, and decidability. Although these are not the usual domain of engineering, in some situations such as mission-critical applications in space or elsewhere, formal analysis of the software's properties could prove useful and may even be essential. Moreover, even when the characteristics of a particular logical formalism are cast in the negative, for example, incompleteness, it is worth noting that these properties can even be known at all. For many other formalisms there are no such results.

Finally, logic has significant expressive power. Although the first-order predicate calculus (as mechanized in restricted form with the Prolog language) is two-valued, logic is not restricted to a two-valued truth-functional language. A few examples are intuitional logics, many-valued logics, modal logics, and tense logics (see Turner 1984). Second, even logic in the limited form of Prolog can readily express information about situations that are incompletely known, so that we need not represent details that are not yet known because it is possible to represent the fact that details are not known.

Reasoning

The most important function of any reasoning scheme—particularly one that is to be carried out by a machine—is to quickly decide the best next step in the problem-solving process. As stated earlier, a good solution, found quickly, can count more than a more elegant but expensive one. It is a good decision about what to do next that permits the operation of the machine to be described as "intelligent." Search and deduction are the core intellectual skills required of a reasoning scheme.

Exhaustive search in any a priori order is unlikely to be considered too intelligent. Instead, a search should take into account what is already known or discovered during the process. The mechanization of data-driven search paradigms originated in the cognitive sciences as a model of the way that human experts solve problems.

On the other hand, it is often important for the reasoning process to have formal properties like consistency and completeness. Properties of this sort, and analyses of the properties, come with more normative models of human problem solving such as logic.

Cognitive Science

Cognitive science is the experimental science whose subject is human problem solving (see Newell and Simon, 1972). The focus of the cognitive sciences is on the human mechanisms for problem solving. The ultimate goal of this program of study is an understanding of the biological basis of cognition. The basic hypothesis is that human cognition is information processing; according to this hypothesis, a cognitive process can be seen as a sequence of internal states successively transformed by a series of information processes. An associated hypothesis is that information is stored in several memories having different capacities and accessing characteristics.

One of the approaches used in the cognitive sciences is the development of models of human cognition, and these include computational models. The computational models complement the experimental work that uses such techniques as thinking-aloud protocols to study the problem-solving behavior of experts. As a consequence of the focus on human problem solving, the architectures of the computational models of intelligence that have been developed are constrained to a certain extent by psychological plausibility.

Architecturally, transfer of control in these models is governed by a "recognize-act" cycle, where the problem solver presumably recognizes a situation based on information stored in the memories and so takes some action. The chunk of know-how used in the recognize-act cycle to drive the problem-solving process forward is called a *rule*. Thus the rule is the model of the subjective psychological notion of learned, appropriate, effective distinctions that people use to make high-level distinctions.

Recognize-act is also called data-driven reasoning or forward chaining. A related model is the stimulus-response association that has been presumed by some to underlie animal behavior, but of course for lower level distinctions in cognitive processes.

The conjecture that human problem solving corresponds to the recognize-act model may or may not be true. Nevertheless it does seem to be the case that human experts use rules as a convenient formalism for expressing problem-solving knowledge.

The practical computer programs that run on these types of models rely on efficient pattern-matching algorithms, a number of which have been developed in recent years. However, the technology has incorporated ideas from a number of other sources. For example, decision tables, a very compact and concrete representation of condition-action rules, have been used for several decades in language analyzers like compilers, in complex transaction processing, and in controllers. The limitations of this approach are that it executes sequentially on the input data in most cases without the ability to use intermediate results, and the conditions that determine a decision are simple Boolean conditions. With this approach, large tables become quite complex to design and maintain, and both the control flow capabilities and ability to describe complex symbolic patterns are very limited.

From the point of view of architecture, though, machines based on the recognize-act model have two facilities that are quite distinct from conventional systems. The first is the pattern matcher, which is used heavily to match rule components against memory that stores current state data. The second is a mechanism that can quickly identify rules that become relevant as the current state changes. Most implementations build these components with software, although hardware units have been proposed to improve the absolute performance of the matcher.

The OPS-class languages such as OPS5, OPS83, or CLIPS are instances of the mechanization in software of the problem-solving models derived from work in the cognitive sciences. Sophisticated expert system-building tools like ART from Inference Corp. or KBMS from the AICorp are based on the same mechanisms as are in CLIPS. Inference and representation mechanisms in CLIPS and similar programs are studied in depth in Chapter 3.

Some of the key strengths of condition-action reasoning paradigms mentioned by Hayes-Roth (1985) include

- Represent problem-solving know-how in a manner suitable for simulation by machine (computer).

- Represent modularization of chunks of knowledge.

- Make decision making more intelligible and explainable.

Some key weaknesses include

- Lack a precise analytical foundation for deciding which problems are solvable.

- Lack a methodology for testing consistency and completeness of a rule set.

- Lack a theory of knowledge organization that facilitates scaling up without loss of intelligibility or performance.

Logic

Logic is the science of human problem solving as it should be. In other words, logicians have always been concerned more with how people *should* reason than with how they do reason. Getting the right answer is not enough—the argument leading to the answer should be correct as well. The goal of formal logic is to represent problem solving as a formal relationship between beliefs and conclusions—to find procedures that can guarantee correct solutions; in other words, to find the *legal* modes of reasoning.

One of the simplest forms of formal logic is the propositional logic invented by Boole. An elementary proposition is a sentence such as: Alarm 5 is triggered." Elementary sentences have no internal structure in propositional logic and are represented by atomic symbols such as A, B, C. The propositional logic describes the correct way in which more complicated sentences can be constructed by combining sentences in a simple fashion using connecting words like *or, not,* and *if.* No sentence of the propositional logic has any internal structure other than that imposed by the logical connectives.

The connectives *and, or,* and *not* are truth functional, meaning that the truth of a sentence depends only on the truth of the individual elements of the sentence that are joined by the connectives. Propositions can be represented by tree structures, in which the nodes are labelled with the logical connectives and the leaves are labelled with the atomic sentences. Assigning truth values to the atomic sentences, a tree structure can also represent the meaning of the proposition. In this case, the meaning is the truth value of the proposition. In these structures, nodes at each level in the tree are labelled with a single atomic proposition. Two arcs from each node are labelled with the truth value assigned to the sentence. The leaves of the tree are labelled with the truth value of the proposition that is computed from the truth values of the atomic propositions as assigned along the arcs from the root to the leaf. Such trees are called *semantic trees*.

Semantic trees can be used to identify those lines of reasoning whose correctness depends only on the way in which the individual propositions are connected, that is, they do not depend on the truth values assigned to the elementary proposition. Such lines of reasoning are termed *Boolean arguments*. The analytical approach to determining the truth of a proposition consists of analyzing the semantic tree. The constructive approach is a procedure for applying *rules of inference* to true propositions to construct additional true propositions. The differences between the two is analogous to the difference between backward and forward chaining.

There are computer theorem provers that implement decision procedures for the propositional logic (the analytical approach); that is, given a formula, it works by deriving the semantic tree and determining whether the formulas are true in all branches of the semantic tree. If it is, the argument is correct; otherwise, it is not.

Some of the simplest expert system technology works basically the same way. The rules of the system are represented as simple propositions of the *A if B* form. The inferencing procedure is then simply a search through the rules—a traversal of the semantic tree, as appropriately represented as some set of data structures for efficient computer execution of the search. With some extensions that we will touch on later, simple propositional inference systems can be a very efficient and effective way to implement decision algorithms in diagnostic systems.

The predicate calculus is another form of logic that is a good deal richer than the propositional logic primarily because the elementary sentences themselves can have structure. Sentences in the predicate calculus are formed from predicates whose arguments are terms, which can be constants, variables, or functions of terms. Constants, variables, and functions of terms all represent things, but in various degrees of detail. A constant represents a specific thing and is analogous to a proper noun. A variable represents some unspecified term. A function of terms is a structured term. Predicates are often written in a functional notation. For example, the earlier sentence, *alarm 5 is triggered,* may be represented in functional notation as *is-triggered(alarm_5)*, where *is-triggered* is the predicate function name, and *alarm_5* is a term. Variables and functions of terms allow the expression of sentences such as *some alarm is triggered* as *is-triggered (x)* and *pressure alarm 5 is triggered,* as *is-triggered (pressure (alarm_5))*.

The formulas of the predicate logic are formed from the sentences and logical connectives as is the propositioned logic together with such quantifiers as *there exists* and *all,* which range over the variables in the sentences.

Correctness of the sentences in the predicate logic is relative to an interpretation of the constituent formulas, a problem much more significant for the predicate logic than for the propositional logic due to the existence of variables. The result is that testing the correctness of predicate formulas cannot be translated into a computer program as easily as it can be for Boolean arguments. The reason is the possible existence of an infinite number of interpretations, where an interpretation is the assignment of values to the logical variables.

There are basically two ways to determine the correctness of arguments (that is, finding a proof) within the formalism of predicate logic:

1. Truth theoretic approaches determine correctness by determining the meaning of the formulas. An example would be a procedure for constructing semantic trees for Boolean forms and thereby determining the truth of the formula or equivalently the correctness of the reasoning.

2. Proof theoretic approaches start with true statements, use *rules of inference* that preserve truth to derive new statements, and continue like this until arriving at the statement to be proved. The simple expert systems based on propositional logic work this way.

Among the more sophisticated rules of inference that have been developed with a eye toward mechanizing the proof process is the procedure known as resolution. The resolution rule is straightforward: Given a sentence with a predicate on the right-hand side of an implication and another sentence with the same predicate on the left-hand side, it is possible to derive a new sentence whose right-hand side is the union of the predicates on the right-hand sides of the original sentences, but with the common predicate deleted, and whose left-hand side is the union of the predicates on the left-hand sides of the original sentences, but with the common predicate deleted. A simple example is

```
sentence 1: is-triggered (alarm_5) if pressure (high).
sentence 2: is-triggered (bell) if is-triggered (alarm_5) and
                  is-triggered (alarm_2).
=>
sentence 3: is-triggered (bell) if pressure (high) and
                  is-triggered (alarm_2).
```

where the net result of applying the resolution rule is to replace the term *is-triggered* (*alarm_5*) in the second sentence with *pressure* (*high*). The preceding resolution example is very simple since the arguments of the predicates may be any valid term, that is, a constant, variable, or a structured term. What is required for the resolution step is that there exist an assignment of values to the variables in the sentences that makes one predicate on the left-hand side of one sentence the same as one predicate on the right-hand side of another sentence. The procedure for finding these variable assignments is called *unification*. (See Kowalski 1979.)

Resolution refutation is an inference procedure based on resolution and unification that starts with the assumption of the negation of the sentence that is to be proved and then proceeds to deduce a contradiction as a result of applying the resolution procedure. This refutation procedure has the properties of being both complete (every true sentence that could be derived from a set of sentences can be derived with the refutation procedure) and consistent (the result of the procedure is guaranteed to be correct).

Prolog is a general-purpose AI language that is in fact an example of an efficient proof theoretic mechanization of a restricted form of the first-order predicate calculus. In other words, Prolog is a computer language with a good deal of the representational power of the predicate calculus. The basic proof procedure underlying Prolog is resolution refutation, where the deductions are performed in a fixed and arbitrary order. We take a close look at a Prolog implementation in Chapter 4.

Programming Languages

Last but not least, just as much as the models of the cognitive sciences and of logic, programming languages can also be viewed as models of human problem solving. The difference is that programming language models have started, not from a theoretical base, but simply from attempts at mechanization in support of reasoning.

Programming languages model a problem-solving process by providing a set of operations with which to specify a sequence of operations that need to be performed in order to solve the problem. The high-level languages that have been developed deliberately impose structure on the problem-solving behavior of the user. This is done in order to make certain problem expressions more natural and to discourage bad programming practice. A good example of a high-level problem-solving concept that is currently incorporated as a matter of course into modern programming languages is recursion. The example of the FORTRAN language, among others, which does not permit recursion, illustrates that this sort of capability was not always considered valuable enough to offset the overhead it brought to the language.

The drawback of any particular programming language relative to any other is that it makes restrictions on the allowed data structures, control structures, and primitives that can make some algorithms more difficult to express than others. Since all programming languages tend to be equivalent in the sense of what they can compute, the expressive power of a language is not meaningfully measured by the class of functions it can evaluate. Expressiveness measures that are couched in terms of the variety of algorithms that can be expressed naturally tend to put the reasoning systems based on cognitive science or logic at the higher end of the scale, particularly with respect to the ability to manipulate symbols.

However, numbers are symbols, too, and some reasoning problems are algorithmic. This is particularly important for embedded systems. Lack of programming language functionality is one of the greatest failures of existing expert system development tools. Lack of numeric processing capability can be one of the greatest failures of existing expert system development languages.

Embedded Systems

Several factors contribute to the difficulty of bringing expert system technology to bear in embedded systems. In the best case, rigorous performance requirements or resource constraints must be met, in addition to the usual factors that make embedding expertise in any system difficult. The net result is that a lot of functionality has to be crammed into a small box, often without a sophisticated computing resource.

In the worst case, formidable programming tasks must be undertaken in a primitive programming environment. For example, special-purpose hardware, such as single-chip digital signal processors or processing units built from bit-slice devices, may represent the only available computing resources, and development support may not extend beyond in-circuit emulators nor development languages beyond the assembly language of the native hardware. Embedded system architectures many times involve specialized sensor and effector devices, and it may be no simple task to reliably program for their control and coordination without operating system or language level support.

The end user is becoming more demanding in specifying delivery hardware and program capability, whether the nature of the application demands it (as in real-time or process control applications) or because of cost and convenience. There is ample evidence that more expert systems are being delivered on hardware familiar to the user—witness the rush to move the technology off special-purpose machines and onto the very conventional mainframes in order to deliver underwriting or financial planning applications to end users. Specialized hardware for embedded systems often addresses particular needs with respect to performance and in many cases requires integration into larger systems. For example, significant integration constraints are imposed by the need for dedicated systems in several areas where knowledge-based technology has been fruitfully applied: monitoring (Fox et al., 1983), self-test (Burns et al., 1986), and calibration (Brand and Wong, 1986).

However, the commercial expert system development environments with effective support for developing knowledge-based systems (irrespective of the delivery machine) are best suited for large and complex systems, involving perhaps thousands of sensors and inference rules and linked to a large central computer (for example, PDS; see Fox et al., 1983). Systems of intermediate size, as might fill the needs of the manufacturing environment and be implemented on low-cost hardware, are difficult to move off the high-end machines once developed. Moreover, they tend to be overengineered, as a natural and understandable consequence of the design expanding to take advantage of the available features. There are even fewer delivery paths to smaller systems such as embedded controllers because these small systems are much more difficult to develop and then deliver in quantity.

More intelligent systems, whatever the hardware platform, are the systems we would like to be able to build. At this stage in the evolution of expert systems technology, the engineering issues, not the AI research problems, are the primary concern. The key is to be able to make use of the knowledgebase technology that has already been developed, in those areas where it is appropriate and valuable.

This book presents a path to effect the transfer of knowledgebase technology to embedded systems while meeting the constraints of embedded applications. This approach addresses the following design goals:

1. Maintain the convenience of standard/conventional knowledge-based development environments and languages.

2. Provide a facility in programming for embedded applications.

3. Do not compromise the performance of the knowledge-based component of the system.

Separate chapters of the book are devoted to each of the major architectural elements of expert systems in practical use today. Each element is described in detail and its implementation illustrated by examining the source code.

Chapter 2 **Virtual Machines**

The Virtual Machine Approach to System Implementation

The game plan for implementing embedded systems with sophisticated functionality—like an expert system—starts with the design of an instruction set architecture for a virtual machine. An instruction set architecture should be expressive enough to enable an efficient description of the problems that the system is designed to solve. By efficient I mean simply that both the things that are being reasoned about and the lines of reasoning themselves should be able to be defined and described in a natural fashion, where the meaning of the description is obvious. There is probably a research result somewhere that states that a reasonable measure of the expressiveness of an instruction set is the verbosity of the resulting code. The more words it takes to say what you want to say, the less expressive the instruction set.

I call the machine with an architecture that is a good fit to the problem a virtual machine because it does not necessarily have any concrete form in hardware. However, if performance is extremely important, then either building special-purpose hardware or, where applicable, modifying processor microcode may well be the only way to achieve the necessary performance.

The virtual machine approach is a good, general design principle no matter what the problem area is because it permits the developer to tailor the machine to the problem. The issue is akin to impedance matching in an electrical circuit, which is required to get the most efficient power transfer from the power supply to the power consumer. If you think of it, most systems are designed and built as layers of machines, each machine defined in terms of the architectures of lower level machines. In the simplest of these, the application itself is built on an implementation language at the top level, which is translated to a machine language that is interpreted in turn by microcode. The design skill required for virtual machine design is the ability to make good tradeoffs between the semantic fit to the problem at the top level and the complexity and execution efficiency of the overall application code.

An instruction set architecture for any machine, virtual or otherwise, includes the following components. There is a description of the instruction format, the data elements and their representation inside the machine, addressing modes, instruction sequencing and interpretation, and program structuring constructs. A good discussion of the relationship between machine instruction sets and high-level languages can be found in Fernandez and Lang (1986).

The instruction format description—one of the lowest level aspects of the architecture—includes a specification of the number of bits in each instruction, and how the bits are divided up into fields whose values characterize the type of the instruction and the types of its arguments. For example, a typical instruction for a microcomputer would have a bit field indicating the type of instruction (for example, arithmetic, logical, or control), a bit field indicating the type and location of the source operand, and a bit field indicating the type and location of the destination operand. (See Figure 2.1.) Computer architectures are classified on the basis of how many operands are referenced explicitly in the instruction. Operands not explicitly referenced are often implicit within a data structure, which is another aspect of the machine architecture. An example of such a structure is a data stack.

The definition of the data elements and their representation specifies what types of things the machine knows at its most primitive level. For example, some instruction sets can handle floating-point numbers, whereas others—most, in fact—specify that fixed-point numbers can be the only arguments of arithmetic instructions. Instruction-sequencing constructs specify the options for changing the flow of control in a program. Examples include instructions for jumps and function calls. Finally, program-structuring constructs add more structure to the program through instructions that implement iteration or conditional execution.

Clearly, the preceding examples that illustrate the components of an architecture are pretty remote, in terms of the objects and reasoning processes, from a machine that solves high-level problems in process control. The design goal for any virtual machine

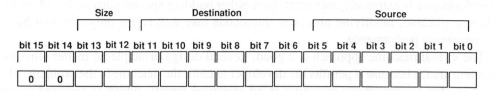

Figure 2.1. Bit Fields in Microcomputer Opcodes

The 16 bits of the MOVE instruction for the 68000 microprocessor are interpreted by the processor as a three-field. The first field specifies the size of the operand to be moved, while the second and third fields specify the source and the destination of the move respectively. The source and destination fields are further subdivided into fields that specify the addressing mode and the address register.

that forms the platform for an intelligent embedded system is to reduce the semantic gap between the high-level operations of the system, for example, specific data acquisition and control processes or essential problem-solving steps, and the much lower level operations that are necessary to control individual system components, in many cases even the embedded hardware components.

Think of this virtual machine design approach as related to designing specialized hardware instruction sets in direct support of high-level languages (for example, LISP machine architectures in support of LISP, Prolog machines for Prolog, or Pascal machines for Pascal—all of which have been designed and built).

The insight behind using a virtual machine design is simply that a specialized vocabulary is often used for talking about a problem by the people who are good at solving these types of problems. The specialized vocabulary serves an important function: to facilitate referencing the important components of the problem as well as the important problem-solving techniques. The net effect is to simplify the description of both the problem and the problem's solution.

The main reason for introducing the virtual machine approach as an integral part of the development of an intelligent embedded system is not just that it is a good design approach in general, but that there are both efficient languages and hardware for building and running virtual machines. Underlying these languages and the related architecture of the hardware is the idea of threaded code.

Threaded Code Languages

There is a class of computer languages called threaded code languages (TCLs) that are good implementation languages for virtual machines of the sort just discussed. The word "threaded" refers to the fact that in most of these languages the object code consists of pointers, and at run-time a very efficient interpreter follows the pointers to the machine code. Pointer following may require decoding many levels of reference. It is this indirect reference and the efficiency with which it is done that gives threaded code its power.

But threaded code languages are more than just a tool with which to build the system, more than just comparable to assembler or C as an implementation strategy. In practice, TCLs also do a very good job of supporting the design process for a virtual machine language by providing a flexible, interactive facility for defining or naming opcodes and for describing the instruction formats of the abstract machine, as well as by providing a mechanism for assembling programs written with these instructions. The resulting computer program, which simulates the virtual machine, is both fast and compact (for a good discussion of the principles of threaded code see Loeliger 1981).

One of the unusual attributes of these threaded languages that is associated with the paradigm of machine design is that they generally provide access to the full range of machines—all the machine layers—on which a system might be built. As a result, tuning the code to squeeze out the last ounce of performance is a natural act with a TCL. The rationale for having to tune in the first place is one of the laws of nature, the 80-20 law: 80% percent of the time is spent in 20% of the code. Thus most of the implementation code can be written at the highest virtual machine level, and only the time-critical portions need be implemented at a level closer to the underlying hardware.

Threaded code languages were invented for, and have been most widely adopted for use in, data acquisition and process control programming—both significant application areas for embedded systems. One reason that threaded code languages have evolved as a mechanism to easily realize abstract machines is that thinking in terms of virtual machine instructions is the natural programming style in data acquisition and control domains. Programmers tend to conceptualize system operation in terms of a high-level, abstract machine, and by so doing can defer having to consider the low-level processes associated with individual system components (even while retaining such access when needed). For example, complex data acquisition procedures can be abstracted to a single type of instruction for some virtual machine, as illustrated in Figure 2.2.

For example, data acquisition, a common operation, could be parameterized by the device to be sampled (a DAC), the number of samples to be taken, and the buffer in

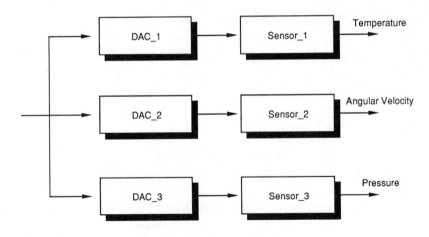

• Code Segment invoking operation in virtual machine code

SAMPLE   DAC_3, 100, BUFFER_2

• Code Segment invoking operation in machine code

```
LOAD    Register_1, DAC_3_Address
LOAD    Register_2, Sample_Count
LOAD    Register_3, Buffer_2_Address
CALL    Sample_Procedure
```

Figure 2.2. Encoding Complex Operations as Virtual Machine Opcodes

which the samples are to be accumulated. Suppose then that the programmer was developing code for a (virtual) machine that had as part of its set of machine code instructions the operator SAMPLE, which takes three arguments representing the device, sample count, and destination parameters. Source code for the application can then simply include the instruction SAMPLE. Object code is produced by an assembler for the virtual machine. Contrast this with code to invoke the same procedure in the native machine code, which may involve loading registers with the arguments prior to calling the subroutine. The advantage to working in terms of the virtual machine is that you can close the gap between the problem that you're trying to solve and the language used for solving it; that is, for sampling problems it is more natural to work in terms of a SAMPLE operation than in terms of register loads and subroutine calls.

This approach allows the programming language to be shifted by the designer up toward the level of the language of the problem domain, while keeping access to the underlying hardware where performance can be tuned. A good example of shifting the language semantics so that they better match the requirements of the problem is a virtual machine architecture into which languages that use pattern matching can be compiled. Suppose there were a machine that would perform the kinds of pattern matching used in the language. Then you might expect to see machine instructions much like instructions for any processor, but taking for this special task two arguments that reference a pattern (*Pattern*) and the item to be matched to the pattern (*Source*), for example,

```
match_pattern   Pattern,Source
```

In fact, the instruction set is likely to be specialized even further to more efficiently handle the different cases that could be recognized at compile time, for example,

```
match_constant   Constant,Source
match_variable   Variable,Source
```

Once a virtual machine with instructions of this sort is designed, it is often very easy to build a compiler for the source language that compiles to the instructions of the virtual machine. Similarly, it becomes easier to port the language to new hardware since only the implementation of the virtual machine instructions need be redone.

The ultimate benefit of shifting the semantics of the programming language in this way, that is, closer to the semantics of the problem-solving language, is productivity, both in development and maintenance. Dramatic productivity increases, which can be so much so that new applications are enabled, are one of the chief long-term impacts of expert system technology on programming languages. Keeping an efficient and accessible hook to the underlying hardware at the same time—no matter what the level of the implementation language—is essential to the embedded systems developer.

Thus a good strategy for achieving the functionality that is required to build embedded knowledge-based systems is to implement standard expert system development languages. The languages are standard in the sense that they are supported by several commercial vendors; that is, they represent the lowest common denominator in terms of development functionality. As part of this strategy, the language is implemented via a threaded code technique, and then the application is built in the expert systems language. Of course, the factors that are important in choosing a particular development language to implement depend to a certain extent on the problem domain. Chapters 3 and 4 will describe the two major inferencing approaches that have been used for the majority of fielded expert system applications.

So after all that has been said about the benefits of using an implementation language that is close to the problem area, why choose to implement a standard language instead of a special-purpose problem-solving language that is tailored to the problem? First, a lot is known about implementing standard languages efficiently, both due to the effort of vendors and the research in the academic community. Second, you can find application programmers who have received some formal training or have some experience developing expert systems in the language; standard languages are often used for training in basic concepts and find widespread use in courses. Finally, you can often easily find solutions to common problems in how-to books, conference proceedings, magazines, or contact with the user community.

Why choose to go to the trouble of implementing language at all? The choice to pursue this solution often has to do with special requirements and engineering constraints associated with the fact that the system must be embedded. Otherwise, reinventing the wheel should be avoided, if possible.

In terms of which wheel to reinvent, follow these selection guidelines: the language should be well known, and a body-of-solutions literature should be available. Rule-based languages of the forward-chaining/situation-action (for example, OPS5) or backward-chaining/logic-based form (for example, Prolog) generally meet these criteria. In addition, they both have small kernels, so it is relatively easy to implement a complete version of either language and embed the result. Both Prolog and OPS5 can be simulated with abstract machines—Prolog on the machine described by David Warren and known as the Warren Abstract Machine (WAM), and OPS5 on the abstract machine described by Charles Forgy. Generally, then, the recommended approach is to construct OPS/Prolog compilers that emit compact code for a highly portable intermediate language. The intermediate language is implemented as a TCL, which brings with it an architecture that is particularly suited to developing embedded applications.

Just a word on a related implementation technique for the intermediate language, namely, byte encoding. As mentioned, TCLs are mostly word encoded, that is, the code consists of pointers. Byte encoding of primitive virtual machine instructions simply means assigning a byte code to the instruction and interpreting the code with an interpreter that fetches the byte, indexes into an instruction table, and then branches to the procedure that does what the referenced high-level instruction is defined to do. The advantages of byte encoding are its relatively efficient interpretation technique and its efficient use of space, although comparisons of code compactness are difficult to make out of the context of a particular application. For example, although byte encoding sets the lower limit of the instruction size at 1 byte, compared to a one-word (usually 16 bits) minimum size for most TCLs, the effective size tends to be larger due to the additional bytes that are needed

to refer to instruction arguments. Small code size is important both where memory resources are limited and, in virtual memory systems, where smaller code means less
paging. (See Figure 2.3.)

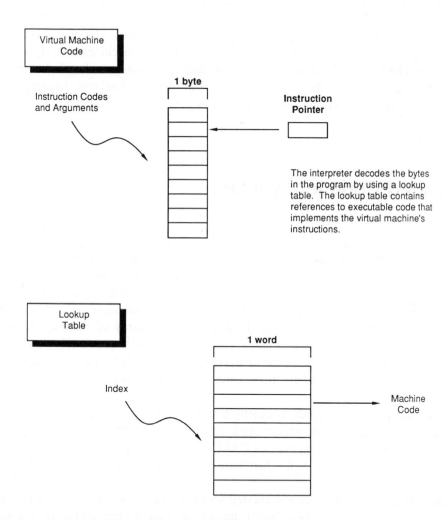

Figure 2.3. Byte Code Encoded Implementations

Byte encoding of the opcodes of the virtual machine can be thought of as a form of threaded code
that is limited to 255 opcodes, that is, the number of different symbols that can be encoded in 8
bits. Opcodes, as encoded in the bytes, must be decoded via a table lookup. Thus the interpreter
for the byte-encoded virtual machine incurs the overhead of fetching a byte, decoding it, and then
jumping to the routine the byte represents. This overhead is in addition to the pointer maintenance
required to maintain control in the program. One advantage that byte encoding may have is
compactness, although the actual difference depends on the program encoded. By contrast,
threaded code uses the address of the routine (a pointer) as its representation. The code may,
therefore, take up more memory since an additional 8 or 24 bits is required to store an address.

A byte encoded intermediate language is the choice of many high-level–language implementors. For example, Warren (1983) has implemented Prolog this way, Deutsch (1973) has done the same for LISP, as have Goldberg and Robson (1983) for Smalltalk. Still others have chosen threaded code for the intermediate language as did Duff (1986) for the object-oriented language Actors. There is no clear evidence that for any given application one scheme is definitely more compact than the other (see Klint (1981) for a study of code size as a function of the implementation technique). Our choice is threaded code, based on experience in using it to implement abstract machines underlying OPS5 and Prolog. The resulting code is compact, fast, and tightly integrated with the programs it is embedded in because they share the same run-time mechanisms. Implementation techniques for these virtual machines are discussed in Chapters 3 and 4.

Threaded Code Interpreters

A small program called a *threaded code interpreter* is the guts of a TCL. Its job is to interpret a data structure that contains both the code, and data and control information. This data structure is a defined code segment and is the end product of the analysis performed by the source language compiler. What this data structure mainly contains for most implementations of a threaded code interpreter—although several alternative approaches are used in threaded code languages—is an array of memory addresses. These addresses point either to executable code segments or to previously defined code segment structures. The threaded code interpreter is responsible for passing control to the executable code segments and for maintaining a set of pointers into the defined code segment structures.

In other words, the interpreter is exactly a slightly higher order version of the procedure-calling mechanism of the underlying hardware, and the threaded code is sequential subroutine calls but without the explicit CALL opcode. The advantage is that lifting the control flow procedures out of the hardware facilitates the use of more sophisticated control structures.

In most TCL designs the compilation step for the language consists of a word-by-word analysis of the source code, where "word" means a delimited string and where the delimiters may in fact change as part of the compilation process. The default delimiter is a space.

Once identified as a separate string, the compiler searches for each word in a lookup table that stores the address of either executable code or the address of a previously defined code segment. During the definition of an code segment, the compiler builds the array of addresses based on table lookup through word-by-word analysis of the input stream.

One way to make sense of the numbers that appear in these defined code segments is to interpret them as the machine codes for the instructions of some computer that realizes the computation specified by the source language statements. After all, they are just numbers to begin with, so one might just as well think of them as opcodes as addresses. The threaded code interpreter is simply simulating this machine in software. The compilation process only needs to compile the source statements to the instructions of the virtual machine, not directly to the instructions of the underlying hardware. The interpreter takes care of the rest at run-time.

One consequence of thinking of the program in these terms is that the program that maps the program statements of the virtual machine into the addresses of the defined code segments or executable code segments that implement the instruction is then equivalent in operational terms to a machine code assembler. Aside from all the other advantages that virtual machines bring, assemblers can be built quickly and assembler code is among the easiest code to debug because of the very direct relationship between the source code and the object code.

One simple refinement of this scheme—the ability to extend the instruction set—means that powerful debugging mechanisms can be constructed. For example, opcodes can be redefined incrementally to operate differently in debug mode. In fact, for most TCLs the compiler itself can be modified so that a single debug flag could control the compilation of the entire body of code, providing an incremental development environment that is extremely flexible.

Given a compiler that can analyze the source statements of a language in the manner described and then produce the intermediate data structures for the interpreter, there may appear to be no need for any other than executable code segments to implement the virtual machine. Each instruction of the virtual machine could be represented by the address of the machine code that implements the instruction. If that were all there was, there would not be a lot of point to the elaborate mechanism of the interpreter since the host processor's subroutine call could do the same thing—transfer control to the code responsible for implementing the instruction—and probably do it much faster. The only tradeoff in this case is space for speed—you save the space occupied by the CALL opcode in return for the overhead of the Threaded Code Interpreter, in which case byte encoding may be preferable.

However, with an interpreter having the capability to both nest control and interpret lists of addresses pointed to by lists of addresses there comes a significant increase in the power of the approach: it makes the virtual machine extensible as well as very portable. Extensibility derives from the ability to define new opcodes in terms of opcodes already defined. Portability comes from the ability of the system to be built up from earlier definitions, all starting with a very small kernel. The kernel becomes the only part of the virtual machine that needs to be implemented in the underlying machine code. Threaded code systems generally require twenty to thirty primitive procedures in the kernel.

Having made the distinction between machine-encoded instructions and those defined from existing definitions, it is worthwhile to introduce some terminology. The machine-encoded instruction definitions are called *primitives*. The rest of the instructions can be implemented using exactly the instructions that are already defined. These are called *secondaries*. The language is extensible because adding a new instruction to the language is as simple as creating a new primitive or secondary. One of the merits of extensibility is that it very naturally leads to the development of layers of machines in the implementation of a very high-level language. The layers of machine ease the transition from the hardware to the high-level language. In this TCLs share much with the LISP language.

The merits of portability are self-evident, and a well-defined and short porting task may enable the relaxation of design constraints that might have existed if porting was not feasible. For example, special-purpose hardware may enable performance requirements to be met, along with sophisticated applications program functionality. If porting were not feasible, for example, an application is in C but no C compiler is available for the target hardware, then this advantage is lost. It is very common for the first language to run on a new piece of hardware to be a threaded code language.

Extensibility enables adding the hooks for performance measurement and debugging, through extension of the compiler and the virtual machine language. For example, any single instruction may be redefined to include trace and reporting capabilities for use in debugging an application. Similarly, since nesting of control is often through a level of indirection, programs may be patched on the fly by modifying a pointer.

Architecture and Operation

The elements that characterize and define a language architecture are the basic data types, the data structures, and the control structures. These are very simple in most of the commercial threaded code languages.

In keeping with their very lean implementation, most of these languages are untyped. That is, the only data elements that can be passed between procedures are 16- or 32-bit signed integers, where the minimum number of bits in an argument is usually determined by the word size of the underlying hardware. Interpretation of the meaning of the integer then depends on the context in which it is used, for example, data may be interpreted as a number, address, or index into a table. Whatever the interpretation, it is determined by the routine in the context of the application and is not a part of the language. Thus, in common with many languages, the program's intention is first and only in the programmer's mind and is not declared in the language. Therefore there is room for error.

By contrast, some languages provide several built-in data types and may in addition permit the user to define other data types. Either the compiler or the run-time environment may perform type checking and thereby catch certain classes of programming error. Although threaded code systems generally provide little built-in capability for typing, because the compiler itself is extensible, such capabilities can be added if and when they are needed. For example, type checking could be controlled by a compiler option, which provides the benefits of both compile-time type checking and run-time type checking.

The only built-in data structure used by threaded languages is the stack. In fact, a threaded interpreter is an example of a stack machine. Generally these languages use two primary stacks, the data stack and the return stack. These are conventional push-down stacks of the sort that are supported in the majority of the modern micro- and minicomputer architectures. The essential difference is that, in most implementations of threaded code languages, these stacks are managed by the software, not the hardware.

The data stack is used to store the operands and return values that are passed between the threaded code programs. These programs are defined in the language without explicit arguments, generally expecting data on the stack in a predefined order and returning results to the data stack. Due to this stack architecture, it is often convenient, though not necessary, to use postfix notation as the basic syntactic convention for a procedure call, that is, naming the parameters last to first followed by the procedure name. The convention then is to think in terms of pushing the operands on the data stack and then calling the procedure. Alternative terminology for the data stack is parameter stack.

The return stack is used primarily to store program control-flow-parameters such as return addresses and loop parameters, but it may also be used for temporary data storage since there is no operational difference between the two stacks.

The data and return stacks and the two basic stack operations (push and pop) may be implemented as data structures and simple procedures, respectively. An example is given in the following C language code. (See Bradley 1986.)

```
/* Define stacks                                        */
long parameter_stack[PSSIZE+1];
long *return_stack[RSSIZE];

/* Define operations on a stack                         */
#define push(whatever)  *--sp = tos;  tos = (long)(whatever)
#define pop      tos;  tos = *sp++
```

As indicated by the code, a parameter stack can be implemented as an array of elements of the type long. The return stack is also an array, but since it primarily stores pointers to secondary definitions, the defined type of the elements in the return stack must be appropriate to the address space. The push and pop operations on the stacks are implemented as manipulations of pointers into the respective arrays.

The control structures commonly found in TCLs support, of course, the transfer of control from one procedure to another as well as both conditional execution and iteration, that is, constructs like *if . . . else . . . then, do . . . loop,* and *begin . . . until.* A discussion of the implementation of these control structures will be deferred until after we take a closer look at how procedure calls work. The structure of definitions is fundamental to the idea of threaded code, and procedure definition is the basic compiler operation.

Definitions are accessed through a data structure termed the *dictionary*. The dictionary entries contain, at the very least, a string that is the name of the procedure, in addition to a pointer to the code. Dictionaries are often implemented as linked lists. A variety of other information might also be contained in the dictionary. For example, version control information such as the creation date and author might be stored with the definitions. In some cases, multiple code pointers are permitted as well. These might be used in conjunction with a modifier word or phase in the source code that is detected at compile time and which results in different code being used in different contexts.

Common TCL implementations, particularly when built with the lower level implementation languages, simply set aside a region of memory to store both the dictionary and the definitions. Thus the basic memory areas—or data structures in the implementation architecture—are the dictionary, the parameter stack, and return stack. A memory map for a generic TCL implementation is illustrated in Figure 2.4.

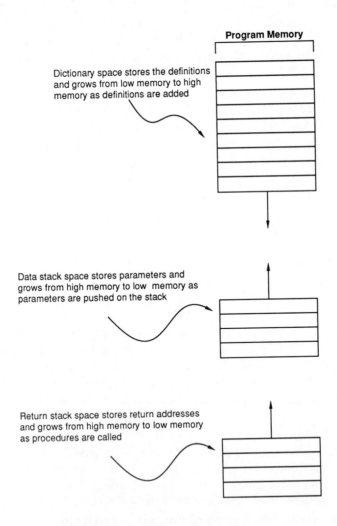

Figure 2.4. Memory Map for Generic TCL Implementation

Three memory areas are required for a minimal TCL: the dictionary space where definitions are compiled, the data stack, and the return stack. By convention, dictionary space grows up to the stack spaces.

To summarize, the basic TCL has the following architectural elements:

Element	Description
Data Stack	A memory with a mechanism to implement a LIFO stack.
Return Stack	A memory implemented like the data stack, with the difference that the return stack stores subroutine return addresses.
ALU	A component that performs arithmetic and logical computations on pairs of data elements.
TOS	A register that maintains a pointer to the top of the data stack.
IP	A register that holds the address of the next instruction to be executed.
Memory	Random access memory for program storage.

Given this architecture, a minimum set of basic operations in the language includes ALU operations such as addition and multiplication as well as bitwise OR, NOT, and AND; stack manipulation operations like duplicate, drop, and swap; memory fetch and store operations; and subroutine call and return instructions. A more fully formed TCL instruction set is reviewed at the end of the chapter.

Representation of Definitions

When a TCL is used to implement a virtual machine, the individual opcodes of the virtual machine that is being simulated are represented in the TCL by a data structure that has at least two fields, the code field and the parameter field. These fields usually occupy contiguous memory locations in the space allocated for the dictionary, although this is not strictly necessary.

The code field contains some representation of executable code, whether direct or indirect. As discussed earlier when the dictionary was introduced, this representation could be as simple as a pointer to the memory location of the code.

As was suggested earlier, dictionary entries for each definition can be built as a linked list, as illustrated in the following C code fragment:

```
struct d_e_t
    {
    struct d_e_t  *link;
     unsigned char flags;
     unsigned char name;
    };
```

In this example, the dictionary entry structure has two fields, one to hold a pointer to the next structure in the linked list (*link*), and a second to hold a pointer to the string that represents the name of the definition (*name*). This structure could be implemented in a similar way with assembly code. Most examples of this approach store some or all of the name string with the definition data structure.

Code Fields

A direct representation of the executable code is usually the code itself. In other words, the code field contains the code. This method of representation results in what is called direct threaded code. (See Figure 2.5.) One of the considerable advantages of direct threaded code is speed of execution. When an instruction of the virtual machine is decoded by the interpreter, control is transferred directly to executable code. Less direct representations of the code, which use pointers to executable code, ultimately represent overhead in the TCL execution cycle, as the interpreter must compute the location of the code.

One disadvantage of direct threaded code is that it takes up more space since some code could otherwise be shared between procedures. Depending on the application, this may not be an issue, and to some extent the increase in space can always be mitigated by sharing code through subdividing the procedure into smaller subprocedures. The net result is that a tradeoff of space for speed can still be made. Direct threaded code is often the better design choice for virtual machines where every last ounce of speed is critical.

An indirect representation of the executable code (indirect threaded code) can be done in a variety of ways. The simplest implementation is to represent the code with a pointer to its address. As mentioned, in this approach the overhead of decoding the address is added to each cycle of the interpreter. (See Figure 2.6.)

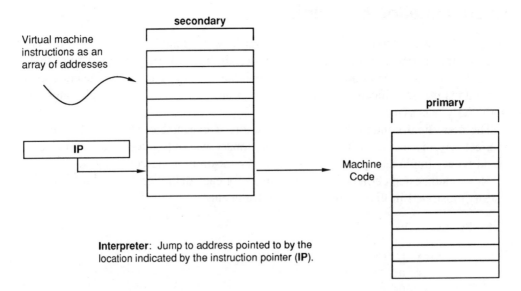

Interpreter: Jump to address pointed to by the location indicated by the instruction pointer (**IP**).

Figure 2.5. Direct Threaded Code

With direct threaded code, the code is represented by its address directly. In other words, when the opcode is interpreted as an address, executable code is found at that address. This design makes the interpreter for the virtual machine very efficient since the basic interpretation loop is fetch and jump.

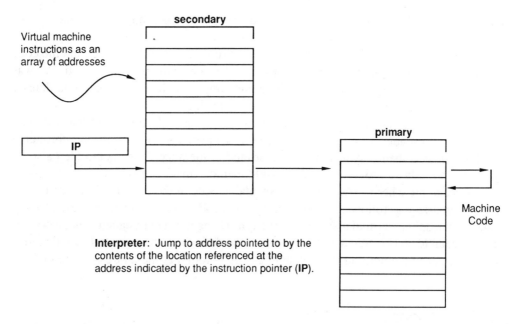

Figure 2.6. Indirect Threaded Code

With indirect threaded code, the code is represented by its address indirectly. In other words, when the opcode is interpreted as an address, that address contains a pointer to executable code. This design makes the interpreter for the virtual machine less efficient than for direct threaded code since the basic interpretation loop is fetch, fetch, and then jump. But this approach is very flexible since the interpretation of any opcode can be changed at run-time, and code can more easily be shared.

One of the advantages of an indirect representation is that it is easy to separate the code and the parameter fields. Some or all of the code fields can be in RAM, for example, while parameter fields are in ROM. Another advantage is that the code fields and therefore the opcode definitions themselves can be altered at run-time, for use in debugging, patching to fix bugs, and so on. Similarly, through indirection, multiple code fields, which are one way to implement context-sensitive definitions, can be made quite space efficient.

Indirection also enables the definition of functions that are of a higher order than procedures. For example, it becomes possible to create definitions for whole classes of procedures. This is done by parameterizing procedures of the class, with the define-time and run-time behavior specified at the time the class is defined. When a member of the new instruction class is used to define an individual procedure, indirection is used to facilitate sharing of code by the members of the class.

An indirect implementation that is slightly more complicated than a pointer to the code but one that can result in very compact code uses a token in the code field; the token is then used to find the executable code. If there are a small number of opcodes or procedures, this approach, also known as token threaded code, can be quite compact. For example, if the limit is 255 or fewer opcodes, an 8-bit token would suffice, and the code would theoretically be more dense than if 16- or 32-bit addresses were used. As was mentioned earlier, in the comments on byte encoding, conclusions about code density based on the minimum instruction size can be misleading.

Token threading can be a very useful technique if the code for the virtual machine needs to be relocatable since the executable code segments are always located through a table lookup. It is then easy to move them around in memory. They could then also be allocated from a heap providing more flexible memory management.

The three approaches to encoding the executable code in the code field of a definition can be summarized as follows. With direct threaded code, executable code is found at the address of the defined virtual machine instruction. Using indirect threaded code, a pointer to the executable code is found at the address of the defined instruction. In token threaded code, a pointer to a pointer to the executable code is found at the address of the defined instruction.

Type	Opcode Definition
Direct	The address of executable code.
Indirect	The address of the address of the code.
Token	An index into a lookup table of code addresses.

Parameter Fields

In the most general implementation approach for TCLs, the parameter field of the definition may contain a mixture of data, pointers to other definitions, and machine code. The data in a parameter field are usually literal values that are used as arguments to procedure calls, or they are control flow parameters that, for example, transfer control to the nth instruction following the current one. The pointers point to the addresses of the code fields of other definitions, and the address interpreter then uses these as its input. Machine code is in the parameter field only in the case of definitions of direct threaded code and, in these instances, only for primitive definitions. Whatever the parameter field contents, the main element of the threaded code interpreter is the address interpreter. It must be able to move through the parameter field as directed by the fields contents.

Address Interpreter

When a TCL is used as the basis of a virtual machine design, it is the address interpreter of the TCL that simulates the virtual machine by interpreting the sequence of opcode addresses in a virtual machine procedure. Interpretation consists of executing the code represented by the code field of the opcode definition. The opcode definition is accessed either directly or indirectly, depending on whether the code field is a direct or indirect representation of the executable code, as described earlier.

Executing the definition consists of executing the code referred to by the code field of the definition. Because each address in a secondary definition's parameter field may point to another secondary definition, one way to look at the parameter field is as a representation of a set of nodes in a call tree for the procedure that is implemented by the definition. (See Figure 2.7.)

The job of the address interpreter is simply to see that the call tree is traversed at run-time as specified in the procedure definition.

In many computer architectures, calls to subroutines are assembled as a CALL opcode, followed by the destination address. The parameter field of a definition for a threaded interpreter can be thought of as a sequence of subroutine calls, but with the

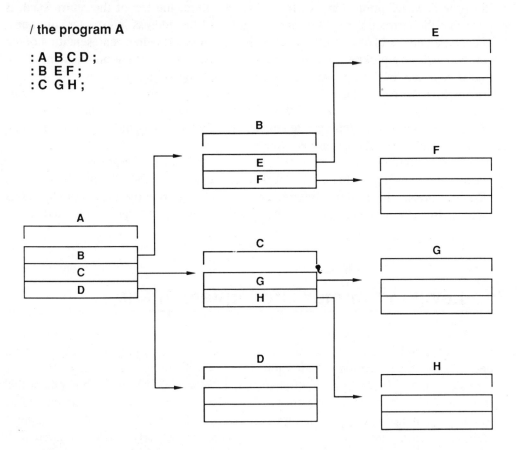

Figure 2.7. Threaded Code as a Tree Representation

A procedure implemented as threaded code can be viewed as a representation of the CALL tree for the procedure, where the tree is traversed at run-time by the opcode interpreter.

subroutine CALL opcodes removed. The result is more compact, somewhat slower, but much more flexible than the in-line code. Studies have shown that the penalty in speed is only 20% on average (see Leoliger, 1981, for a discussion of overhead in TCLs).

The main reason an address interpreter is slower than in-line code is that some of the processing of control information, including pointer manipulation, that the processor handles at the hardware level must now be handled by the software of the address interpreter. For some hardware, this difference is very slight.

As the address interpreter traverses the call tree, it maintains a virtual instruction register (it may just be a cell in memory that is used for storing the pointer) that points to the next element in the current definition. If the definition being called is itself a secondary definition, the contents of the virtual instruction register are saved on the return stack, and then the instruction register is reset to the first address in the parameter field of the new definition. On exit from this definition, the top of the return stack is popped into the instruction register, and execution of the address interpreter continues.

If the parameter field of a definition were simply a tree-structured representation of the subroutine calls of a program, we would achieve compactness as the only benefit of the threaded code approach. But we can do more, using opcodes for altering the flow of control within the parameter fields. Examples of the kinds of control flow operations usually available are *if . . . else . . . then, begin . . . end, begin . . . until,* and *do . . . loop.* Each of these are implemented using a small set of control flow primitives: conditional and unconditional jumps. (See Figure 2.8.)

The address interpreter is often referred to as the inner interpreter of the TCL. However, these languages are designed as interactive development environments, and so another interpreter, the top-level interpreter, is used to interpret the stream of characters that comes from the top-level input device, whether that is a terminal, or file, and so on.

Top-Level Interpreter and Implementation

Most threaded code interpreters use a very simple mechanism, implemented in threaded code, to enable the execution of definitions from a terminal command line or from any other means of supplying a stream of characters as input. The ability to implement this sort of mechanism in a very compact way means that a command line interpreter can be left embedded in the system. This in turn becomes an extremely useful feature in support of debugging during the development of the system, particularly when compared with much more limited capabilities offered by typical byte-encoded language implementations. For example, individual routines can be run by invoking the command line interpreter. New routines are defined and existing routines modified in the same way.

There are limitations to this approach. Since the input stream is interpreted one word at a time, the set of control flow instructions that can be used at the command line level

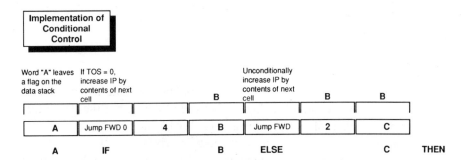

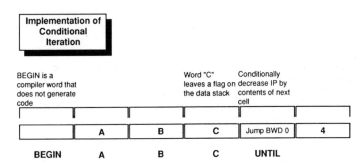

Figure 2.8. Implementation of Control Instructions

Rather than be limited to tracing out the CALL tree left-right and depth first, a simple set of control-flow primitives are used to modify subtree traversal order at run-time.

is very limited. In practice this is not a significant limitation because most implementations include components of the compiler along with the command line interpreter. With the ability to access the compiler from the top level, any test definition with complex control can be created as a single instruction, which is then invoked. Patch definitions may be created in a similar way.

The top-level interpreter is the familiar read-evaluate loop. In a threaded interpreter, the loop becomes

1. Parse a token from the input stream.

2. Decode the token to the address of the routine.

3. Execute the routine.

4. Repeat.

A token is taken here to mean some set of characters that are read in sequence from the input device. A space is the default delimiter between tokens, but the delimiter can be changed on the fly, so that token becomes a very flexible notion.

Before looking at the details of the threaded code interpreter itself, let's make the idea of the command line interpreter concrete by examining some C code that might be used to implement it. The code supports the claim that an interpreter can be made very compact and at the same time quite flexible. The basic control flow of the command line interpreter is outlined in the following code (from Bradley 1986):

```
outer_interpreter()
    {
    unsigned char *thisword;

/* V_STATE is a state variable that has two modes - interpreting or compiling      */
    V_STATE = (long)INTERPRETING;

/* initialize the global parameter stack pointer to the top of the parameter stack  */
    xsp = (&parameter_stack[PSSIZE]);

/* go into an infinite loop                                                          */
    while (1)
        {
/* initialize the return stack pointer to the top of the return stack               */
        xrp = &return_stack[RSSIZE];
        prompt();

/* TIB is "terminal input buffer" The cexpect function reads characters into the buffer */
        V_NUM_TIB = V_SPAN = cexpect(tibbuf, (long)TIBSIZE);
        V_TO_IN = 0;

        while ( (((thisword = blword())[0]) != 0)
            && interpret_word(thisword) )
            {
/* reset the parameter stack pointer if underflow                                    */
            if ( xsp > (&parameter_stack[PSSIZE]) )
                {
                xsp = (&parameter_stack[PSSIZE]);
                error("Stack Underflow \n");
                break;
                }

/* reset the parameter stack pointer if overflow                                     */
            if ( xsp < parameter_stack )
                {
                xsp = (&parameter_stack[PSSIZE]);
```

```
                    error("Stack Overflow /n");
                    break;
                    }
                }
            }
        }
```

The function that does the work in the command line interpreter is the interpret_word function. Its job is to take a blank delimited string from the input stream and then decide what to do next. Everything else is either stack bookkeeping or token parsing.

Interpret_word's action depends on the machine state and the instruction type. The machine can be in either compile or interpret mode. A token can reference either a primitive or a secondary definition. If the machine is in interpreter mode, the referenced routine is executed; otherwise, the address of the routine is compiled in the dictionary space. In the following implementation, if the routine is a primitive routine, a reference number is stored instead of its address. The reference number is a token in its own right. It is decoded by a switch statement, which transfers control to the appropriate code. This switch construct is discussed later.

Code for a C language implementation of the interpret_word function is as follows:

```
interpret_word(str)
    unsigned char *str;
    {
    long tp = (long)canonical(str);
    int immed;

/* the function finf searches an array for the word                              */
    if ((immed = find(&tp)) != 0)
        {
/* If the word we found is a primitive, use its primitive number instead of its cfa   */
/* The constant MAXPRIM indicates the maximum number of primitives                 */
        if ( *(long *)tp < MAXPRIM  &&  *(long *)tp >= 0 )
        tp = *(long *)tp;

/* if the state is interpreting, execute the definition                          */
        if ( immed > 0 || V_STATE == (long)INTERPRETING )
            execute_one(tp);
        else
/* otherwise enclose the token in the dictionary                                 */
        *dp++ = tp;
        }
    else if ( !handle_literal(str) )
        {
        where();
        if ( V_STATE == (long)COMPILING )
            {*dp++ = (long)LOSE;}
        else
        return(0);
        }
    return(1);
    }
```

The *immed* parameter that is referenced in this piece of code needs some explaining. When the interpreter is in compile mode, definitions that are classed as immediate are executed immediately and not compiled into the definition. This is how compiler directives are implemented. As it turns out, this is the means to make the compiler extensible as well, since any new definition can be declared to be immediate and the new immediate words can be used to add to the compiler capabilities.

Whether at compile-time or at run-time, a definition is executed by calling the inner-interpreter, through the execute_one routine from the function interpret_word. The design of the inner-interpreter is illustrated by the following C code:

```
inner_interpreter(ip)
    register long *ip;
    {
    register long *sp = xsp;
    register long *token;
    register long tos = *sp++;
    register long **rp = xrp;

    register long scr;
    register unsigned char *ascr;
    unsigned char *ascr1;
    long lscr, lscr1;

    while(1)
        {
        token = *(long **)ip++;
        doprim:
        if ((long) token >= MAXPRIM)
        goto docf;
        switch ((int)token)
            {
            case 0:
            error("Tried to execute a null token\n");
            goto abort;
            case NOT:     tos =           ~ tos; continue;
            case AND:     tos = *sp++ & tos; continue;
            case OR:      tos = *sp++ | tos; continue;
            case XOR:     tos = *sp++ ~ tos; continue;
```

As mentioned earlier, the inner-interpreter is essentially a large case statement that handles the primitive routines as known cases and simulates function calls to handle the defined routines. In the parameter field of a definition, references to a primitive appear as the primitive number, which is used by the switch statement at run-time to get to the right code. The set of primitive routines can be extended simply by inserting the appropriate code into the switch statement. The operation, as described, makes for the most efficient code, with tradeoffs available in terms of space, and in many cases portability, if the primitive routines are coded in machine code. The usual practice is to extend the set of primitives only after analysis of the application to determine the procedures that consume the bulk of the processing time.

The secondary definitions are handled via the same switch mechanism. This happens in one of several ways, depending on the kind of definition. There are at least four kinds of definition, as follows:

Definition Type	Switch
Constant	DOCON
Variable	DOVAR
Procedure	DOCOLON
Code	DOCODE

Consider the following example of C code that handles the several cases of defined (secondary) procedures. This segment appears as the default in the main switch construct that handles the primary definitions.

```
        default:
        docf:
        if ((scr = (long)*token++) >= MAXCF)
            goto dodoes;
        switch ((int)scr)
            {
            case DOCOLON:  *--rp = ip; ip = token;     continue;
            case DOCON:    push ( *(long *) (token) );  continue;
            case DOVAR:    push ( token );              continue;
            case DOCODE:   (*(int (*) ())token)();     .continue;

            dodoes:
/* Push parameter field address                                */
                push ( token );
/* Use the code field as the address of a secondary definition */
                *--rp = ip;
                ip = (long *)*--token;
                continue;
            }
        }
    }
```

The simplest case illustrated here is the code for handling defined constants. When executed, the contents of the following memory location (the first element of the parameter field) are pushed on the parameter stack. A related case is the code for defined variables; on execution the address of the next memory location is pushed onto the parameter stack. This is like a defined constant but with a level of indirection.

What gives the threaded interpreter its power is the threading of segments of code that is handled at run-time by the third case, DOCOLON. In this situation, the current contents of the instruction pointer are saved to the return stack, and the instruction pointer is reset to point to the first memory location of the parameter field. In effect this is a CALL to the defined procedure as execution proceeds. The term "colon" refers to the token that in most threaded languages invokes the compiler and begins the definition of a new subroutine.

The DOCODE procedure is used much like DOCOLON except that the subsequent code in the parameter field is machine code. DOCODE differs from the machine code in a primary definition in that it appears as one of the instructions in the parameter field of a definition, and it indicates that the next section of code is to be interpreted immediately as a primitive.

The last case is *dodoes,* which handles higher order procedure definitions. The parameters of these sorts of definitions are compiled into the parameter field when the procedure is defined. The code field points to the run-time procedure that applies to all procedures of the class. The parameters of the individual instance of the class are passed to the run-time code via a pointer on the data stack.

The name of the *dodoes* instruction suggests its semantics. The syntax of the *dodoes* procedure is *do . . . does . . .* which specifies what to *do* when an instance of the instruction is created, and what a member of the class *does* at run-time. For example, the class of pattern-matching instructions used in the virtual machine outlined in the second section of this chapter might be defined in the code for the compiler/assembler using the *dodoes* construct. The *do* part of the definition would be used to capture type information about the instruction that would then be passed at run-time (during execution of the assembler) to a single procedure defined by the *does* part of the definition.

With this approach, the compiler/assembler becomes very compact because code is reused as much as possible. It is also readily extensible since defining new members of a class of instructions is very easy. Finally, the assembler itself is interactive and allows the developer to assemble the code line by line from a development terminal. The ability to do this can be very important for debugging or building system patches.

FORTH Language

The FORTH language is the best known and most widely available of the popular high-level languages implemented with the threaded code technique. There are a number of large commercial suppliers of the language, and several professional computer programming and engineering associations support FORTH interest groups. FORTH interest groups also communicate through electronic bulletin boards on public networks like Compuserve and GENIE. There is a journal, *The Journal of FORTH Application and Research* (JFAR), that publishes research on software and hardware topics related to FORTH four times a year.

Major FORTH conferences are held at least twice a year in the United States, in Rochester, N.Y., in June and at Asilomar, Calif. in November. Conference sponsors include the IEEE and major research laboratories. The conferences are international in scope, with attendees from Europe, Australia, and the Far East. In addition, there is usually one international conference per year, most often in Europe, but FORTH conferences have been held in Australia and China. Conferences are usually organized around a theme, and Artificial Intelligence, Object-Oriented Systems, and Embedded Systems have been recent topics. *Embedded Systems Programming* magazine features mainly FORTH and C as the major programming languages for embedded systems implementation.

There are two major dialects of FORTH and several derivative languages. An ANSII standard for FORTH is under development. The progress of the standards committee is regularly reported on the bulletin boards and in the monthly FORTH magazine, *FORTH Dimensions*.

FORTH played a major role in the early stages of the evolution of software for the Apple Macintosh computer and the products of Sun Microsystems. The Macintosh example is testimony to the ease with which FORTH can be ported to new machines and operating environments. The compactness and extensibility of threaded code languages were the major features exploited by Sun Microsystems.

In common with others of the threaded code language class, FORTH has extensive support for the virtual machine approach to systems development. The language itself is built around an extensible, interactive compiler that can be implemented in a minimum amount of memory—some in less than 2K bytes for a full interpreter and compiler.

As in any threaded language, a FORTH program is built as a hierarchy of small subroutines. Each subroutine is termed a word in the FORTH terminology. There does exist a small set of words that forms the basic word set in a "standard" FORTH implementation. For a good introduction to the language, see Haydon (1983) and Brodie (1982, 1984).

A glossary of the FORTH basic word set is presented here. Each definition is followed by a "stack picture," designed to illustrate the state of the parameter stack before and after the word is executed. In this formalism, N represents a number, FLAG represents a logical constant (-1 if true, 0 if false) and ADDR represents an address. The format of the stack picture is (before–after), thus the input parameters are on the left and the output is on the right. Where multiple elements are on the stack, the top of the stack is to the right.

FORTH Glossary

0	(-- 0)	Push the integer 0 onto the stack.
0<	(N1 -- FLAG)	Return TRUE if N1 is less than 0.
0=	(N1 -- FLAG)	Return TRUE if N1 is equal to 0.

0>	(N1 -- FLAG)	Return TRUE if N1 is greater than 0.
0BRANCH	(N1 --)	If N1 is FALSE (0), branch to the address in the next memory location.
1+	(N1 -- N2)	Add 1 to N1.
1-	(N1 -- N2)	Subtract 1 from N1.
2+	(N1 -- N2)	Add 2 to N1.
2*	(N1 -- N2)	Multiply N1 by 2.
2/	(N1 -- N2)	Divide N1 by 2.
4+	(N1 -- N2)	Add 4 to N1.
<	(N1 N2 -- FLAG)	Return TRUE if N1 is less than N2.
<>	(N1 N2 -- FLAG)	Return TRUE if N1 is not equal to N2.
=	(N1 N2 -- FLAG)	Return TRUE if N1 is equal to N2.
>R	(N1 --)	Push N1 onto the return stack.
>	(N1 N2 -- FLAG)	Return TRUE if N1 is greater than N2.
!	(N1 ADDR --)	Store N1 at location ADDR.
+	(N1 N2 -- N3)	Add N1 to N2.
<	(N1 N2 -- FLAG)	Return TRUE if N1 is less than N2.
+!	(N1 ADDR --)	Add N1 to the value pointed to by ADDR.
-	(N1 N2 -- N3)	Subtract N2 from N1.
:	(--)	Start the definition of a subroutine.
;	(--)	End the definition of a subroutine.
?DUP	(N1 -- N1 N1)	Duplicate N1 if N1 is nonzero.
	(N1 -- N1)	N1 if N1 is zero.
@	(ADDR -- N1)	Fetch the number stored at ADDR.
ABS	(N1 -- N2)	N2 is the absolute value of N1.
AND	(N1 N2-- N3)	Bitwise N1 and N2 to give N3.
BRANCH	(--)	Unconditionally branch to the address in the next memory location.
DROP	(N1 --)	Drop N1 from the stack.
DUP	(N1 -- N1 N1)	Duplicate the top of the stack.
I	(-- N1)	Return the index of the currently active loop.
I'	(-- N1)	Return the limit of the currently active loop.
J	(-- N1)	Return the index of the outer loop in a nested loop.
LEAVE	(--)	Force an exit from a loop.
NEGATE	(N1 -- N2)	N2 is the two's complement of N1.
NOP	(--)	Do nothing.
NOT	(FLAG1 -- FLAG2)	Synonym for 0=.
OR	(N1 N2-- N3)	Bitwise or of N1 and N2 to give N3.
OVER	(N1 N2-- N1 N2 N1)	Push a copy of the second element of the stack onto the stack.
PICK	(... N1 -- ... N2)	Push a copy of the N1-th element of the stack on the stack.
R>	(-- N1)	Pop the top element of the return stack.
R@	(-- N1)	Copy the top element of the return stack.
ROLL	(... N1 -- ... N2)	Move the N1-th element of the stack to the top of the stack.
ROT	(N1 N2 N3 -- N2 N3 N1)	Move the third element of the stack to the top of the stack.

SWAP	(N1 N2 -- N2 N1)	Swap the order of the top two elements of the stack.
U<	(U1 U2 -- FLAG)	Return TRUE if U1 is less than U2 (unsigned).
U>	(U1 U2 -- FLAG)	Return TRUE if U1 is greater than U2 (unsigned).
U*	(U1 U2 -- U3)	Multiply U1 by U2 to give U3 (unsigned).

Conclusion: Virtual Machines for Expert Systems

The most popular high-level languages that are based on the fundamental reasoning and representation technologies used to build expert systems are OPS5 and Prolog. Although related systems are founded on the underlying inference procedures, OPS5 and Prolog are the most fully formed of their respective classes. OPS5 is perhaps the leading member of the class of languages based on forward chaining as the reasoning paradigm. Prolog is undoubtably the most widely used language based on backward chaining as the problem-solving approach.

In addition, OPS5 represents an approach to mechanizing reasoning based on research in cognitive science. Prolog represents models based on systems of formal logic.

Both these languages have well-understood virtual machines, with a literature on their architecture and a series of implementations extending over approximately twenty years. The virtual machines contain instruction sets useful for implementing classes of languages of which OPS5 and Prolog are instances.

In the following chapters we take a close look at these virtual machines as well as the design approaches that underlie their implementation in various languages. Where the instructions of the virtual machine are the object language, taking a close look at the instruction set may suggest extensions or restrictions of values for particular applications. By the same token, taking a close look at the implementation could uncover opportunities to further tune and compact the implementation, which may in turn enable embedding expertise in new applications.

Implementation via a threaded code approach has the advantage of the conciseness, interactivity, and portability that are the strengths of threaded code development systems. Direct implementation in a higher level language like C may have some advantages where performance is absolutely critical and alternative hardware solutions are not an option, although this is tough to decide ahead of time, being dependent as it is on the quality of the C compiler.

In the chapters that follow, we use a mix of C and FORTH approaches to implementation. A review of FORTH usage in AI programs can be found in the article by Trelease (1987).

Chapter 3 **Production Systems**

Introduction

The original production systems were designed to be models of human problem solving. Researchers in the cognitive sciences developed the basic architecture of the models. Computer scientists then built the programs. The work on these architectures and their efficient implementation eventually led to the OPS class of programming languages.

The problem-solving approach used in the OPS languages is often called forward chaining. Forward chaining is a useful computational mechanism that is particularly good for search procedures, its merits as a cognitive model aside. Forward chaining, as used in production systems, is also a major technology of Expert Systems.

The languages that descended from OPS have evolved into fully formed development languages. These include much of the software that is firmly at the high end of the commercial expert system toolkits. A number of these toolkits provide the means to incorporate application code in embedded systems. Three of these are ART, from Inference Corporation; the Goldworks system from Gold Hill; and the public domain CLIPS system developed under contract by NASA. They represent the high-end of expert system development tools, PC-based tools, and public domain systems, respectively.

This chapter starts with a brief discussion of production systems in general and their use in embedded systems. Next we take a close look at the implementation of a production system language, using a threaded code approach. This particular production system is called FORPS (FORTH-based Production System). FORPS is very simple but fast and was designed for and has been embedded in control systems. It serves as a good case study of the implementation of the most basic functionality of the technology, with an eye towards using it in embedded systems.

FORPS is an example of one of the simplest approaches to building forward-chaining reasoning. CLIPS is an example of a production system language with many more features, and the complexity of its implementation in comparison with the simpler threaded code approach is worth some study. CLIPS (C Language Integrated Production System) uses C as the implementation language.

Understanding the implementation of a computer language, particularly a sophisticated language technology like production systems, is necessary to properly guide its use, control its side effects, and have confidence in its results. All of these are essential in embedded systems programming. This is the reason for studying these implementations in depth.

Production Systems Overview

The basic components of a production system language are a set of rules, a working memory, and an inference mechanism. The inference mechanism is based on a recognize-act cycle. Thus the problem-solving process that is to be applied to a particular problem (for example, diagnosing a fault or planning an action) is modeled by the rules developed for the application. Information about a problem instance is kept in the working memory while the problem is being solved, and the process is driven by the recognize-act cycle. There are many good discussions of the basic technology to draw from for more background information, example applications, and design approaches. For example, see the book on OPS5 by Brownston et al. (1985).

Now you might ask, if you understand the information you need and the process required to solve a problem, why not just write the program in a procedural language? The fact is that some real-world problem-solving processes can get pretty complex— more complex than procedural languages were designed for. After all, procedural languages were by and large designed to crunch numbers, not symbols.

With a procedural language, the programmer directs the problem-solving process from a model that is determined before the program runs—generally a program in a procedural programming language does not have to recognize the situation it's in before deciding where to transfer control. Instead, every possible situation and all the processes for dealing with them are spelled out in a system specification beforehand. When being able to adjust to the situation on the fly is important, production system languages can be very useful. The same holds true if many special situations need to be considered, and a developer cannot be expected to know them all in advance. (An example of this appears at the end of the chapter.)

This is not to say that careful specification and the other methods of conventional software engineering can be laid aside when building production systems. In general, adding rules ad hoc to handle new situations does not work for any but the smallest systems. What the production system technology does bring is a more natural means of programming for complexity.

So, the distinguishing characteristic of a production system is the inference mechanism, which provides pattern-directed control of the problem-solving process. The elements of the working memory model the state of the problem search space as the problem-solving process progresses. As an aside, it is worth mentioning that this working memory representation of the problem search space is problematic for most production systems because they do not allow you to build very sophisticated models—but more about that later. First let's talk about the most important element of the production system, the rule. Rules are what describe and guide the pattern-directed search.

Rules

Rules are also called *productions*. A production is a way to represent the pairing of a condition and an action, which underlies the pattern-directed search. Rules usually have the following syntax with the corresponding meaning:

```
IF the condition holds THEN perform the action
```

The condition and the action in the preceding prototype rule can be defined via logical connectives in terms of simpler conditions and actions. The terms "production" and "rule" are used interchangeably in this chapter to refer to the same IF . . . THEN . . . source code structure.

The role of the condition part of the production—the left-hand side of the rule, or LHS—is to describe the problem situations in which the actions may be relevant in solving the problem. For example,

```
IF the engine won't start
   and the spark plugs have an irregular spark THEN . . .
```

One very common way of encoding the situation description in the LHS is with a pattern. Patterns on the LHS can include variables to provide an existential semantics (something exists that satisfies a condition) as well as a parameterization of the rules. The LHS may also use general predicates outside the pattern-matching procedure.

Variables in production system languages are used like variables in procedural languages as a handy way to refer to the same piece of information within the scope of a production. Predicates are tests that can be used to evaluate the current situation outside the operation of the pattern matcher. The simpler production systems do away with the overhead of a pattern-matching mechanism and allow only predicates functions in the LHS.

The action part of the production—the right-hand side of the rule, or RHS—defines the problem-solving steps associated with solution of a problem in a particular situation. The problem-solving steps are generally procedures. In the preceding example, the action(s) necessary to solve the problem might be *change the spark plugs*.

The good news is that a production system provides a straightforward encoding of expertise with very natural semantics. Therefore, the expression of the problem-solving strategy is straightforward. The bad news is that in existing production system languages the pattern description language that can be used in productions to represent situations is quite limited in power. This means ultimately that encoding a representation of the knowledge about objects in a form that the expert might use is very difficult, and the system's ability to handle complex situations is limited. The source of this limitation is threefold:

1. The permitted representations of the state of the world have limited expressiveness. The lowest level of representation includes the memory elements, but in most cases these are just N-tuples. N-tuples are interpreted as relations (rows in a table, as in a relational database) over atoms and numbers. For example, a memory element representing an integrated sensor element in some system might be

   ```
   (sensor A25-X blood_pressure low 35mv 10:15:45)
   ```

   where the first term is interpreted as the name of the relation (that is, sensor), and the remaining terms are the values of the fields in this instance of the relation (field names from left to right are *sensor_id*, *sensor_type*, *reliability*, *most_recent_reading*, and *time_of_reading*).

2. The pattern descriptions on the LHS are built only from the logical connectives AND, OR, and NOT plus the simple relations that constitute the working memory. There is thus both little internal structure to the relations and a limited set of connectives to use in forming more complicated structures. However, the evaluation of functions may be allowed in the LHS of a production to determine field values for a candidate match.

3. The matching process is not intelligent. This is a common characteristic of practical commercial pattern matchers and is a limitation that is accepted for the sake of efficiency. A pattern matcher might be considered intelligent if it considered $2+2$ to match the number 4.

The main reason for using the built-in test mechanism based on pattern matching is to make the programming style more declarative. A declarative style should make it easier for the programmer to state what should happen and not to worry about how it happens. This could be done with a good description language and a powerful inference mechanism. However, in most cases, the simplicity of the pattern description language defeats this purpose, and procedural tests are ultimately more useful. They are more flexible and faster.

When the LHS of the production is matched with the contents of working memory and/or the indicated tests are successful, the actions on the RHS of the production are performed. The conventional terminology used here is to say that the rule is "fired." The result of at least one of the RHS actions is usually to alter the contents of working memory by asserting or retracting an element of working memory. This changes the description of the situation and enables other rules to fire. However, the "action" on the RHS of the production can be any computer program, and therefore the application may in theory be connected with any number and kind of device in the outside world, including effectors such as motors or relays or sensors on the front end of data acquisition devices.

Working Memory Elements

The contents of the working memory area are called, simply, working memory elements (WMEs). As noted earlier, in expressive power, the WMEs are usually fairly primitive, that is, they are able only to represent simple relations between things, and things are represented only by their reference atom. For example, a machine might have many attributes like mass, volume, and power conversion efficiency, and relations to many other objects like its power supply or other machines to which it might be supplying power. Yet a WME might only be able to represent that machine in a relation by an atomic reference or name, like *machine_1*.

It is common practice to refer to the information in WMEs as *facts,* although the term *working memory element* is more descriptive. They are data structures after all. In reality facts are much richer than bits and bytes, the constituent elements of WMEs.

The working memory area, by virtue of all the data it contains, should constitute a detailed and complete description of the current state of the problem-solving process. It is exactly this (potentially very large) state description that is matched against the condition pattern of the productions. Alternatively the state might be tested through some procedure. These descriptions and tests are used in any combination to select the appropriate problem-solving actions. The *actions* parts of productions may then alter the contents of working memory to reflect either the new state that exists as a result of the action, or a new description of the state enabled by a recognition of a pattern.

For example, if the collection of WMEs in working memory constitutes an alarm condition, and that condition is recognized by a production, one of the actions of the product may be to add a WME to indicate that the alarm condition has been recognized. This statement of recognition, perhaps in conjunction with some other statements of recognition, may then match the LHS of some other production. This other production fires in turn.

WMEs are the grist for the basic inference procedure of the production system—the recognize-act cycle.

The Recognize-Act Cycle

The pure production system model uses a simple control mechanism, the recognize-act cycle. The recognize-act cycle is the problem-solving process. During the recognize phase of the cycle, the patterns in memory are matched against the conditions of all the productions in the system, the specified tests are performed, and the productions that have their LHS satisfied are collected in a set. This collection is called the conflict set because now there can be a conflict if there is more than one production with a satisfied LHS. One of the productions in the set is selected in a separate step called conflict resolution, and the action part of the production is performed—the production is "fired." After the selected production has fired the recognize-act cycle is repeated. The program terminates when no rule conditions are satisfied by the contents of working memory, or on an explicit terminate action.

The recognize-act cycle is efficient enough for practical use when based on the RETE (Latin for *net*) match algorithm. The RETE match algorithm effectively trades space for time by saving the match state between recognize-act cycles. Only incremental changes need be evaluated on the recognize cycle.

The creation of WMEs triggers a comparison between the new WME and all condition elements in all the rules in the program, and links are made between the WMEs and all the condition elements they match. The net result is that only net additions or deletions to working memory are matched on each recognize-act cycle. The assumption, of course, is that only small changes to working memory are being made on each cycle. Large changes such as updating all sensor readings on each cycle may magnify the impact of slight inefficiencies in the matching process on overall performance.

But you may not need or want to trade space for time. If so, the RETE net may not be the best choice. Some of these alternatives are discussed later when we describe a very simple production system based on a threaded code virtual machine.

To match WMEs efficiently, the condition elements of all the productions are compiled into a memory network of test nodes called the RETE net. Each node in the net is the internal representation of one of the tests (patterns) in a condition element. Within the network, nodes are connected in the order in which the tests occur in the condition element. Part of the pattern-matching procedure involves following pointers through the network and performing the tests that they point to.

The condition elements share nodes in the network where possible in order to efficiently use the available memory. The amount of sharing that can be used depends on the sophistication of the network compiler, which takes the source code (of productions), analyzes it, and generates the data structures representing the net.

When a WME is created, a reference to the WME is passed to the top node in the network and the pattern-matching component of the inference engine takes over. The pattern matcher is responsible for determining whether or not the WME passes the test represented by each node. For example, in a monitoring application a test in rules about blood pressure might look to see if the third element of the WME is the atom *blood_pressure*.

If the WME passes the test at the top node, the reference is passed on to the next node for the next test and so on, until either the test fails or until a terminal node of the network is reached. Reaching a terminal node signifies the successful match of all the condition elements of a production. Thus, if this point is reached, the action part of the production is placed on a list, in order of its priority, with the action parts of all the other productions that have been activated. This list is called the *agenda,* and rules on the agenda are referred to as *instantiations.*

The basic compilation strategy for production system rules is therefore to build an internal network representation of the tests in the condition elements of the productions.

Some of the early production system languages (notably OPS5) used elaborate conflict resolution strategies to determine which of the activated productions to fire. These resolution strategies were designed with the modeling of human cognitive processing in mind. The following criteria are commonly used in conflict resolution strategies:

Criterion	Description
Refraction	Refraction is a term from the neurosciences referring to the relative inexcitability of a neuron immediately after it has fired. In production systems it refers to a conflict resolution criterion that is virtually a necessity in order to prevent infinite loops. Refraction is designed to ensure that the same instantiation never fires more than once.
Recency	Recency chooses the instantiations that have been matched by the most recent WMEs. Both recency and refraction strategies require time tags for both WMEs and instantiations.
Specificity	With this criterion more specific rules are given priority over the less specific. Specificity is defined in terms of the LHS complexity. A LHS with more condition elements is deemed more specific than a LHS with fewer conditions.
Arbitrary choice	When all else fails, toss a coin.

These criteria are incorporated into the two conflict resolution strategies of OPS5, LEX (lexographic sort) and MEA (means-ends analysis). The LEX strategy uses the conflict resolution criteria in a four-part process:

1. Eliminate rules that have already fired (refraction).

2. Order instantiations based on recency, and select the most recent.

3. Order the most recent instantiations by specificity.

4. Choose arbitrarily from the set with highest specificity.

The MEA analysis adds one more step to the process, a step that is useful in implementing control strategies for rule sets:

1. Eliminate rules that have already fired (refraction).

2a. Order instantiations based on recency of the WMEs matching the first condition element.

2b. Order instantiations based on recency of all matching WMEs, and select the most recent.

3. Order the most recent instantiations by specificity.

4. Choose arbitrarily from the set with highest specificity.

These conflict resolution strategies result in some interesting behaviors but at the cost of the speed of the problem-solving process. Much simpler strategies can be used. For example, the conflict might be resolved by choosing the first rule to enter the set. This would certainly be quick. Another alternative, and this is the strategy used by most commercial systems with the exception of OPS5, is to have the programmer assign each rule an associated priority number. The rule with the highest priority is selected from the conflict set.

Issues for Embedded Production Systems

The pure production system model is not necessarily well suited to embedded applications where asynchronous peripheral events may logically influence the recognize-act cycle during operation. This is especially true where the time taken for the recognize-act cycle is longer than the mean time at which new information becomes available externally. For example, in a situation where consideration of the most up-to-date information may be critical to deciding on the proper actions, data acquisition processes may need to be continually acquiring data and creating working memory elements.

Typical rule-firing rates for production systems are on the order of one to several hundred rules per second, implying a recognize-act cycle time that is on the order of milliseconds. This imposes a practical lower limit on the characteristic times of the peripheral processes. This limit would, for example, restrict the applicability of production systems for use in feedback controllers, where delays in the feedback path can turn negative feedback into positive feedback.

Process and machine control applications provide a number of good examples of systems where there is a need to react very quickly to changes in the environment. Yet, even from the brief discussion in the last section, it should be clear that the recognize-act cycle might not be easily interrupted to take advantage of any new information that might be available.

The analogy is with more conventional system operation where the options for input handling are polling or interrupts. Interrupts are the best way to handle inputs that could occur at any time, and where it is important not to lose data. Keyboard handlers are one example. Polling is useful for handshake data transfers, where the system can control the input data rate. Most production systems designs for data acquisition or control find polling is the only practical alternative. Either interrupt handlers do not exist or the data must be buffered. In either case, response to changes is slower than the changes themselves.

A good example is the system for space shuttle telemetry monitoring developed with CLIPS (Muratore et al. 1989). Buffer layers are used in the system to match the data rates with the capabilities of the individual processing components of the system. Data acquisition is performed with special purpose hardware that can handle input at 200 kilobits per second rates. Data conversion software then produces aggregate information at a rate of 2000 parameters per second. Procedural programs then implement algorithms for detecting and signaling conditions associated with the problem. For example, an alarm might be signaled if a voltage falls below a predetermined level. The algorithms produce changes in CLIPS working memory at a rate of 350 facts per second. The CLIPS program is then able to make assessments at rates near 1 per second.

Other approaches to the problem of embedding production systems in real-time operating environments have been explored. Most use production systems like CLIPS that are implemented in languages other than LISP (see Skapura 1989).

A related issue for embedded production systems is the problem of accessing WMEs outside the scope of a rule, as might be necessary to integrate data acquisition subsystems. A few commercial production systems permit this by providing hooks to the RETE net maintenance procedures. Other solutions to this problem have also been described (Dress 1986 a and b). A workaround for the commercial systems like OPS5 that do not have convenient hooks would be to have most, if not all, rules invoke an action that incorporated information from the external sources as a natural part of each cycle.

A second and related issue is the consistency of the RETE net, which cannot be guaranteed in the event that WMEs are created and processed out of synch with the regular recognize-act cycle. Thus synchronization of external sources of data with the recognize-act cycle is preferred.

These problems arise in part from the complexity of the mechanism involved in managing the RETE net. This mechanism exists primarily to increase the recognize-act cycle's efficiency of operation where there are large working memories and large numbers of rules—where it therefore becomes impractical to test every condition of every rule on every cycle. However, for small rule sets that may not need an explicit working memory, the production system can be streamlined considerably.

An example of such a system is FORPS (FORTH-based Production System). It is a forward-chaining rule-based system with no formal representation of a working memory, and it represents a very stripped down production system mechanism.

Introduction to FORPS

FORPS is a production system language developed under NASA contract. The system is implemented in threaded code using FORTH. It was developed as part of the Advanced Integrated Maintenance System (AIMS) at Oak Ridge National Laboratory, and it was first applied as part of an obstacle avoidance system embedded in a Servo-Manipulator.

Since the system was embedded, and part of a controller, speed and compactness were of primary importance in the design. Under the assumption that the number of rules in the production system would be relatively small, the space required by the RETE-net was traded off against the time required to do an exhaustive search of the rules on each recognize-act cycle. To support the search, rule information is stored in a table (Figure 3.1).

This rule table contains the basic information for each rule: identifying number, a pointer to the LHS code, a pointer to the RHS code, the activation state of the rule, and the rule priority. The table structure makes the top-level code for the inference procedure straightforward, as illustrated by the following FORTH code:

```
: FORPS ( -- )  \evaluate conditions - actions until none fire
   ThisRule @ LastRule !
   Cycle OFF                    \ counts number of times through the rules
   begin
       1 Cycle +!
       SetDefault               \ clear activation fields
       TestRules                \ run all conditions (antecedents)
       DoBestRule               \ execute best action (consequent)
   until  ;                     \ until no activity
```

The first action in the inference procedure is to set a pointer to the last rule in the table and to clear the cycle counter. On each cycle, the contents of the activation state field of the rule table is cleared for all rules, and then the condition of each rule is executed. In this production system, evaluation is simply a matter of running the code pointed to by the contents of the condition field in the rule table. The result of running a condition is placed in the corresponding activation field.

After all the rules are tested, each activation cell contains either a TRUE or a NIL flag, indicating whether the rule is activated or not. The conflict resolution strategy is then executed to determine which rule to fire.

RULE #	C-PFA	A-PFA	Activation	Priority
RULE 1	4020	4134	0	8
.	.	.	.	.
.	.	.	.	.
.	.	.	.	.
.	.	.	.	.
RULE N	4908	5030	-1	0

The internal representation of rules in FORPS is a simple table that stores the parameter field addresses of the condition and the action code (C-PFA and A-PFA, respectively), the priority of the rule, and the status of the rule in the current cycle (-1 is interpreted as an activated rule).

Figure 3.1. The Rule Table in FORPS

Rules in FORPS are compiled into a table. Each table entry contains pointers to the code for the LHS and the RHS of the rule, as well as an activation flag and information about the priority of the rule.

As mentioned earlier, the strategy in FORPS is to simply pick the activated rule with the highest priority. Alternate conflict resolution strategies could be used. Some of these may require changing the structure of the rule table.

The top-level loop continues until there are no active rules at the end of a cycle or until a HALT instruction is executed as an action in a preceding rule.

FORPS uses a simple syntax for rules:

```
RULE: <name>            \ define the rule with name "<name>"
PRIORITY: <number>      \ define the priority as <number>
    *IF*                \ start of LHS condition
    <condition1>        \ start of a FORTH program returning
                        \ TRUE or FALSE
    <condition2>        \ each condition is a single FORTH
                        \ procedure
                        \ these are implicitly ANDed
      .
      .
    <conditionN>        \ end of LHS
    *THEN*              \ start of RHS actions
    <action1>           \ a FORTH program
    <action2>           \ likewise
      .
      .
    <actionN>
    *END*               \ end of RHS
```

The rule syntax in FORPS is a good example of how the FORTH compiler can be modified to directly support a new language as an extension of FORTH. The RULE: word is an extension of the : (colon) in FORTH word. It defines a new FORTH definition with the given name and installs a new entry in the rule table. The PRIORITY: word is an immediate word, meaning that it is executed instead of being compiled. Its effect is to change the priority of the rule in the rule table from the default of zero to the indicated priority.

The word *IF* is also immediate and has the effect of installing the address of the rule's condition cell in the rule table. *IF* also compiles into the rule definition a routine that, at run-time, places a marker on the top of the data stack. This marker delimits the start of the conditions and is used at the end of the LHS when the results of all the conditions are ANDed together to form the conjunction of the conditions in the LHS. The conditions following the *IF* and up to the *THEN* are compiled into the definition just as they would be in a FORTH definition.

When the top-level loop tests the condition of a rule, it reads the condition address from the rule table and transfers control of the threaded code interpreter to that address. Thus the rule compiler acts like the conventional compiler but uses multiple code fields, one for the conditions, the other for the actions.

The word *THEN* is an immediate word that installs the address of a rule's action cell in the rule table. *THEN* ends the compilation of the condition code and compiles into the rule definition a routine that, at run-time, ANDs together the results of the tests in the RHS and stores the result in the activation flag of the rule in the rule table. THEN* compiles the word EXIT into the definition, followed by the contents of the code field of a conventional FORTH definition. The net effect is that, at run-time, the rule code exits after computing and storing the result of the test on the LHS.

As the FORTH compiler continues to compile the action part of the rule, it is as if a second but separate FORTH definition were being compiled within one rule definition. This second definition is what is executed if the rule is fired.

The word *END* is identical to the ; (semicolon) word in FORTH with some additional bookkeeping for the rule table.

The code for the rule-defining words is as follows:

```
: Rule: ( name ( — )    \create a new named rule
    ThisRule @ Rules? < not abort" No rule space"

    \ Enough space in RuleTable for new rule, begin object-area stuff
    [compile] :                        \acts like ordinary : def'n

    \ Erase any previous rule's flotsam
    CurrentRule ARule erase    sets all fields to 0's

    \ the new token evaluates condition (antecedent)
    latest 2- >w@<                     \ get token from vocabulary
                                       \ (interpreter implementation dependent)
    CurrentRule ^Rule.condition w! ;   \ save in current rule

: Priority: ( word ( — )   \set the new rule's priority
    \ evaluate the following word: a number, a constant, or other value
    find                               \ is it a defined word?
    ?dup if     execute                \ found: evaluate it
    else        pocket number          \ not found: assume it's a number
    then
    CurrentRule ^Rule.priority ! ;
immediate                              \ executes during rule definition


\ **** Words used to define conditions and actions
\        (antecedents and consequents)

VARIABLE StackDepth                    \ used by <*if* and <*then*

: <*if* ( rule# — rule#\ true )        \ begin condition (antecedent)
    true                               \ also leave a default flag
    depth StackDepth ! ;               \ will always be >= 2

: *IF* ( — )  \begin compilation of condition (antecedent)
    !CSP                               \ mark stack for error check
    ThisRule @ [compile] literal       \ compile rule# as literal
```

```
        compile <*if*  ;                        \ followed by *IF* primitive
    immediate

VARIABLE HighestPriority                        \ highest-priority so far
VARIABLE BestRuleAction                         \ holds best action

: <*then* ( rule#\ true  [..flags..] -- )       \ end of condition (antecedent)
    true
    depth  StackDepth @ do                      \ AND all flags together
        and
    loop

    \ decide now whether the rule fired or not, and if the priority is high
    \ enough, remember the action (consequent) for later invocation.

    \ If rule fired, does its priority warrant remembering?
    if
        thRule                                  \ point to this rule
        dup ^Rule.priority @                    \ get this rule's priority
        dup HighestPriority @ > if
            \ this rule has higher priority
            HighestPriority !                   \ keep new priority
            ^Rule.action w@
            BestRuleAction !                    \ keep new action, too
        else
            2drop
        then
    else
        drop
    then  ;

: *THEN*  ( -- ) \ end compilation of condition, begin compiling action
    ?CSP                                        \ is stack balanced?
    compile <*then*                             \ *THEN* primitive
    [compile] ;                                 \ end of condition (antecedent)

    here make.token                             \ token does following action
    CurrentRule ^Rule.action w!                 \ put action-token in rule-table
    Colon-CFA ,                                 \ action phrase is a colon-def'n

    smudge                                      \ to be unsmudged by *END*
    state on ;                                  \ now compile the action (consequent)
immediate

: *END*  ( -- ) \ end of action (consequent); end of rule
    1 ThisRule +!                               \ point to next free rule in RuleTable
    [compile] ; ;
immediate
```

The following Glossary describes the major words used in the FORPS implementation.

Glossary:

Rule   This is a defining word that is used to start the compilation of a new rule. Because it defines a new compilation capability, it is a good illustration of the extensibility of the FORTH compiler.

Priority   This word is an extension to the compiler that looks at the next token in the input stream and uses it to compute the priority of a rule. The result is inserted into the rule table.

<*if*   The rule compiler compiles this routine at the start of a set of conditions. If there are no conditions the result of the evaluation is true by default.

IF   This is an extension to the compiler that incorporates information about the current rule and then compiles the run-time routine <*if* into the definition of the rule.

<*then*   The rule compiler compiles this routine at the end of a set of conditions. This routine is a loop that AND's the results of the evaluations of the conditions. If the rule is activated, <*then* compares the priority of the rule against the current highest priority activation and saves a reference to the rule with higher priority.

THEN   This is an extension to the compiler that compiles <*then* and updates the rule table with a pointer to the starting address of the rule action.

END   Marks the end of the action part of a rule. Updates the pointer into the rule table and ends the compilation of the rule.

One benchmark of the performance of this limited production system design is the Towers of Hanoi problem. The Towers of Hanoi problem shares the problems of all benchmarks: confusing the effect of inference engine architecture with the effect of processor architecture, compiler performance, and application characteristics. This said, on a 68000 processor operating at 10 MHz, the FORPS program solving the Towers of Hanoi problem operates at 220 inferences per second, or roughly 4.5 milliseconds per rule. Another way to look at it is that the minimum overhead for executing a rule in this system is 0.7 milliseconds. The actual overhead depends on the specific problem and is a function of the overall complexity of the conditions and actions that are required to solve the problem.

The tradeoff between the FORPS approach and the RETE net, therefore, comes at the point where scanning the entire rule set on each inference cycle becomes too expensive relative to the cost of building and maintaining the RETE net.

The FORPS architecture does admit strategies that reduce the per-cycle scanning required and delay the point at which the RETE becomes the better alternative. Examples of these strategies are recency control (limits the rules that are tested to those that access only more recent facts) and rule phasing (divides the rule set into multiple rule tables). A more straightforward strategy, but one with less flexibility, is to order the rules in priority order, so that on each cycle, the rule that is activated first is the rule that is fired.

Another advantage of the FORPS architecture for embedded systems is particularly apparent when resources are very limited. FORPS requires very little RAM. At the very minimum, only the rule table and the return and data stacks are required in RAM. All rules can be in ROM. Depending on the application, additional scratchpad RAM needed for calculations could be very limited.

Introduction to CLIPS

CLIPS is a production system written in the C language and developed under a NASA contract. Source code for CLIPS is available to NASA contractors free of charge and to the general public for a nominal fee. (See Giarratano 1988, 1989.)

In terms of basic production system functionality, CLIPS is more fully formed than FORPS. In fact, it stands up quite well in comparison to the commercial production systems. In addition, its C language implementation and the availability of the source code make it quite attractive for the embedded system's developer. We will take a close look at the CLIPS source code here as a basis for exploring production system implementation issues. Let's begin with a brief overview of CLIPS syntax for its two major language constructs, rules and facts.

Defining Constructs

CLIPS uses two defining constructs, the *deffacts* construct, which defines a collection of facts; and the *defrule* construct, which defines rules. The collection of facts that are named in a *deffacts* construct is asserted (that is, added to the working memory area) when the system is started, after the rules have been read and the RETE net built. The *deffacts*-construct is thus useful for setting the initial state of the system after the productions are defined and before entering the first recognize-act cycle. The syntax for *deffacts* constructs is as follows:

```
(deffacts <name> ["<comment">]    ; define the set of facts
                                  ;   with name "<name>"
```

```
( <<fact 1>>)                          ; first condition pattern
    •
    •
    •
(<<fact n>>) )                         ; end of LHS
```

Other than the availability of memory, CLIPS sets no limit to the number of initial facts and there may be multiple *deffacts*-statements in a program.

Similarly, there may be any number of productions in the system, subject only to memory limits, with each production defined by a *defrule* construct. The syntax for the *defrule* construct is

```
(defrule <name> [<"comment">]         ; define the rule with
                                      ; name "<name>"
   ( <<first pattern>>)               ; first condition pattern
     •
     •
     •
   (<<nth pattern>>)                  ; end of LHS
  =>                                  ; THEN
   (<<first action>>)
     •
     •
     •
   (<<last action>>) )                ; end of RHS
```

The syntax of the *defrule* construct is very much like the Rule: construct in FORPS. The biggest difference in semantics is that CLIPS can use patterns on the LHS, whereas FORPS cannot.

There is no practical limit to the number of conditions or actions that a single rule may have in CLIPS. The physical limit is available memory. The arrow symbol (=>) is used to indicate the boundary between the LHS and the RHS or a rule, like the *THEN* in FORPS. The next section describes the categories for patterns that can be used on the LHS of a rule in CLIPS.

LHS Patterns

The conditions that must be satisfied before a CLIPS rule can be fired are generally represented by patterns, which must then match some working memory element to be satisfied. However, there is provision for general predicates implemented via procedures, as in FORPS.

Condition elements have the same form as WMEs, that is, they are N-tuples. Individual fields within the condition elements on the LHS of CLIPS rules may be of several types, as indicated in the following table.

Pattern Type	Element	Use
Literal	\<name\>	Defines the exact atom that must appear in the WME.
Single wildcard	?	Match any value in a single field.
Multifield wildcard	$?	Match any value in zero or more fields.
Single variable	?\<name\>	Capture any value in a single field.
Multifield variable	$?\<name\>	Capture any value in zero or more fields.

On their first occurrence in a pattern, the variables are bound to (that is, are given a value equal to) the value of the corresponding field of the WME being matched. A literal value in a field constrains the pattern to an exact match with a WME at that position.

The individual fields within a condition element may also be given more structured constraints as to the values they can match. Constraints are of two basic types, logical and predicate function. The constraints on fields are listed in the following table.

Constraint Type	Symbol	Use
Logical	&	Constrain to \<value1\> and \<value2\>
Logical	|	Constrain to \<value1\> or \<value2\>
Logical	~	Constrain to not \<value1\>
Predicate Function	&:	Constrain to (\<function\>\<\<arguments\>\>)
Predicate Function	|:	Constrain to or (\<function\>\<\<arguments\>\>)
Predicate Function	~:	Constrain to not (\<function\>\<\<arguments\>\>)
Pattern Expansion	=	Constrain to (\<function\>\<\<arguments\>\>)

The last constraint type listed in the table is called pattern expansion, which constrains the matching field in much the same way that literal field elements do. The pattern expansion constraint relies on a function evaluation at run-time to determine the value to which the WME field is constrained.

Evaluation of any multiple constraints in a pattern element occurs from left to right. Logical constraints may be combined in any manner or number. Predicate function constraints may also be used to apply an arbitrary test to the value of a field in a WME. As mentioned earlier, pattern expansion constrains the field in the matching WMEs to be equal to the value returned by the function at the corresponding position in the condition element.

Finally, the reserved word "test" can be used at the beginning of a condition element for user-defined comparisons of variable values bound in earlier condition elements. The syntax for the *test* pattern is

```
(test (<function>[<<arguments>>])).
```

The functions within a test are nested and are evaluated from inside out.

The condition elements on the LHS of a rule are assumed to be connected by an implicit *and* as in FORPS, though it is possible to change this default by defining logical pattern blocks. Three types of pattern blocks are used, inclusive *or,* explicit *and* and explicit *not.* The syntax of the inclusive *or* block is

```
(defrule <name> [<"comment">]      ; define the rule with
                                   ; name "<name>"
    ( <<additional patterns>>)
    (or (<<pattern>>)              ; rule will fire multiple times
              •                    ; once for each satisfied
                                   ; condition in the or block
              •
        (<<pattern>>))
    (<<additional patterns>>)      ; end of LHS
    =>                             ; THEN
        (<< actions>>))            ; end of RHS
```

The explicit *and* can be used to mix *and* and *or* blocks.

```
(defrule <name> [<"comment">]      ; define the rule with name
                                   ; "<name>"
    ( <<additional patterns>>)
    (or (and (<<pattern>>)         ; rule can fire
              •                    ; if all conditions in the
                                   ; and block are satisfied
              •
        (<<pattern>>))
        (<<other patterns>>))
    (<<additional patterns>>)      ; end of LHS
    =>                             ; THEN
        (<< actions>>))            ; end of RHS
```

Finally, the *not* function may be used with only one condition element at a time, as follows.

```
(defrule <name> [<"comment">]      ; define the rule with
                                   ; name "<name>"
    ( <<preceding patterns>>)
    (not (<<pattern>>))            ; rule can fire if <<pattern>>
                                   ; not matched
    (<<additional patterns>>)      ; end of LHS
    =>                             ; THEN
        (<< actions>>))            ; end of RHS
```

The CLIPS parser handles logical pattern blocks by expanding the source code for the rule into multiple rules in the internal rule representation.

The final and a very important type of LHS pattern element is the pattern binding. Pattern bindings bind a WME to a variable (in contrast to conventional variable bindings, which assign an element of a WME to a variable) and are used in conjunction with certain RHS operations, like retract, that operate on an entire fact. The syntax for a pattern binding is

```
?<fact-var-name> <- (<<fields>>)
```

Once bound, the binding name *?<fact-var-name>* can be used on the RHS to refer to an entire WME.

RHS Actions

The basic actions used on the RHS of a CLIPS production are used to assert and retract WMEs. Their syntax is straightforward:

```
(assert (<<pattern>>) [(<<additional patterns>>)])
(retract ?<fact-var> [?<<fact-vars>>] | <fact-num>
     [<<fact-nums>>])
```

The *fact-num* argument type lets the programmer refer to a WME by its reference number. Assert actions add a WME to the working memory area; retract actions remove a working memory element.

External functions may be called within an assert statement to set the value of a particular WME field. The pattern expansion operator (=) is used to indicate to the parser that evaluation of the function is what is to happen. A number of built-in functions for I/O, variable manipulation, and mathematics are provided in CLIPS, as in most production systems. In addition, CLIPS provides a general call-out interface to external functions.

In a system like FORPS, by contrast there is a minimal distinction between the production system and the implementation language. There is no need for interfaces or an identified set of built-in functions because the underlying implementation language is completely accessible. This can translate into an environment that is much more flexible for some embedded systems development because the compile edit, link, cycle is broken.

In CLIPS two special RHS constructs, *if . . . then . . . else* and *while,* permit testing and looping on the RHS.

```
(defrule <name> [<"comment">]
   [ ( <<preceding patterns>>)]
=>
   (if (<predicate-function><< args>>)       ; if given condition
                                             ; is satisfied
   then                                      ; perform the
                                             ; following actions
   [<<action-1>>)
   •
```

```
(<<action-n>>)]
[else                                    ; optionally
[<<action-1>>)                           ; perform these
                                         ; actions
       •

(<<action-n>>)])
```

The while structure may include nested *while* and *if . . . then . . . else* structures.

```
(defrule <name> [<"comment">]
   [ ( <<preceding patterns>>)]
=>
   (while (<predicate-function><< args>>)  ; while given
                                           ; condition is
                                           ; satisfied
   [do]                                    ; perform the
                                           ; following actions

   [<<action-1>>)
        •
   (<<action-n>>)])
```

These two constructs are concessions to the procedural representation of knowledge and enable control flow slightly outside of the strict recognize-act cycle. However, the scope of these constructs is still within a single rule. Production systems often deal only awkwardly with a clear-cut need to govern control flow over the rule set as a whole. For example, there may be a clear need for either sequential execution in a defined order through a set of rules or *do . . . while . . .* control flow over a set of rules. CLIPS is silent on these strategies as are most production system designs, leaving the developer to resort to coding control patterns into the LHS of the rules, an often counterintuitive and opaque representation of the control strategy.

Production System Compilation in CLIPS

In FORPS, rule compilation is largely table building, and there is not distinct working memory for the production system. In CLIPS, both the rules and the fact patterns end up compiled into a network. This section describes the structure of the network and how the compilation process works.

Compilation Step 1. Compile Rules to a Network

To explain the RETE network and the way rules are compiled into the net, let's look at the simplest case, rules with a single condition on the LHS.

Example 3.1: RETE net for the rule "activate-goal."

```
(defrule activate-goal                    ; define the rule with name
                                          ; "activate-goal"
    (goal pending)                        ; find condition: there is
                                          ; a WME = "(goal pending)"
=>                                        ; THEN
    ( ... ) )                             ; actions
```

Three types of network nodes are needed to compile the rule of example 1:

1. A root node, which is just the entry point into the net.

2. A single input node (sometimes termed an alpha or pattern node) for each test that is required at run-time to match the pattern (goal pending) with potential matching WMEs.

3. A terminal node that puts the activation on the agenda if the match is successful.

This simple net is illustrated in Figure 3.2.

When working memory is changed by the addition of a new working memory element, potential matching nodes in the network are passed a data structure (called a *token*) that

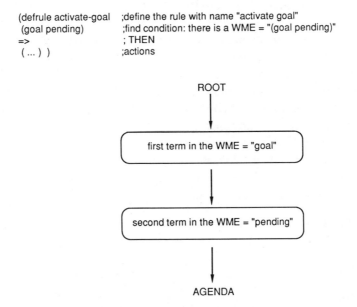

Figure 3.2. RETE Net with One-Input (alpha) Nodes

Individual condition elements of a production are compiled into a pattern network that performs pattern tests against the individual fields of the working memory elements.

contains a reference to the WME that has been added. The reference is usually implemented at least as a pointer to the memory location in the working memory area where the WME is stored. Each node in the net has associated with it a test to be performed on any WMEs referenced by tokens passed to it. If the test is successful at a given node, the token is copied and passed on to the next node in the net.

In the example of Figure 3.2, if the WME (goal pending) is added to the working memory area during the act cycle, then on the recognize cycle a token is created and sent to the root node of the network. The root node passes the token to the first node, which tests that the first field of the WME is the atom *goal*. Since this test is successful in the example, the token is copied and sent to the next node, which tests whether the second field of the fact is the atom *pending*. Passing this test, the token is copied and sent on to the remaining node, which adds the activation to the agenda. Once on the agenda, the production's actions may be executed on the act cycle (depending, of course, on the priority level of the rule relative to the rules already on the agenda).

Not all the matching done within a WME is a test for equality of atoms. For example, a match may be required between an atom in the WME and the result of the evaluation of an expression at the current node in the network. Matches involving multifield variables and wildcards add another level of complexity. Multifield variables use the pattern matcher to recursively evaluate all possible matches.

Note that, as described earlier, a RETE net built from one-input nodes corresponds to one node, one test, and each path through the net represents one condition. Rules that have more than one condition element in the LHS may need to use an additional type of node in the RETE net in order to handle internode tests. These two-input nodes (termed *beta nodes* or *joins*) are more complicated structures than the one-input nodes since it is at these nodes that the inference procedure will need to maintain a representation of the state of the partial match. One-input nodes either match each WME or they don't. Two-input nodes may be partially satisfied. In practice this means that a list of all the tokens that have entered the node at either input must be maintained by the node, just in case some later change in working memory might provide the missing element in the match. A simple example of a rule whose RETE net representation requires a beta node to handle an interelement test is given in Example 3.2.

Example 3.2: Rules "Plus_X" and "Times_X"

```
(defrule Plus_X                ;define the rule with name "Plus_X"
      (goal simplify ?N)       ;find condition: there is a WME =
                               ;"(goal simplify ?N)"
      (expression ?N 0 + ?X)   ;find condition: there is a WME =
                               ;"(expression ?N 0 + ?X)"
  =>                           ;THEN
      (...))                   ;actions

(defrule Times_X               ;define the rule with name "Tims_X"
      (goals simplify ?N)      ;find condition: there is a WME =
```

```
                                    ; "(goal simplify ?N)"
        (expression ?N 0 * ?X)      ; find condition: there is a WME =
                                    ; "(expression ?N 0* ?X)"
    =>                              ; THEN
            ( . . . ))              ; actions
```

Rules with multiple conditions, like those in Example 3.2, are compiled into the net by first compiling each element of the condition separately into a series of one-input nodes. Next, the individual condition nets are joined through two-input nodes. The resulting net is illustrated in Figure 3.3.

Each two-input node keeps track of all tokens referencing WMEs that satisfy the corresponding condition elements. This match of a WME to a condition is made independent of other pattern elements (tokens that pass from the root node through the right side of the network). The memory structure that stores tokens for WMEs matching the alpha nodes in the pattern net is termed *alpha memory*.

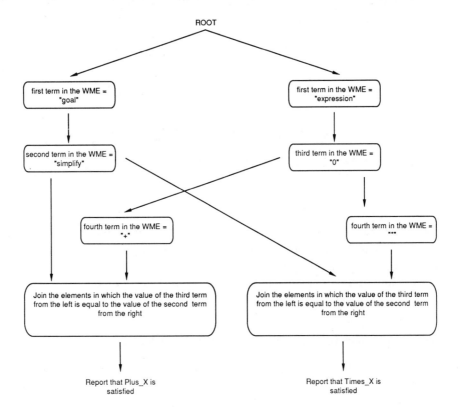

Figure 3.3. RETE Net with Two-Input (Beta) Nodes

In the case where individual conditions of a production have joint pattern elements, two-input network elements are used to implement the tests. The two-input elements of the network appear after the pattern network elements.

Two-input nodes also keep track of all tokens that pass from beta elements higher in the net. The memory that stores tokens for WMEs matching the beta nodes in the net is termed *beta memory*. On each combination of tokens, one from alpha memory, one from beta memory, the node performs the interelement test specified in the condition. In this particular example, the test determines whether the third field of any of the memory elements matching the initial pattern also matches the second field of the memory elements matching the second pattern. The variable ? N in the source code refers to both these fields.

Pairs that pass the interelement test are packaged in a new token and sent down to any subsequent nodes in the network. The subsequent node in this particular example is a terminal node, which puts the activation for this rule on the agenda.

Although the implementations of tokens have not been discussed in any detail, it should be no surprise that the token structures that are passed through the net must contain more information than just the reference to the WME. For example, to handle retraction of WMEs, the tokens must contain a flag indicating whether the referenced WME has been added or removed from working memory. Other information about the WME may be packaged with the token, for example, whether the token was added by an action of a rule or by some external procedure such as an asynchronous sensor monitor.

Compilation Step 2. Implement Working Memory, RETE, and Agenda Mechanisms

Having named the basic constructs of the production system language and described how the rules and facts are compiled into a network structure for efficient matching, let's now look at CLIPS, a particular implementation of a production system in the C language.

Three major tasks are involved in the implementation of the production language, each task corresponding to the implementation of one of the basic components of the production system's architecture:

1. To develop a machine representation of WMEs or facts.

2. To develop a data structure for the RETE net and efficient procedures for building the net and matching patterns in the net following changes in working memory.

3. To implement the inference engine itself.

Most of the work done by the inference engine is a function of the pattern matcher working with the RETE net during the recognize phase of the recognize-act cycle. What remains of the inference engine after matching is the agenda mechanism. The agenda mechanism is responsible for scheduling and then executing the actions.

Internal Representation of Facts

Working memory elements in CLIPS are implemented as C record structures. The working memory area per se is implemented as a doubly linked chain of WME structures (Figure 3.4). There does not seem to be much leverage to be gained from working on more efficient storage mechanisms for WMEs (for example, hashing on the first element

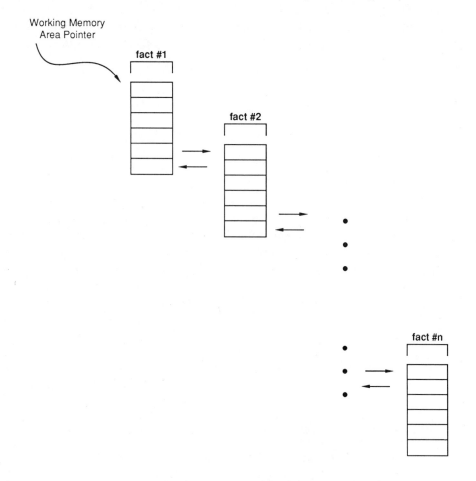

Figure 3.4. CLIPS Implementation of Working Memory

In CLIPS, the working memory elements are C structures, whose fields contain the basic infor- mation about the structure of the fact. New facts are allocated from free memory and linked together to form a list. References back to specific working memory elements are contained in the RETE network, so even for large working memories, accessing the individual elements need not be inefficient.

to improve access time) since matching operations in the RETE net dominate the time taken by processes that manipulate working memory. This is certainly true for those embedded systems where working memory is in core. On the other hand, very large working memories that exceed available RAM are conceivable. Similarly, working memory elements may need to be stored in more permanent memory, and so an allocation/deallocation mechanism for memory management may be necessary and may need to be efficient. These requirements could mean a different design for WMEs.

Facts are syntactically and semantically pretty simple, and the information from the source code that needs to be stored internally about them is minimal. The CLIPS *fact* record type stores link information (links to other member of working memory), a unique fact id number that is assigned when the fact is created, and information about the fact's internal structure. The structure definition in C for CLIPS facts is as follows:

```
struct fact
        {
        struct element *atoms;      /* pointer to fact elements       */
        struct match *list;
        long int ID;                /* unique fact id#                */
        int fact_length;            /* number of fact elements        */
        struct fact *next;          /* next fact in working memory     */
        struct fact *previous;      /* previous fact in working memory */
        };
```

A fact's internal structure is simply represented by a length and a pointer to a list of the elements in the fact. Each element of the fact has its own distinct internal representation. Again reflecting the inherent simplicity of facts, fact elements can be one of two types, either numeric or character. The type is indicated in the element record by a type field. The value of the element has its own field in the record. Atoms are stored in a separate space in memory. Finally, the *next* field stores the links that connects the list of elements for a particular fact.

```
struct element
        {
        int type;                   /* type of element = CHAR or NUM  */
        union
        {
        struct draw *hvalue;
        float fvalue;
        } val;                      /* element value                  */
        struct element *next;       /* next element in fact           */
        };
```

Facts also contain a chain of references to the condition elements that they match in the pattern network. This chain is used when WMEs are removed from the working memory, so that the RETE network can be efficiently updated. The match structure is a simple linked list, as indicated by the following structure definition:

```
struct match
        {
        struct match *next;         /* next member of match list      */
        struct pat_node *slot;      /* element matched in pattern net  */
        };
```

The *pat_node* structure pointed to within each match element is the basic building block of the pattern net. The pattern net is one of the two nets that make up the RETE network in CLIPS.

RETE Network

The network described in the following section is one instance of a network of feature recognizers used in the service of a recognize-act inference cycle. There are both simpler and more sophisticated approaches than the CLIPS RETE net, but it is a good point of departure.

The RETE net in CLIPS is actually built from two building blocks, the pattern node and the join (the one-input node and two-input node, respectively, in Forgy's terminology [see Forgy 1982]). Matching between WMEs and the conditions in the LHS of a rule takes place first in the network of the pattern nodes (the *pattern net*). WMEs that complete a match in the pattern net are then passed down to the network of joins (the *join net*) for further tests, but at this point the tests are between elements of different WME's or, equivalently, between elements in the different conditions that make up the LHS. The pattern net thus corresponds roughly to the individual patterns of the condition on the LHS, whereas the join net reflects the structure of the LHS as a whole. (See Figure 3.5.)

Representation of Pattern Nodes   The pattern nodes perform a single intraelement test on a fact. For example, there might be a test in the pattern net to determine whether the third element of a WME is equal to a given atom. The pattern net is built from pattern nodes, and each path through the net, from the root node to a terminal node, represents an individual condition element on the LHS of a single production.

When the LHS of productions are compiled, sharing in the pattern net is utilized wherever possible. The rules for sharing are as follows:

1. All previous fields in the pattern must be shared in the pattern network.

2. Any test expression in a new pattern must be identical to an expression in place at the current level in the existing network.

The result of these sharing rules is a tree-structured pattern network. (See Figure 3.6).

A)
```
(defrule Plus_X         ; define the rule with name "Plus_X"
  (goal simplify ?N)    ; find condition: there is a WME = "(goal simplify ?N)"
  (expression ?N 0 + ?X) ; find condition: there is a WME = "(expression ?N 0 + ?X)"
  =>                     ; THEN
  ( ... ) )             ; actions
```

CLIPS Joins are represented as boxes; beta memory is represented as a filled circle
CLIPS Pattern Net terminal nodes are represented as open circles

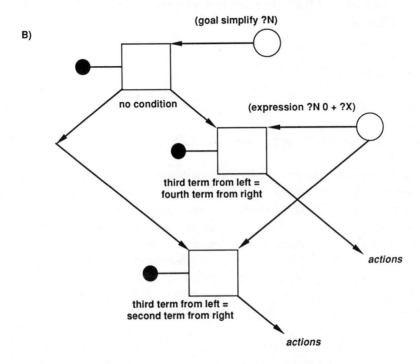

Figure 3.5. RETE Structures Corresponding to CLIPS Productions

In the example, the production (A) is compiled into the collection of structures (B).

In contrast to an implementation strategy like that used by CLIPS, where nodes are implemented as structures, the internal representation of the nodes may instead directly reflect the fact that the nodes in the pattern network represent tests. In this case, the test program becomes (is identical to) the internal representation of the pattern network, an implementation approach that is described by Forgy. Implementation of the network in Forgy's machine is based directly on an architecture for a virtual machine that performs the network tests. The virtual machine is then simulated in software and a program using the instructions of the virtual machine is executed by an interpreter. The instruction set of Forgy's virtual machine is given in Table 3.1.

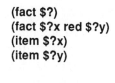

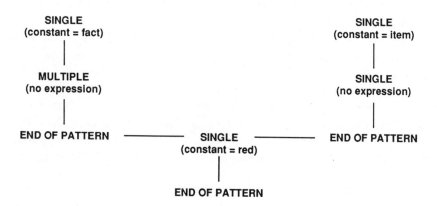

Figure 3.6. The Pattern Net

The patterns in each individual condition of a production are compiled into a tree structure. The branches of the tree are shared between patterns as much as possible.

Table 3.1 The Forgy Virtual Machine Instructions

Instruction	Description
TEQA *location,atom*	Test: WME field *location* = atom
TEQN *location,num*	Test: WME field *location* = num (integer)
TEQF *location,num*	Test: WME field *location* = num (floating point)
TEQS *location1,location2*	Test: WME field *location* 1 = *location* 2
TNEA *location,atom*	Test: WME field *location* ≠ atom
TNEN *location,num*	Test: WME field *location* ≠ num (integer)
TNEF *location,num*	Test: WME field *location* ≠ num (floating point)
TNES *location1,location2*	Test: WME field *location* 1 ≠ *location* 2
TXXA *location,atom*	Similar to above; XXLT for less than, etc.
AND *left-loc* = *right-loc*	Test: WME field *left-loc* = *right-loc*
TERM *production*	Terminal node for *production*
FORK *label*	Jump to *label* saving return address
MERGE *label*	Jump to *label*

One of the differences between the Forgy and the CLIPS approaches to the RETE net involves the translation of source-level instructions. Forgy translates the source-level instructions into the machine code of a RETE machine. CLIPS translates them into data structures that are less machine architecture than an alternate form of the source code. Thus CLIPS is closer in philosophy to an interpreter for production system code. The approach Forgy uses compiles the source code to the instruction set of a virtual machine. The CLIPS approach makes the network compiler much less complex, since the relation between the source code and the internal representation is relatively direct. Data structures are also easier to incrementally change than code segments. There can be a speed-space tradeoff too, since interpreted code is often more compact but slower than compiled code.

In CLIPS, the pattern network nodes are implemented as record structures in the C language. The pattern node records contain links to the other pattern nodes in the network (for example, the *same_level, prev, next_level,* and *last_level* fields). These links are used for navigating through the network during pattern matching. Clearly, pointer following is not as efficient as the encoded jumps used in the virtual machine implementation proposed by Forgy.

The node record also contains both information about the node type (used by the pattern matcher to mark nodes during traversal of the network) and a reference to the test to be performed on the WME as part of the pattern match at this point in the net. If the node is a terminal node in the pattern net, the alpha field of the node record references the WMEs that have matched (this is termed the *alpha memory* of the RETE net). The CLIPS record structure for a pattern node, therefore, looks like this:

```
struct pat_node
        {
        struct pat_node *same_level;
        struct pat_node *prev;
        struct pat_node *next_level;
        struct pat_node *last_level;
        int type;
        struct test *eval;
        struct list *path;
        struct flink *alpha;
        };
```

The *list* record structure is as follows:

```
struct list
        {
        struct internode *path;
        struct list *next;
        };
```

The *test* and *flink* record types are defined later. In the CLIPS approach, program and data structures are kept quite separate. The composition of test procedures in conditions are deferred until run-time. Therefore, efficiency may be less than the equivalent compiled form in the Forgy design, where the program and the internal net representation are the same.

Construction of Pattern Net In CLIPS, the pattern net is built using a procedure called *place_pattern*. This procedure takes a set of pointers as input parameters: the current position in the rule pattern, the current position in the pattern net, and the last position added to the net. Information about the pattern expressions is developed from a rule analysis routine. The procedure place pattern returns a pointer into the pattern net referring to the most recently added pattern node of the pattern net.

The following code segment defines the procedure parameters and their types:

```
static struct pat_node *place_pattern(pattern_list,upper_level,
        pat,elem,last_elem,top_pat_node)
    struct pat_node *pattern_list;
    struct pat_node *upper_level;
    int pat, elem;
    struct pat_node **top_pat_node;
    {
    struct test *basic_list;
    struct test *tmp_basic;
    struct pat_node *cur_elem, *new_elem;
    struct pat_node *last_look = NULL;
    struct var_info *var_ptr;
    int same_type, cn_test;
    int pn_type;

/* Initialize local variables                                          */
    cur_elem = pattern_list;
    basic_list = get_pn_expr(pat,elem);
```

The following WHILE loop ensures that the pattern can be shared with elements in the current pattern wherever possible:

```
    while (cur_elem != NULL)
        {
/* if we've reached the end of the existing path, return               */
        if ((cur_elem->type == STOP) && (elem > last_elem))
            { return(cur_elem); }
```

Otherwise, the program gets the type of the pattern element and compares it with the type of the element at this level in the existing net. If they are the same type and apply the same test, we can share the existing net at this level. Otherwise, the program drops to the next level in the net and continues.

```
        pn_type = get_node_type(pat,elem);
        if (cur_elem->type == pn_type)
            { same_type = TRUE; }
        else
```

```
                { same_type = FALSE; }
        if ( ( same_type == TRUE ) &&
           ( same_thing( cur_elem->eval , basic_list ) == TRUE ) )
              {
              returntests( basic_list );
              cur_elem = place_pattern( cur_elem->next_level , cur_elem ,
              pat , elem+1 , last_elem );
              return( cur_elem );
              }
        else
/* otherwise see if we can share some other node at the same level              */
              {
              last_look = cur_elem;
              cur_elem = cur_elem->same_level;
              }
        }
```

Once all the possibilities for node sharing have been exhausted, the procedure needs to create new pattern net nodes and integrate them into the network, as follows:

```
    cn_test = FALSE;
    if ( basic_list != NULL )
         {
         if ( basic_list->val.fun_ptr == PTR_CONSTANT )
             { cn_test = TRUE; }
         }

/* initialize a new pattern node and insert into the network at the current level */

    new_elem = get_struct( pat_node );
    new_elem->last_level = upper_level;
    new_elem->next_level = NULL;
    new_elem->same_level = NULL;
    new_elem->prev = NULL;
    new_elem->eval = NULL;
    new_elem->path = NULL;
    new_elem->alpha = NULL;

    if ( last_look == NULL )
         {
         if ( upper_level == NULL )
             { *top_pat_node = new_elem; }
         else
             { upper_level->next_level = new_elem; }
         }
    else
         {
         if ( cn_test == TRUE )
             {
             last_look->same_level = new_elem;
             new_elem->prev = last_look;
             }
         else if ( upper_level != NULL )
             {
             new_elem->same_level = upper_level->next_level;
```

```
   if (upper_level->next_level != NULL)
        {upper_level->next_level->prev = new_elem; }
   upper_level->next_level = new_elem;
   }
else
   {
   new_elem->same_level = *top_pat_node;
   if (*top_pat_node != NULL)
        {(*top_pat_node)->prev = new_elem; }
   *top_pat_node = new_elem;
   }
}
```

If the end of the pattern has been reached, the node in the pattern net is marked as a terminal node and control is returned to the caller.

```
if (elem > last_elem)
   {
   new_elem->type = STOP;
   new_elem->eval = NULL;
   return(new_elem);
   }
```

If this element of the pattern was a segment variable, then the pattern node will perform a multiple bind when pattern matching. Otherwise a single bind will occur.

```
pn_type = get_node_type(pat,elem);
new_elem->type = pn_type;
```

Otherwise, if the end has not been reached, the program installs the test in the node (note that a nop is stored as NULL), and then goes on to place the next level of the pattern into the net.

```
new_elem->eval = basic_list;
test_install(basic_list);
new_elem = place_pattern(NULL,new_elem,pat,elem+1,last_elem);
return(new_elem);
}
```

Once the individual elements of the LHS of a rule have been analyzed and represented in the pattern net, the internal representation of the interelement structure is constructed. This internal representation is a network of nodes that join pairs of patterns.

Representation of Join Nodes The second major building block of the RETE net is the join node. Its function is to perform interelement tests between the pattern elements on the LHS of a production. When the LHS of a production is compiled, join sharing is used whenever possible. The rules for join sharing are as follows:

1. All previous joins (to a given point on the LHS of the rule) must be shared.

2. The test expression for the join must be identical to an expression in place at the current level of addition in the join network.

3. The join to be shared must be entered from the same location in the pattern network.

Example 3.3 illustrates the principles of join sharing. These rules are very similar to the rules for sharing in the pattern net, with the exception of the third condition, which reflects the directional nature of the join net.

Example 3.3: Join Sharing.

(a) The following productions share pattern nodes for testing of the constant *data*, in addition to sharing all pattern elements for the first pattern in the condition. The join for the first pattern can also be shared, whereas the joins for the second patterns cannot—they violate the rule that joins must be entered from the same pattern.

```
(defrule example1
    (data red ?x)
    (data green ?x)
    =>)

(defrule example2
    (data red ?x)
    (data blue ?x)
    =>)
```

(b) The following production shares with production example2 both pattern and join nodes for the first two patterns. A third join must be added for the last pattern.

```
(defrule example3
    (data red ?y)
    (data blue ?y)
    (info ?z)
    =>)
```

In CLIPS the joins that represent the interelement tests are implemented using record structures in C. These structures are designed in much the same way as pattern nodes; that is, there are fields in the structure for storing links in the network and references to the tests to be performed at run-time.

For comparison, note that, as in the case of the pattern nets, the function call for the test at a join node is composed at run-time that is, the procedure and arguments are only put together at run-time. Therefore testing conditions are less efficient in an explicit network than in the scheme described by Forgy, in which the tests are compiled to executable code. In the Forgy code the network arcs are represented implicitly in control transfer statements appearing in the code (Example 3.4.)

Example 3.4: Forgy Virtual Machine Implementation of the RETE Net.

The following productions are compiled into a sequence of instructions for a virtual machine that implements the pattern matching of the RETE net. The passing of control between elements of the code implements the RETE topology.

```
(defrule Plus0x
        (Goal Simplify ?x)
        (Expression ?x 0 + ?y)
=> ..)

(defrule Time0x
        (Goal Simplify ?x)
        (Expression ?x 0 * ?y)
=> ..)
```

The instructions used to implement the net in this example are FORK, AND, and TEQA/N (Test Equal Atom/Number). The FORK instruction indicates that a given node has more than one successor, the AND instruction indicates a two-input node for nonnegated patterns, and the TEQA/N indicate tests at one-input nodes. MERGE functions like an unconditional jump and indicates the rejoining of two-input nodes.

```
ROOT    FORK L003            ; root node of the network
        TEQA 0,Goal          ; is the zero-th element = "Goal"
        TEQA 1,Simplify      ; is the first element = "Simplify"
        FORK L002
L001    AND (2) = (1)        ; is the second element of first pattern
                             ; equal the first element of second pattern
        TERM Plus0x          ; if so, Plus0x is satisfied
L002    AND (2) = (1)        ; is the second element of first pattern
                             ; equal the first element of second pattern
        TERM Time0x          ; if so, Time0x is satisfied
L003    TEQA 0,Expression    ; is the zero-th element = "Expression"
        TEQN 2,0             ; is the second element = "0"
        FORK L004
        TEQA 3,+             ; is the third element = "+"
        MERGE L001
L004    TEQA 3,*             ; is the third element = "*"
        MERGE l002
```

The CLIPS join node record structure is composed as follows. The first field of the CLIPS record structure points to the beta memory of the join. The last field points to the pattern node in the pattern network through which the alpha memory is accessed. Recall that the pattern network tests the match of a WME to a single condition element in isolation. The CLIPS architecture is slightly different from the conventional RETE net in that each pattern corresponds to its own join, whereas in the standard topology, if only one pattern exists, it is represented as a single one-input join in the net. (See Figure 3.5.)

Other fields in the internode structure store information about the join logic (that is, whether the pattern is *not'* ed or not). The logic of the join determines how the join test is used. Finally, in the node record, there are link fields containing information about the relative position of the node in the network, and there are fields containing references to the join tests.

The internode structure is defined as follows:

```
struct internode
    {
    struct flink *beta;    /* Bindings from left-hand side       */
    char lhs_log;          /* Left-hand side logic: '+' or 'e'   */
    char rhs_log;          /* Right-hand side logic: '+' or '-'  */
    struct test *eval;
    struct test *not_eval;
    long int id;           /*Not id if "e -" join                */
    struct list *next;     /* The next join to enter             */
    struct internode *join_above;
    struct pat_node *entry_pat;
    };
```

Construction of the Join Net The RETE net is built using a procedure called *construct_joins*. This procedure takes as its input a logical representation of a production, which is produced by a rule analysis procedure. The *construct_joins* procedure then builds the set of linked joins representing the LHS and returns to the calling routine the last join constructed, which then functions as a link between the join net and the right-hand side actions of the rule. The *construct_joins* procedure calls *place_pattern* to build the pattern net.

The procedure takes as input a pointer to the root node of the pattern net and a pointer to the rule information produced by the analysis module. The *rule_info* structure is defined as follows:

```
struct ruleinfo
    {
    char *name;
    struct ruleinfo *next;
    struct patptr *pats;
    char *pp_form;
    };
```

The types of the procedure arguments and the local variables of the procedure are as follows:

```
struct internode *construct_joins(top_pat_node,rule_ptr)
    struct pat_node **top_pat_node;
    struct ruleinfo *rule_ptr;
    {
    struct internode *last_join, *join;
    struct pat_node *last_pat;
    struct var_info *bind_ptr;
    int first_join = TRUE;
    char logic = '+';
    int cur_pat;
    int try_to_reuse = TRUE;
    struct list *temp_list, *old_join_list, *list_of_joins;
    char lhs_log;
    int total_joins, join_number;
    struct test *join_test, *not_test;
```

After initializing local variables, each of the patterns and/or test constructs of the rule LHS is processed. After processing by the rule analysis procedure, there should be no lower level *and* or *or* logic structures.

```
    last_join = NULL;
    total_joins = count_joins();
    join_number = 1;

    while (join_number <= total_joins)
        {
        logic = get_join_logic(join_number);
        if (first_join == TRUE)
            { lhs_log = 'e'; }
        else
            { lhs_log = '+'; }

        last_pat = place_pattern(*top_pat_node,NULL,
                join_number,1,get_elem_count(join_number),top_pat_node);

        if (first_join == TRUE)
            { list_of_joins = last_pat->path; }
        else
            { list_of_joins = last_join->next; }

        join_test = get_join_expr(join_number);
        not_test = get_not_expr(join_number);

        if ((try_to_reuse == TRUE) &&
            ((old_join_list =reuse_join(list_of_joins,lhs_log,logic,
```

```
              join_test,not_test,last_pat->path)) != NULL) )
      {
      add_pat_list(last_pat,old_join_list,rule_ptr);
      last_join = old_join_list->path;
      returntests(join_test);
      returntests(not_test);
      }
   else
```

If there is no sharing, a new join is initialized:

```
      {
      try_to_reuse = FALSE;
      join = get_struct(internode);
      join->beta = NULL;
      join->eval = NULL;
      join->not_eval = NULL;
      join->join_above = NULL;
      join->entry_pat = NULL;
      join->next = NULL;
      join->lhs_log = lhs_log;
      join->id = 0;

      if (lhs_log == '+')
         {
         temp_list = last_join->next;
         last_join->next = get_struct(list);
         last_join->next->next = temp_list;
         last_join->next->path = join;
         }

      conn_pat_to_join(join,last_pat,logic,rule_ptr);
      join->join_above = last_join;
      join->entry_pat = last_pat;
      last_join = join;
      join->eval = join_test;
      test_install(join_test);
      join->not_eval = not_test;
      test_install(not_test);
      }
```

On returning to the caller, the program sets a pointer to the next pattern and the expressions associated with the join for that pattern.

```
      join_number++;
      first_join = FALSE;
      }

   return(last_join);
   }
```

Representation of Alpha and Beta Memory The memories that are maintained at the nodes in the RETE net are used to keep track of the partial matches that have been made to that point in the net. The alpha memories store references to WMEs that match a single pattern in the LHS of a rule and are accessed from the terminal nodes of the pattern net. The beta memories store references to WMEs that have matched earlier joins, that is, have passed both the individual pattern tests and the interelement join tests. Beta memories are accessed from the individual joins. Both alpha and beta memories have the same representation in terms of their definition as structures in the C language.

```
struct flink
    {
    struct fbind *binds;
    long int count;
    struct flink *next;
    };
```

The count field of the *flink* structure is used by the beta memories to keep count of the number of partial matches that a particular WME participates in, for use with *not*' ed patterns. A *not*' ed pattern only generates a successful partial match if the count is zero at the end of all memory comparisons.

The *fbind* structure is used in the memories to keep track of WMEs.

```
struct fbind
    {
    struct fbind *next;
    long int whoset;
    struct fact *origin;
    struct fact_marker *marker;
    };
```

The marker structure is a specialized WME reference that is used to represent segment matches. A marker indicates that a single pattern element match spans more than one fact field in a WME. Fact markers are often built as linked lists since segment patterns can match a given WME in a number of ways. The structure definition for a fact marker is as follows:

```
struct fact_marker
    {
    int element;
    int start;
    int end;
    struct fact_marker *next;
    };
```

Once all the rules have been compiled into the RETE net, the system can be run in a forward-chaining inferencing mode using the underlying recognize-act inference cycle.

To repeat the fundamental aspects of the inference procedure, the first part of the cycle is responsible for determining matches between the rules and new WME that have been either added or removed. This process works by driving the new WME through the RETE net as far as it can go. If a terminal node of a join is reached, a production has been activated, and as a result its actions can be scheduled on the agenda. The second part of the cycle is to select and then execute one of the procedures on the agenda.

Matching

The matching procedure is responsible for traversing the RETE network when there is a change to the contents of working memory. The first part of the RETE network that is traversed is the pattern network, and this initial traversal must find all patterns that match the WME that has been added or removed. Therefore, in practice the entire pattern net must be searched.

Pattern Net Matching The *compare* procedure compares the elements of a fact to the nodes in the pattern network. The arguments to *compare* are a pointer to the fact being compared (*fact_ptr*), a pointer to the list of atoms in the fact (*elem_ptr*, which is a redundant argument because it can be derived from *fact_ptr*), the current position index into the pattern being matched (*pat_pos*), and the index of the current atom being pointed to in the fact (*cur_elem*). The markers argument is the list of segment markers generated during the pattern match.

The types of both the procedure arguments and the local variables, and a description of the procedure logic are given in the following C code:

```
compare(fact_ptr,elem_ptr,patn_ptr,pat_pos,cur_elem,markers,end_mark)
    struct fact *fact_ptr;
    struct element *elem_ptr;
    struct pat_node *patn_ptr;
    int cur_elem;
    struct fact_marker *markers, *end_mark;
    {
    struct list *drive_list;
    struct flink *var_list;
    struct match *list_of_matches;
    int finish_match, length, end_epos;
    struct fact_marker *new_mark, *old_mark;

    if (patn_ptr == NULL) return;
    current_pattern_fact = fact_ptr;
    current_pattern_marks = markers;
    length = fact_ptr->fact_length;
    while (TRUE)
        {
        finish_match = FALSE;
```

If there are no elements in the fact left to match, and the pattern net element being matched against is not an end-of-pattern marker or a multiple element binder, the pattern-matching attempt for this pattern has failed. In other words, once the end of the WME is reached, there can only be a match if the end of the pattern net is reached at the same time, or if the pattern net at the current point matches multiple elements.

```
if ((cur_elem == length) &&
  (patn_ptr->type != STOP) &&
  (patn_ptr->type != MULTIPLE))
    { finish_match = TRUE; }
```

If there are elements in the fact left to match, and the pattern element being matched against is an end-of-pattern marker, the fact is too long for the pattern and the pattern-matching attempt has failed.

```
else if ((cur_elem < length) && (patn_ptr->type == STOP))
    { finish_match = TRUE; }
```

If there are no elements in the fact left to match, and the pattern element being matched against is an end-of-pattern marker, the pattern has matched. The pattern is added to the list of matching patterns for the WME.

```
else if ((cur_elem == length) && (patn_ptr->type == STOP))
    {
/* Add the pattern to the list of matches for this fact.              */
        list_of_matches = fact_ptr->list;
        fact_ptr->list = get_struct(match);
        fact_ptr->list->next = list_of_matches;
        fact_ptr->list->slot = patn_ptr;
```

Once a pattern matches, we need to get the fact bindings associated with this pattern and "drive" them to the joins connected to this pattern.

```
        var_list = get_struct(flink);
        var_list->next = NULL;
        var_list->count = 0;
        var_list->binds = get_struct(fbind);
        var_list->binds->whoset = fact_ptr->ID;
        var_list->binds->origin = fact_ptr;
        var_list->binds->next = NULL;
        if (markers != NULL)
            { var_list->binds->marker = copy_marks(markers); }
        else
            { var_list->binds->marker = NULL; }

        var_list->next = patn_ptr->alpha;
        patn_ptr->alpha = var_list;

        drive_list = patn_ptr->path;
```

```
     while (drive_list != NULL)
         {
         drive(var_list,drive_list->path,RHS);
         drive_list = drive_list->next;
         }
     finish_match = TRUE;
     }
```

If the match was successful or if the search for a match on a particular path is complete, we must reset the pattern net pointers before continuing the search through the net.

```
if (finish_match == TRUE)
    {
    while ((patn_ptr->same_level == NULL)||
      (patn_ptr->type == BLOCKED))
        {
        if (patn_ptr->type == BLOCKED) patn_ptr->type = SINGLE;
        patn_ptr = patn_ptr->last_level;
        if (patn_ptr == NULL)
            { return; }
        else if (patn_ptr->type == MULTIPLE)
            { return; }
        pat_pos--;
        cur_elem--;
        }
    patn_ptr = patn_ptr->same_level;
    }
else if (patn_ptr->type == SINGLE)
    {
```

Now we compare the pattern element with the fact element. At this point the pattern element that could match is a constant. The program checks that the fact element is the same type and value and, if it is, proceeds to the next level of compare.

```
    if (patn_ptr->eval == NULL)
        {
        cur_elem++;
        pat_pos++;
        patn_ptr = patn_ptr->next_level;
        }
    else if (pat_compute(&elem_ptr[cur_elem],patn_ptr->eval) != FALSE)
        if (patn_ptr->eval->val.fun_ptr == PTR_CONSTANT)
            { patn_ptr->type = BLOCKED; }
        cur_elem++;
        pat_pos++;
        patn_ptr = patn_ptr->next_level;
        }
    else
        {
        while ((patn_ptr->same_level == NULL)||
          (patn_ptr->type == BLOCKED))
            {
```

```
              if (patn_ptr->type == BLOCKED) patn_ptr->type = SINGLE;
              patn_ptr = patn_ptr->last_level;
              if (patn_ptr == NULL)
                  { return; }
              else if (patn_ptr->type == MULTIPLE)
                  { return; }
              pat_pos--;
              cur_elem--;
              }
        patn_ptr = patn_ptr->same_level;
        }
   }
else if (patn_ptr->type == MULTIPLE)
   {
```

At this point the pattern element that could match is a '$?'. So the type or value of the
fact element does not matter. However, multiple paths of comparison have to be followed
since the $? can bind to zero or more fact elements. A special case is if the next level in
the pattern net is the end of the pattern and there are no other nodes in the net at the same
level that $? appears, in which case $? binds to all elements.

```
        old_mark = markers;
        if ((patn_ptr->next_level->type == STOP) &&
          (patn_ptr->next_level->same_level == NULL))
            {
            new_mark = get_struct(fact_marker);
            new_mark->element = pat_pos;
            new_mark->start = cur_elem 1;
            new_mark->end = length;
            new_mark->next = NULL;
            if (end_mark == NULL)
                { markers = new_mark; }
            else
                { end_mark->next = new_mark; }

            compare(fact_ptr,elem_ptr,patn_ptr->next_level,
                pat_pos1,length,markers,new_mark);
            }
            else
            {
/* Bind to no elements                                                */
            new_mark = get_struct(fact_marker);
            new_mark->element = pat_pos;
            new_mark->start = cur_elem + 1;
            new_mark->end = cur_elem;
            new_mark->next = NULL;
            if (end_mark == NULL)
                { markers = new_mark; }
            else
                { end_mark->next = new_mark; }
            compare(fact_ptr,elem_ptr,patn_ptr->next_level,
                pat_pos1,cur_elem,markers,new_mark);
```

Now consider the rest of the bindings:

```
                    end_epos = cur_elem;
                    while (end_epos < length)
                        {
                        new_mark->element = pat_pos;
                        new_mark->start = cur_elem + 1;
                        new_mark->end = end_epos + 1;
                        new_mark->next = NULL;
                        end_epos++;
                        compare(fact_ptr,elem_ptr,patn_ptr->next_level,
                            pat_pos+1,end_epos,markers,new_mark);
                        }
                    }
                rtn_struct(fact_marker,new_mark);
                if (end_mark != NULL) end_mark->next = NULL; markers = old_mark;
                current_pattern_marks = old_mark;
                while ((patn_ptr->same_level == NULL)
                    (patn_ptr->type == BLOCKED))
                        {
                        if (patn_ptr->type == BLOCKED) patn_ptr->type = SINGLE;
                        patn_ptr = patn_ptr->last_level;
                        if (patn_ptr == NULL)
                            { return; }
                        else if (patn_ptr->type == MULTIPLE)
                            { return; }
                        pat_pos--;
                        cur_elem--;
                        }
                patn_ptr = patn_ptr->same_level;
                }
            }
        }
```

Once the new fact has matched a pattern in the pattern network, a reference to it is stored in the alpha memory of the terminal node of the pattern net, and it is sent to the join network. Matching in the join network is accomplished with the *drive* procedure. The *drive* procedure is called from the *compare* procedure.

Join Net Matching The *drive* procedure pushes a set of fact bindings through the join net. Input variables to this procedure are *join* (a pointer into the join net), *binds* (the set of fact bindings being passed to the *join*), and *enter_direction* (the direction, left or right, that binds are entering the *join*. Drive alters and uses binds. Thus, if the calling routine does not want binds altered, it makes a copy of them before calling drive. Like the pattern net matching, the join net is searched recursively.

The types of the procedure arguments, the local variables, and a description of the procedure logic is given in the following coding:

```
int drive(binds,join,enter_direction)
    struct flink *binds;
    struct internode *join;
```

```
int enter_direction;
{
struct fbind *lhs_binds, *rhs_binds, *tracer;
struct flink *compare_side, *linker, *clinker;
char entry_logic, opp_logic;
struct list *list_of_joins;
int join_test;
```

A terminating condition for the search is reaching the end of the network. If there is no next node, the terminator join has been reached and the rule is ready to fire. This join is connected in the RETE net to the list of actions for the rule about to fire, so if this point in the net is reached, the action of the rule can be added to the agenda.

```
if (join->next == NULL)
    {
    add_activation(symbol_string(join->eval->val.hvalue),
        join->eval->next_arg->val.index,
        join->eval->next_arg->next_arg,
        binds);
    return(1);
    }
```

Now the bindings should be stored on the appropriate side of the join.

```
if (enter_direction == RHS)
    {
    binds->next = join->entry_pat->alpha;
    join->entry_pat->alpha = binds;
    }
else if (enter_direction == LHS)
    {
    binds->next = join->beta;
    join->beta = binds;
    }
else
    {
    clips_system_error(301);
    cl_exit(5);
    }
```

Initialize a group of variables to indicate which facts the new facts are to be compared with. Also initialize the logic of each side of the join.

```
if (enter_direction == RHS)
    {
    compare_side = join->beta;
    opp_logic = join->lhs_log;
    entry_logic = join->rhs_log;
    rhs_binds = binds->binds;
    }
else
    {
```

```
compare_side = join->entry_pat->alpha;
opp_logic = join->rhs_log;
entry_logic = join->lhs_log;
lhs_binds = binds->binds;
}
```

If the opposite side of the join that was entered has positive logic, but has no fact bindings, no binds will be passed down to the next join. In other words, there was nothing on the other side to match with, so the process can terminate.

```
if ((opp_logic == '+') && (compare_side == NULL))
   { return(1); }
```

If the opposite side of the join that was entered is empty (either there is no pattern or the upper level join enters through that side), perform the appropriate action for the RHS join logic.

```
if (opp_logic == 'e')
   {
   empty_drive(join,binds->binds);
   return(1);
   }
```

Compare each set of binds on the opposite side of the join with the set of binds that entered this join. If the binds match, perform the appropriate action for the logic of the join.

```
while (compare_side != NULL)
   {
   join_test = FALSE;
   if (enter_direction == RHS)
       { lhs_binds = compare_side->binds ; }
   else
       { rhs_binds = compare_side->binds; }
```

Evaluate the join expression for this combination of RHS and LHS bindings.

```
if (join->eval == NULL)
       { join_test = TRUE; }
   else
       { join_test = join_compute(join->eval,lhs_binds, rhs_binds); }
```

If the join expression evaluated to true (that is, there were no conflicts between variable bindings, all tests were satisfied, and so on), perform the appropriate action given the logic of this join.

```
if (join_test != FALSE)
       {
       if ((entry_logic == '+') && (opp_logic == '+'))
```

```
                { pp_drive(lhs_binds,rhs_binds,join); }
            else if (entry_logic == '-')
                { pn_drive(join,compare_side); }
            else if (opp_logic == '-')
                { binds->count++; }
        }

    compare_side = compare_side->next;
    }
```

If a join with a positive LHS and a negative RHS was entered from the LHS side of the join, and the join test failed for all sets of matches for the new bindings on the LHS side (the counter on the LHS is set to zero), the LHS bindings should be sent down to the joins below along with a marker that represents the instance of the negated pattern that was satisfied.

```
if ((opp_logic == '-') && (binds->count == 0))
    {
    if (join->not_eval != NULL)
        {
        join_test = join_compute(join->not_eval, binds->binds,NULL);
        if (join_test == FALSE) return(1);
        }
    linker = get_struct(flink);
    linker->binds = copy_binds(binds->binds);
    linker->count = 0;
    linker->next = NULL;
    tracer = linker->binds;
    while (tracer->next != NULL)
        { tracer = tracer->next; }
    tracer->next = newnid();
    binds->count = tracer->next->whoset;
```

Send binding to all joins below this join.

```
    list_of_joins = join->next;
    while (list_of_joins->next != NULL)
        {
        clinker = get_struct(flink);
        clinker->next = NULL;
        clinker->count = 0;
        clinker->binds = copy_binds(linker->binds);
        drive(clinker,list_of_joins->path,LHS);
        list_of_joins = list_of_joins->next;
        }

    drive(linker,list_of_joins->path,LHS);
    }
return(1);
}
```

Evaluation of Tests   The test evaluations at the nodes are performed by composing a function call at run-time. Information about the test function and its arguments are represented using the *test* structure.

```
struct test
    {
    int type;
    union
        {
        float fvalue;
        int index;
        struct funtab *fun_ptr;
        struct draw *hvalue;
        char *s_ptr;
        } val;
        struct test *arg_list;
        struct test *next_arg;
    };
```

Tests are evaluated using a generic evaluation procedure called *generic_compute*. This evaluation procedure composes the function call given the test structure as input. The procedure returns the results in a *values* structure.

```
struct values
    {
    int type;
    char *name;
    union
        {
        struct draw *hvalue;
        float fvalue;
        } val;
    struct fact *origin;
    int begin;
    int end;
    struct values *next;
    };
```

The *generic_compute* procedure is essentially a large switch statement to handle the different problem types.

```
int generic_compute(problem,compute_result)
    struct test *problem;
    struct values *compute_result;
    {
    struct values *vresult;
    float result;
    char *sresult, *fun_name;
```

```
struct draw *dresult;
struct test *temp_arg;
char (*cp)();
char *(*sp)();
struct draw *(*dp)();
float (*fp)();
struct values *(*vp)();
char cbuff[2], rc;
struct test *old_arg;

switch (problem->type)
{
case STRING:
case WORD:
compute_result->type = problem->type;
compute_result->val.hvalue = problem->val.hvalue;
break;

case NUMBER:
compute_result->type = NUMBER;
compute_result->val.fvalue = problem->val.fvalue; break;

case FCALL:
fun_name = problem->val.fun_ptr->fun_name;

old_arg = new_fctn_args;
new_fctn_args = problem;

switch(problem->val.fun_ptr->fun_type)
    {
    case 'v' :
    (*problem->val.fun_ptr->ip)();
    compute_result->type = RVOID;
    compute_result->val.fvalue = 0.0;
    break;

    case 'i' :
    result = (float) (*problem->val.fun_ptr->ip)();
    compute_result->type = NUMBER;
    compute_result->val.fvalue = result;
    break;

    case 'f' :
    fp = (float (*)()) problem->val.fun_ptr->ip;
    result = (*fp)();
    compute_result->type = NUMBER;
    compute_result->val.fvalue = result;
    break;

    case 's' :
    dp = (struct draw *(*)()) problem->val.fun_ptr->ip;
```

```
            dresult = (*dp)();
            compute_result->type = STRING;
            compute_result->val.hvalue = dresult;
            break;

            case 'w' :
            dp = (struct draw *(*)()) problem->val.fun_ptr->ip;
            dresult = (*dp)();
            compute_result->type = WORD;
            compute_result->val.hvalue = dresult;
            break;

            case 'c' :
            cp = (char (*)()) problem->val.fun_ptr->ip;
            rc = (*cp)();
            cbuff[0] = rc;
            cbuff[1] = EOS;
            compute_result->type = WORD;
            compute_result->val.hvalue = add_symbol(cbuff);
            break;

            case 'm' :
            (*problem->val.fun_ptr->ip)(compute_result);
            break;

            case 'u' :
            (*problem->val.fun_ptr->ip)(compute_result);
            break;

            default :
            clips_system_error(1202);
            cl_exit(5);
            break;
            }

    new_fctn_args = old_arg;
    break;

    case BWORDS:
    case BWORD:
    cl_print("werror"," n*** ERROR *** /n");
    cl_print("werror","Variables cannot be accessed at this level /n");
    break;
    }
    return;
    }
```

Clearly, composing the procedure at run-time in this fashion is not going to be as efficient as compiling the test code as part of the net, as done in the Forgy approach.

User-defined functions are defined for use by the system with the *define_function* procedure. Information about these functions is stored in a function table, implemented as a linked list. Table entries are structures of type *funtab,* where each entry records the function name (*fun_name*), the type of the return value (*fun_type*), and a pointer to the function code (*ip*).

```
struct funtab
    {
        char *fun_name;
        char *def_name;
        char fun_type;
        int (*ip)();
        struct funtab *next;
    };
```

The *define_function* procedure is used to define a system or user function so that CLIPS can access it.

```
define_function(name,return_type,pointer,defn_name)
    char *name, *defn_name;
    char return_type;
    int (*pointer)();
    {

    struct funtab *new_function;

    if ( (return_type != 'i') &&
         (return_type != 'f') &&
         (return_type != 's') &&
         (return_type != 'w') &&
         (return_type != 'c') &&
         (return_type != 'v') &&
         (return_type != 'm') &&
         (return_type != 'u') )
         {
         cl_print("werror","ERROR: Illegal function type passed to define_function  n");
         cl_print("werror","Legal values are i, f, s, w, c, v, m, and u. /n");
         return(0);
         }

    new_function = get_struct(funtab);
    new_function->fun_name = name;
    new_function->fun_type = return_type;
    new_function->ip = pointer;
    new_function->next = fctn_list;
    new_function->defn_name = defn_name;

    fctn_list = new_function;
    return(1);
    }
```

The Agenda Mechanism

The agenda mechanism handles the *act* part of the recognize-act inference cycle. The representation of an activation on the agenda is as follows:

```
struct activation
    {
    struct flink *basis;
    struct test *actions;
    long int id;
    char *rule;
    int salience;
    struct activation *next;
    };
```

Each activation structure stores information about the pattern matches that resulted in the activation (*basis*), the actions that will be performed if this activation is selected from the activations on the agenda (*actions*), and the salience of the rule, for use by the agenda mechanism in selecting the next activation to fire. The agenda itself is implemented as a linked list of activations.

The inference engine control flow, incorporating the agenda mechanism, is illustrated in Figure 3.8.

The CLIPS function *run* executes the activations on the agenda. If the input parameter *run_limit* is <0, rules execute until there are no more rules to be run. If *run_limit* is >0, up to *run_limit* number of rules will be executed. The *run* function returns the number rules that have been executed.

```
run(run_limit)
    int run_limit;
    {
    struct test *commands;
    struct fbind *local_vars;
    struct activation *rule_to_fire;
    int rules_fired = 0;
    char print_space[20];
    struct values result;
    struct exec_func *exec_ptr;

/* Fire rules until the agenda is empty, the run limit           */
/* has been reached, or a rule execution error occurs.           */

    EXECUTION_ERROR = FALSE;

    while ((AGENDA != NULL) &&
      (run_limit != 0) &&
```

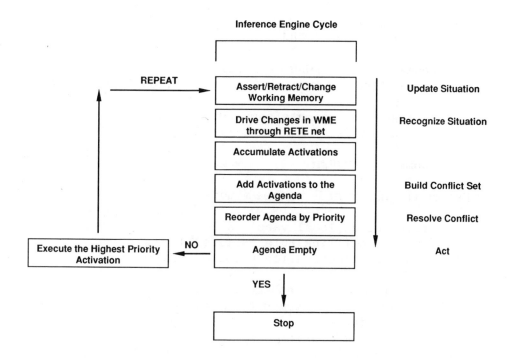

Figure 3.7 Inference Engine Control Flow

Control flow in the inference engine proceeds from changes in the working memory through modification of the RETE net, which in turn may result in the modification of the activations list on the agenda. The agenda is a stack where the stack elements are activations that are ordered according to their priority.

```
(EXECUTION_ERROR == FALSE))
   {

/* Bookkeeping and Tracing.                                          */

      currentrule = AGENDA->rule;
      rules_fired++;
      if (run_limit > 0) { run_limit--; }

/* Execute the rule's right hand side actions.                       */

      change_agenda = TRUE;
      rule_to_fire = AGENDA;
      commands = AGENDA->actions;
      local_vars = AGENDA->basis->binds;
      AGENDA = AGENDA->next;
```

```
        gbl_lhs_binds = local_vars;
        gbl_rhs_binds = NULL;

        commands = commands->arg_list;
        while ((commands != NULL) && (EXECUTION_ERROR == FALSE))
             {
             generic_compute(commands,&result);
             commands = commands->next_arg;
             }
        commands = NULL;

/* Return the agenda node to free memory.                              */

        returnbinds(local_vars);
        rtn_struct(flink,rule_to_fire->basis);
        rtn_struct(activation,rule_to_fire);

/* Remove retracted facts, ephemeral symbols,                         */
/* variable bindings, and temporary segments.                         */
        rmv_old_facts();
        rem_eph_symbols();
        flush_bind_list();
        flush_segments();

/* Execute exec list after performing actions.                        */
        exec_ptr = exec_list;
        while (exec_ptr != NULL)
             {
             (*exec_ptr->ip)();
             exec_ptr = exec_ptr->next;
             }
        }
        EXECUTION_ERROR = FALSE;
        return(rules_fired);
     }
```

Conclusion

One of the most important results of the cognitive science research of the last several decades has been the production system model for human performance in solving problems. The production system model has been used to describe human problem solving in a number of areas, including game playing, applied mathematics, and computer programming.

At the least, the production system offers a general framework for implementing search procedures. Among its major advantages is the separation of knowledge and control, where the control is provided by the recognize-act cycle, and the knowledge is provided by the rules. The chief advantage here is the ease of program extension. The main disadvantage is the inability to modify and therefore the exposure to the limitations of the built-in control mechanisms.

Production systems do readily map onto a state space search, which is a natural way to think about control systems, many of which are embedded systems. The productions in this case represent the set of possible state transitions, with the conflict resolution strategy selecting between possible branches. Use of rules in this way can simplify the design, implementation, and debugging of the controller, in addition to adding to its functionality.

Another unique aspect of the production system architecture is the use of pattern-directed control, which enables the system to respond by using the rules in any sequence. The result is a mechanism for heuristic search.

Knowledge-based systems have been used in open loop control of space shuttle flight operations. These systems monitor the shuttle, detect faults, and advise flight operations personnel. Data-directed reasoning systems implemented in CLIPS (Muratore 1989) are used to help the flight controllers interpret flight data, a task that had required two to three years of controller training. System requirements put a premium on performance and mean that the expertise has to be embedded within hardware and software systems for real-time telemetry monitoring. Future efforts include knowledge-based programs for monitoring mechanical systems and electric power systems in addition to expert systems for guidance, navigation, and control.

The next chapter takes a close look at the control processes underlying the systems with a strong basis in formal logic. This chapter closes with a look at a simple but representative production system application in CLIPS.

Sample Application

A simple CLIPS application is presented here.

The phase control rules are executed first, and they direct the operation of the system through two phases of processing. In the first phase the user is queried about certain facts of the engine state. These facts could also be asserted through a monitoring subsystem. The second phase suggests possible repairs. Repairs are suggested during processing and are asserted as WMEs.

The rules that control the query process are labeled as Query Rules. The rules responsible for listing repairs appear under the heading Repair Listing Rules. Both sets of rules have as their first conditions a pattern that is designed to test the current processing phase. These conditions are (query phase) and (list-repairs) for the query and repair-listing phases respectively.

```
;;;******************************
;;;* AUTOMOTIVE EXPERT SYSTEM   *
;;;******************************


;;;**********************
;;;* ENGINE STATE RULES  *
;;;**********************

(defrule normal-engine-state-conclusions ""
    (working-state engine normal)
=>
    (assert (spark-state engine normal))
    (assert (fuel-level gas-tank sufficient))
    (assert (charge-state battery charged))
    (assert (rotation-state engine rotates)))

(defrule unsatisfactory-engine-state-conclusions ""
    (working-state engine unsatisfactory)
=>
    (assert (fuel-level gas-tank sufficient))
    (assert (charge-state battery charged))
    (assert (rotation-state engine rotates)))

;;;***************
;;;* QUERY RULES  *
;;;***************

(defrule determine-engine-state ""
    ?rem <- (query phase)
    (not (working-state engine ?))
=>
    (retract ?rem)
    (printout t "What is the working state of the engine:" t)
    (printout t " (normal/unsatisfactory/does-not-start)? ")
    (bind ?response (read))
    (assert (working-state engine ?response)))

(defrule determine-rotation-state ""
    ?rem <- (query phase)
```

```
   (working-state engine does-not-start)
   (not (rotation-state engine ?))
=>
   (retract ?rem)
   (printout t "Does the engine rotate (yes/no) ? ")
   (bind ?response (read))
   (if (eq ?response yes)
      then
      (assert (rotation-state engine rotates))
      (assert (spark-state engine irregular-spark))
      else
      (assert (rotation-state engine does-not-rotate))
   (assert (spark-state engine does-not-spark))))

(defrule determine-sluggishness ""
   ?rem <- (query phase)
   (working-state engine unsatisfactory)
   (not (symptom engine sluggishness | not-sluggishness))
=>
   (retract ?rem)
   (printout t "Is the engine sluggish (yes/no)? ")
   (bind ?response (read))
   (if (eq ?response yes)
      then
      (assert (symptom engine sluggishness))
      else
      (assert (symptom engine not-sluggishness))))

(defrule determine-misfiring ""
   ?rem <- (query phase)
   (working-state engine unsatisfactory)
   (not (symptom engine misfiring | not-misfiring))
=>
   (retract ?rem)
   (printout t "Does the engine misfire (yes/no)? ")
   (bind ?response (read))
   (if (eq ?response yes)
      then
      (assert (symptom engine misfiring))
      (assert (spark-state engine irregular-spark))
      else
   (assert (symptom engine not-misfiring))))

(defrule determine-knocking ""
   ?rem <- (query phase)
```

```
    (working-state engine unsatisfactory)
    (not (symptom engine knocking | not-knocking))
=>
    (retract ?rem)
    (printout t "Does the engine knock (yes/no)? ")
    (bind ?response (read))
    (if (eq ?response yes)
        then
        (assert (symptom engine knocking))
        else
        (assert (symptom engine not-knocking))))

(defrule determine-low-output ""
    ?rem <- (query phase)
    (working-state engine unsatisfactory)
    (not (symptom engine low-output | not-low-output))
=>
    (retract ?rem)
    (printout t "Is the output of the engine low (yes/no)? ")
    (bind ?response (read))
    (if (eq ?response yes)
        then
        (assert (symptom engine low-output))
        else
        (assert (symptom engine not-low-output))))

(defrule determine-gas-level ""
    ?rem <- (query phase)
    (working-state engine does-not-start)
    (rotation-state engine rotates)
    (not (fuel-level gas-tank ?))
=>
    (retract ?rem)
    (printout t "Does the tank have any gas in it (yes/no)? ")
    (bind ?response (read))
    (if (eq ?response yes)
        then
        (assert (fuel-level gas-tank sufficient))
        else
        (assert (fuel-level gas-tank empty))))

(defrule determine-battery-state ""
    ?rem <- (query phase)
    (rotation-state engine does-not-rotate)
    (not (charge-state battery ?))
=>
```

```
    (retract ?rem)
    (printout t "What is the state of the battery (charged/dead)? ")
    (bind ?response (read))
    (assert (charge-state battery ?response)))

(defrule determine-point-surface-state ""
    ?rem <- (query phase)
    (or (and (working-state engine does-not-start)
             (spark-state engine irregular-spark))
        (symptom engine low-output))
    (not (point-surface-state points ?))
 =>
    (retract ?rem)
    (printout t "What is the surface state of the points " t)
    (printout t "(normal/burned/contaminated)? ")
    (bind ?response (read))
    (assert (point-surface-state points ?response)))

(defrule determine-conductivity-test ""
    ?rem <- (query phase)
    (working-state engine does-not-start)
    (spark-state engine does-not-spark)
    (not (charge-state battery dead))
    (not (conductivity-test ignition-coil ?))
 =>
    (retract ?rem)
    (printout t "What is conductivity test for the ignition coil" t)
    (printout t " (positive/negative)? ")
    (bind ?response (read))
    (assert (conductivity-test ignition-coil ?response)))

;;;***************************
;;;* REPAIR SUGGESTION RULES   *
;;;***************************

(defrule no-repair-needed ""
    (working-state engine normal)
 =>
    (assert (repair "No repair needed.")))

(defrule charge-battery-repair ""
    (rotation-state engine does-not-rotate)
    (charge-state battery dead)
 =>
    (assert (repair "Charge the battery.")))
```

```
(defrule timing-adjustment-repair ""
    (working-state engine unsatisfactory)
    (symptom engine knocking)
 =>
    (assert (repair "Timing adjustment.")))

(defrule replace-ignition-coil-repair ""
    (working-state engine does-not-start)
    (spark-state engine does-not-spark)
    (conductivity-test ignition-coil negative)
 =>
    (assert (repair "Replace the ignition coil.")))

(defrule distributor-lead-wire-repair ""
    (working-state engine does-not-start)
    (spark-state engine does-not-spark)
    (conductivity-test ignition-coil positive)
 =>
    (assert (repair "Repair the distributor lead wire.")))

(defrule point-gap-adjustment-repair ""
    (working-state engine unsatisfactory)
    (symptom engine misfiring)
 =>
    (assert (repair "Point gap adjustment.")))

(defrule replace-points-repair ""
    (working-state engine does-not-start)
    (spark-state engine irregular-spark)
    (point-surface-state points burned)
 =>
    (assert (repair "Replace the points.")))

(defrule clean-points-repair-1 ""
    (working-state engine does-not-start)
    (spark-state engine irregular-spark)
    (point-surface-state points contaminated)
 =>
    (assert (repair "Clean the points.")))

(defrule clean-points-repair-2 ""
    (working-state engine unsatisfactory)
    (symptom engine low-output)
    (point-surface-state points contaminated)
 =>
```

```
    (assert (repair "Clean the points.")))

(defrule clean-fuel-line-repair ""
    (symptom engine sluggishness)
=>
    (assert (repair "Clean the fuel line.")))

(defrule add-gas-repair ""
    (rotation-state engine rotates)
    (fuel-level gas-tank empty)
=>
    (assert (repair "Add gas.")))

;;;***********************
;;;* REPAIR LISTING RULES   *
;;;***********************

(defrule no-repairs ""
    (list-repairs)
    (not (repair ?))
=>
    (assert (repair "Take your car to a mechanic.")))

(defrule print-repair"'
    (list-repairs)
    (repair ?item)
=>
    (format t " %s%n" ?item))

(defrule spaces-at-end ""
    (declare (salience -10))
    (list-repairs)
=>
    (printout t t t))

;;;***********************
;;;* PHASE CONTROL RULES    *
;;;***********************

(defrule system-banner ""
=>
    (printout t t t)
    (printout t "The Engine Diagnosis Expert System")
    (printout t t t))
```

```
(defrule initiate-query ""
    (declare (salience -10))
    (not (query phase)))
=>
    (assert (query phase)))

(defrule initiate-repair ""
    (declare (salience -10))
    (query phase)
=>
    (printout t t t)
    (printout t "Suggested Repairs:")
    (printout t t t)
    (assert (list-repairs)))
```

Chapter 4 **Logic Systems**

Introduction

In this chapter we'll take a close look at systems that use logic as their model of intelligence. If you recall, the production system languages have an underlying model of human problem solving whose essence is captured in the recognize-act cycle of the inference engine. Systems based on logic have really approached the task of mechanizing intelligence in the same vein—logic is just a model of human problem solving that dates from way back. Make no mistake though. Despite the surface similarities of the rules (for example, their IF . . . THEN . . . syntax), the pure production system and the pure logic system philosophies are radically different.

The simplest way to describe the differences is to note that the production system's recognize-act cycle is meant to be descriptive of the human problem-solving process. The rules of inference that are fundamental to the logic system's operation are prescriptive. They attempt to describe a formal system that captures the rules for the proper way to reason about a problem.

These differences are not captured by the common terminology for problem-solving strategies. Forward chaining is a strategy that best serves data-directed problems. The idea here is to reason from observations to conclusions. Backward chaining is a strategy that best serves a goal-directed, divide-and-conquer approach. This strategy reasons from goals to supporting facts, in the form of a proof.

Production systems are most often forward-chaining systems, though this categorization says more about how their inference engines work than it does about the sorts of problem-solving strategies that can be implemented with the system. A similar statement is true for logic systems. Although they are backward chaining in basic operation, forward-chaining problem solving is quite easily handled. Thus the IF . . . THEN . . . rule syntax is common to both kinds of systems, which gives them their surface similarity and congruent capabilities.

A pretty narrow definition of logic, which helps to understand how logic systems work, is the following: logic is the study of the kinds of argument that are valid simply by virtue of their structure. Once you take this view, any sort of rule language based on logic that is to run on a machine (that is, a mechanical theorem prover or inference engine) needs at least two elements, an internal representation of the form of argument, and a procedure that can efficiently use this representation to decide the validity of the argument.

Rule languages of this sort can be distinguished on the basis of how much structure they allow the rules to have. You can think of structure in terms of data structure because this is exactly what rule structure translates into inside the computer. The simplest rule languages are based on the propositional logic, where complex arguments are described only in terms of the atomic sentences of which they are made. These sentences are called *propositions*.

The requirements of an internal representation of an atomic proposition in a rule language based on propositional logic are met by a token for the proposition (for example, a pointer to the string representing the proposition's text). If this is all you need for each proposition, clearly the rule data structure will be very compact, as will the entire rulebase. A series of very compact and very fast propositional logic languages has been developed by Park (1984). An early version, published in 1984, is entirely backward chaining. This system, called Expert-2, is written in FORTH, and Expert-2 is to FORPS as Prolog is to CLIPS.

Prolog, by contrast with Expert-2, is a mechanical theorem prover for predicate logic, which attaches meaning to the internal structure of the atomic propositions, for example, the predicate name and the number and structure of its formal parameters. A predicate is formally a function of any number of arguments that evaluates to one of the logical values true or false. Thus a predicate is often interpreted as a property or a relation that might hold between things.

Because the internal structure of propositions is significant in the predicate logic, an interpreter for Prolog must run its argument validation process over more complex data structures than those used by an interpreter for propositional logic. This added complexity tends to limit the performance of Prolog interpreters, certainly relative to interpreters for propositional languages.

The principle underlying Prolog compilation is the combination of the validation process and the proposition (also known as the clause) structure, so that the internal representation of each proposition is in fact executable. What is executed is the procedure that determines the validity of the proposition. Compilation in this sense can make a predicate calculus language like Prolog very efficient. In other words, the trick to compiling Prolog and increasing the execution performance is to make the code itself an executable description of the clause.

This chapter introduces the basic architectural elements of a Prolog Virtual Machine (PVM) and discusses two examples. The PVM described in the following section illustrates quite well the basic operation of the Prolog machine, and virtual machines for logic languages in general. It has the tremendous advantage of conceptual simplicity as well as the practical simplicity of a small instruction set. This simplicity can be advantageous for embedded systems under constraints of memory resources. However, as usual, there is a space-time tradeoff, and another abstract Prolog machine known as the Warren Abstract Machine (WAM) is more complex but about a factor of two faster. These measurements are based on the implementations described here. The WAM is described later in this chapter.

The simplicity of the PVM is best illustrated by the observation that the instructions of the virtual machine are of only two types, those that alter the flow of control and those that denote the structures in Prolog clauses (in keeping with the theme of compiled Prolog as description). Compilation to the virtual machine instructions becomes a simple matter of composing a description of the clause, which can easily be done by hand. Implementation of the virtual machine is a straightforward programming task.

The compiler technology presented here is based on the simple compiler described by Bowen, Byrd, and Clocksin in their 1983 paper. The C code for the virtual machine is given in Appendix A. Code for the compiler (in Prolog) is given in Appendix B. The last section of this chapter covers Prolog compilation in more detail, including a more complete Prolog compiler and the instruction set for a version of the Warren Abstract Machine.

Introduction to Prolog

Prolog is a simple language with a straightforward syntax and program structure (Figure 4.1).

Its declarative semantics (what each clause in a program means when read as a statement, as in logic) is also straightforward. Each Prolog procedure may be read as an

```
A Prolog program is a set of procedures
A Prolog procedure is a set of clauses
 - each clause is of the form "P :- Q1,Q2, ... Qn."
   read: P is true if
        Q1 is true  and
        Q2 is true  and ... and
        Qn is true.
 - if n = 0 the clause is written as  "P."
   read: P is true.
Some terminology:
     P        :-      Q1,Q2,Q3 .
   |___|    |___|   |_____| |_|
   head     neck      body     foot
```

Figure 4.1. Prolog at a Glance

assertion that the specified relation holds between its arguments. The procedure name is the relation name.

The simplest case of a clause is the unary relation. You can think of a unary relation as asserting set membership or stating a type for an individual. For example, the type of individual devices in a circuit may be specified by the predicates *inverter* and *and_gate*, as in the Prolog clauses:

```
inverter(device_1).
inverter(device_2).
and_gate(device_3).
```

Predicate definitions may also be conditional, as in the following clauses:

```
fault(X,inverter) :- inverter(X),input(X,Y),output(X,Y).
open_circuit(X,Y) :- connected(X,Y),output(X,Z),
                     not (input(Y,Z)).
```

The first clause is read as "inverter X is faulty if X is an inverter and the input to X is Y and the output of X is also Y." The second clause is read as "there is an open circuit between devices X and Y if X is connected to Y and the output of X is Z and the input to Y is not Z." The terms X,Y, and Z in these definitions are logical variables, meaning that they reference some unknown individual device or value. The scope of a variable reference is the clause in which it is used.

What is unusual and makes Prolog useful as a programming language is its procedural semantics. Understanding how a Prolog program works involves understanding the search mechanism that is part and parcel of procedure invocation (and this search procedure may result in backtracking). The way information is passed between procedures through pattern matching (called *unification*) is also unique to Prolog and provides the language with a good bit of its power.

Aside from the search and pattern-matching capabilities, Prolog procedures execute much like any conventional language. However, one consequence of the built-in search mechanism is that any procedure call can invoke more than one procedure, or even none at all. Since the Prolog machinery needs to search through the candidate procedures, one good way to visualize Prolog procedure execution is as a search tree, or as what might be more aptly called a *proof* tree in the case of a successful search (Figure 4.2). This is exactly analogous to a call tree for a conventional program, except that the path taken is not determined until run-time, nor is it deterministic. There may be more than one proof tree that a Prolog program could trace out.

Prolog procedures can also have parameters (Figure 4.3). Unlike parameters in conventional languages, Prolog parameters are neither strictly input nor strictly output parameters. This is a consequence of the pattern-matching procedure. Rather, the role played by a parameter depends on the procedure call. One of the very unusual things about Prolog parameters is that they can be used both to pass information to a procedure and to return information to the caller. Which is which depends on the context of the call.

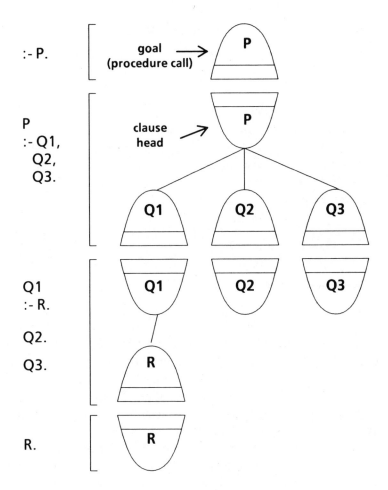

:- P.

P
:- Q1,
Q2,
Q3.

Q1
:- R.

Q2.

Q3.

R.

Figure 4.2. Proof Tree for the Prolog Procedure P

Given the Prolog program on the left, successful execution of the procedure P, as invoked by the goal :- P., can be represented by the tree on the right. Each upper half circle represents a procedure call, whereas the lower half circle represents a matching procedure. The Prolog machine must search through the program, matching the call against candidate procedures. The expense of the search and the associated pattern-matching limit the Prolog performance. (The tree diagram has been called a Ferguson diagram by van Emden.)

This aspect of Prolog parameters is a side effect of one of the more interesting of the ideas about computing that have been realized in the Prolog language. The idea is "call by description." You get this effect if you interpret each parameter of a procedure as a description, and do the same for each argument supplied by a procedure call. These descriptions can be more or less general depending on whether or not they contain variables.

On procedure invocation, the argument terms of the caller (the goal) are matched with the parameter terms of the called procedure. The pattern-matching process implemented

Prolog procedures can have terms as parameters

A term may be:
 - a constant
 - a variable
 - a structure

Constants are atomic objects

Variables stand for arbitrary objects
(by convention variable names begin with an uppercase letter)

Structures consist of a functor applied to terms as arguments
(eg. "p(a,b)")

Some terminology:

$$\underbrace{\textbf{p}}_{\text{functor}} \quad \underbrace{\textbf{(a,b)}}_{\text{arity} = 2}$$

Figure 4.3. Prolog at a Glance

in the unification procedure tests whether two terms can be matched by assigning values to some of the variables in the terms. In a sense, unification is an attempt to find a view of the two descriptions under which they describe the same thing. In Prolog, a successful unification of two terms results in the most general description covered by both original descriptions. The resulting description may be a specialization of the originals (Figure 4.4).

The pattern-matching procedure used in unification can be expensive, primarily because so many cases need to be considered (Figure 4.5).

When the structure analysis performed by the pattern-matching procedure is delayed until run-time, as in an interpreter (either Prolog or OPS interpreters for that matter), performance suffers. Searching for candidate matching clauses during a procedure call can also be expensive. These costs, together with the fundamental role of structure analysis in logic languages, lead to the basic insight underlying all compilation strategies for Prolog. The strategy for compiling Prolog is as follows:

1. *Specialize the unification for each clause.* Unification involves an analysis of structure, so move as much of the analysis as possible from run-time to compile-time.

2. *Reduce the set of candidate clauses.* Index clauses by their structure. Common indices are main functor, arity, and type of first parameter.

The focus of this section is primarily the implementation of the first strategy. It is relatively easy to see how to approach the implementation of the latter. For example, if all procedures with the same main functor were chained together and accessed through a pointer from the main functor word, there would be a substantial reduction in the search

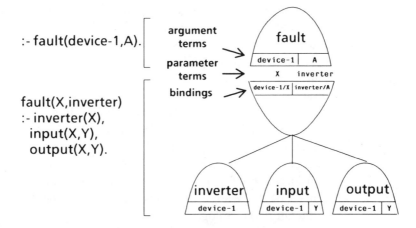

:- fault(device-1,A).

fault(X,inverter)
:- inverter(X),
   input(X,Y),
   output(X,Y).

Figure 4.4 Procedure Invocation by the Goal ":-fault(device_1,A)."

Read the bindings "*a/b*" as "*a* is substituted for *b*." Following the first successful unification of the goal with the head of the procedure, the variable X in the procedure has been specialized to the constant *device-1*. The variable A in the goal has been specialized to the constant *inverter*.

	Constant C_p	Variable X_p	Structure S_p
Constant C_a	Succeed $C_a = C_p$	Succeed $X_p = C_a$	Fail
Variable X_a	Succeed $X_a = C_p$	Succeed $X_a = X_p$	Succeed $X_a = S_p$
Stucture S_a	Fail	Succeed $X_p = S_a$	Succeed if *

* S_a and S_p have the same functor and arity, and the corresponding arguments of S_a and S_p unify

Figure 4.5. Cases Considered by the Unification Process

Subscripts refer to the arguments passed by the caller (for example, structure S_a) and the parameters for the procedure (for example S_p). Variables are pointers, so if a variable has been bound it must be replaced by the bound value prior to comparison. The process of following a chain of pointers from a variable is called dereferencing the variable. Unification is a recursive procedure.

space. A discussion of indexing of clauses to speed up the search for candidate clauses will be deferred until later, during discussions of the Warren Abstract Machine.

The best approach to describing compilation is to break down the process of compiler building into two steps. In the first step, we build a compiler that compiles Prolog source code statements to the instruction set of a Prolog Virtual Machine (PVM). The PVM described here has several advantages. It is easy to understand and implement because the set of instructions is small (there are only seven instructions). In addition, the compilation procedure is straightforward because there is essentially a one-to-one correspondence between clause structure and the object (PVM) code. Moreover, the PVM is a stack machine, which reduces the complexity of the compiler, since issues like register allocation need not be considered. Finally, this PVM serves as a good introduction to the operation and instruction set of the Warren Abstract Machine (see the 1983 paper by Warren) and the current literature on Prolog compilation.

The second step involves the implementation of the PVM. Implementation of a virtual machine is a common approach to compiler building, as was discussed in considerable detail in Chapter 2, with the tradeoff being speed for portability and more compact code.

Prolog Compilation Step 1. Compile Prolog to PVM Instructions

To explain the compilation procedure, let's look first at the compilation of Prolog structures, probably the simplest case. Remember that the strategy is to approach the compiled code as if it were a description of the structure of the source code. The descriptive words that are needed as building blocks are the names of the types of Prolog terms—the unstructured terms such as variables and constants, and the structured terms like lists. The term types suggest that there should be PVM instructions named *var* and *const* in the code for unstructured terms, and a *functor* instruction for structured terms, with an instruction like *pop* used to indicate the termination of a structured term description. These instructions are eventually implemented as individual C procedures.   •

Given the four instructions, the procedure for compiling Prolog structures to PVM instructions is simply to compose a description of the structure using *const, var, functor,* and *pop*.

In the following two examples of the compilation of Prolog structures note the near one-to-one correspondence between the Prolog objects that comprise the structure and the PVM instructions the structure compiles into.

For a simple technical reason, the object code does not reference logical variables by their names in the source code. The reason is that variables occurring in a clause must be unique to each use of the clause. Thus there can be no unique reference to the variable X. With each procedure invocation, new procedure variables are created and associated

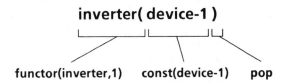

Example 4.1: Compilation of the structure "inverter(device-1)"

The PVM code describes the term "inverter(device-1)" as a structure with functor = inverter, arity = 1, and whose single formal parameter is a constant = device-1. The PVM instruction *pop* terminates the description.

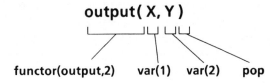

Example 4.2: Compilation of the structure "output(X,Y)"

The PVM code describes the term "output(X,Y)" as a structure with functor = output, arity = 2. The two formal parameters of the structure are variables, referenced by an index into an array of variables.

with the procedure's stack frame. So the compiler renames variables as they appear in a clause—first variable, second variable, and so on—and the numbers are used as indices into the area allocated for a procedure's variables. Thus variables are referenced by a number (index) in the object code.

If you feel comfortable with the compilation process for structures, it's only a short step to compiling complete procedures. However, there are some additional steps and some subtleties of which you should be aware.

The main additional step that's required to compile a procedure is to use the PVM instructions *call, enter,* and *return* to mark the transfer of control in the object code.

The chief subtlety involved in understanding how the resulting code works is the difference between the way PVM instructions operate in the head and the body of a clause. In the head of a clause, PVM instructions perform the operations of unification, as specialized for that clause. In the body of a clause, PVM instructions must prepare arguments for a procedure call. In other words, PVM instructions must operate in at least two modes; "match" mode in the head of a clause and "arg" mode (short for argument) in the body. This brief discussion previews some implementation issues, and the reason for mentioning these issues here is to provide a rationale for the different forms of description used in the head and body of a clause.

A second subtlety is the effect of clause indexing on the compilation of the head of a clause. Let's assume that clauses can be indexed by their main functor and arity, that is, if the procedure fault/2 (that is, functor = fault, arity = 2) is being invoked, candidate clauses can be found by looking, say, at the place where the atom *fault* is stored and following a chain of pointers to the fault/2 clauses. This means that the whole Prolog program does not need to be searched and that the functor and arity of the clause can be left off the description of the clause head. There are more sophisticated indexing schemes, but we'll keep with the simple one for the time being.

With these additional facts in mind, we first consider the compilation of Prolog clauses without bodies—unit clauses.

Compilation of Unit Clauses

The chief differences between the compiled forms of structures and unit clauses are first the indication, via the word *return*, of transfer of control at the end of the unit clause. The second difference is the fact that the functor and arity of the clause are not part of the object code emitted by the compiler. For example, continuing and extending the description of the compilation procedure, the clause

```
inverter(device-1).
```

is compiled as follows. First the compiler notes that the functor/arity of the clause is "inverter/1." A pointer to the compiled code is stored in a list of pointers to other clauses in the same procedure. The compiler also notes that the clause has a single constant, "device-1." Next, a description of the clause is put together as before. This is the program (description) for "inverter(device-1)" that is stored with the collection of clauses for functor/arity = "inverter/1."

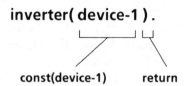

A more complicated example is the clause

```
inverter(connected(device-2,Y)).
```

There is one variable, one constant, and a structure in this clause, and the PVM code emitted by the compiler is

```
functor(connected, 2)    % connected
const(device-2)          % (device-2
var(1)                   % Y
pop()                    %          )
return()                 %
```

The connection between the source code and the object code is illustrated in the following compilation example.

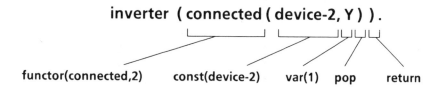

Lists may be represented in this PVM by a structured term with functor/arity = cons/2 (Table 4.1). The first parameter of cons/2 references the first element of the list and the second parameter of cons/2 references the rest of the list. Other representations of lists could be used to save both space and time, at the (slight) cost of increasing the size of the PVM instruction set.

Table 4.1. Prolog List Syntax

Prolog source code has several syntactic forms for lists. Generally, a list is enclosed by square brackets. The empty list [] is a constant; and the character | separates the beginning of a list from the rest of the list. There is a single internal representation of a list, which, in the examples here, is a structure of functor = cons, arity = 2.

External Form	Internal Form
[]	nil
[a]	cons(a,nil)
[a|[]]	cons(a,nil)
[a,b]	cons(a,cons(b,nil))
[a|[b]]	cons(a,cons(b,nil))
[a|b]	cons(a,b)

As a final example of the compiled form of a unit clause, consider

```
append([a,b],L,[a,b|L]).
```

This clause has only one variable. The PVM code emitted by the compiler is

```
functor(cons,2)          % [
    const(a)             %  a,
    functor(cons,2)      %
        const(b)         %    b
        const(nil)       %
        pop()            %
    pop()                % ],
```

```
var(1)                    % L,
functor(cons,2)           % [
    const(a)              % a,
    functor(cons,2)       %
        const(b)          %      b
        var(1)            %          |L
        pop()             %
    pop()                 % ]
return()                  % .
```

The compiled code can be read as a description of the structure of the clause "append([a,b],L,[a,b|L])." With the PVM instruction set implemented in C, the description constitutes the program that is executed when "append/3" is called.

Compilation of Nonunit Clauses

Compilation of nonunit clauses requires two additional PVM instructions: *enter* and *call*. *Enter* is the object code representation of the "neck" (:-) of a clause. Its chief purpose is to switch the PVM execution mode and adjust certain pointers. The PVM instruction *call* takes a reference to the clause to be called as its argument. Its purpose is to transfer control to the called procedure and to save the control information.

Call is compiled following the compiled description of the procedure arguments. As mentioned earlier, the compilation of a procedure call is slightly different from the compilation of a structure. For example, consider the clause

```
fault(X,inverter):-inverter(X),input(X,Y),output(X,Y).
```

The head of the clause is compiled the same way unit clauses are compiled. The neck of the clause is then marked in the object code by the instruction *enter*, and a procedure call is compiled after a description of the arguments to the procedure (see the example on the next page).

As a final example, consider the clause

```
append([X|L1],L2,[X|L3]) :- append(L1,L2,L3).
```

The clause has four variables. The PVM code for this clause is

```
functor(cons,2)          % [
    var(1)               % X
    var(2)               %    |L1
    pop()                %         ],
var(3)                   % L2,
```

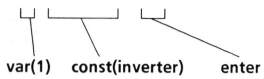

fault(X, inverter) :-

var(1)   const(inverter)   enter

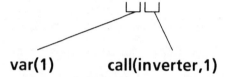

inverter(X) ,

var(1)   call(inverter,1)

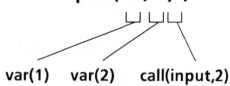

input(X ,Y) ,

var(1)   var(2)   call(input,2)

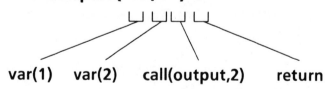

output(X ,Y) .

var(1)   var(2)   call(output,2)   return

```
functor(cons,2)        % [
    var(1)             % X
    var(4)             %      |L3
    pop()              %             ],
enter()                % :-
    var(2)             % L1
    var(3)             % L2
    var(4)             % L3
call(append,3)         % append(L1,L2,L3)
return()               % .
```

Prolog Compilation Step 2. Implement the Prolog Machine.

Having named the instructions of the basic Prolog machine and described how to compile Prolog clauses to Prolog machine code, what remains is the implementation of the machine. This section describes the simulation of the Prolog machine in software. There are three main architectural components of the simulation:

1. The internal representation of Prolog terms (for example, constants, variables, and structures) and of references to these objects.

2. The structure of the stacks required to support Prolog computation.

3. The procedural semantics of the PVM instructions—what the instructions do.

Side issues like the memory map, implementation registers, and scratch stacks will be touched on here, but in less depth than the architecture.

Internal Representation of Terms and References to Terms

The first topic is how to represent references to Prolog terms. Since there are three primitive types of Prolog terms, one form of internal representation could be a 32-bit memory cell with the two high-order bits set aside to indicate the type of the term and the remaining bits containing a pointer to the term (this is just a generalization of the idea of pointer). The two fields of the reference are called the "tag" and the "val," following the convention used by Clocksin (1985). The following list represents a sufficient set of references to primitive objects:

Tag	Val	Purpose
1	Pointer to a variable binding	Variable
2	Pointer to an atom record	Atom
3	Pointer to a structure record	Structured term

For the sake of run-time efficiency, it may be desirable to increase the number of types of terms that can be referenced. For example, it is usually worthwhile to have a special type of reference for integers, even though integers could very well be referenced like any atom. Similarly, you might wish to reference lists in a way that is distinct from the way general structures are referenced. This usually means using a different tag for lists. The same considerations apply to references to bound and unbound variables.

The simplest of the internal representations of terms is the representation of variables, if only because the structures representing variables and references to variables are identical. The val field of a variable reference always points to some reference to a Prolog term, whereas an unbound variable is often indicated by a reference structure that has the tag field of a variable and a val field that points to itself. With this scheme, an unbound variable can be easily recognized.

Unlike variables, the internal representations of Prolog constants and structures are data structures that are distinct from the representations of references to these types of term. Both constants and structures are represented by different kinds of record, with distinct fields in the record holding relevant information about the term. For example, the record representing a structure will hold the information about its functor and arity, as well as references to its parameter terms. The constant record can contain information about the constant, including its print name (a string) and perhaps a pointer to a chain of procedures whose principal functor has the same name as the constant.

Constant and structure representations are built in very different areas of memory. Structures reside exclusively in an area of memory called the *structure stack* (sometimes called the *global stack*). This stack constitutes the necessary dynamic memory allocation required for Prolog computation, and it simplifies the garbage collection problem somewhat since stacks can grow and shrink with the computation.

Constants also reside in a special area of memory. For a simple C implementation of Prolog, you can use an array to implement the constant space. Each Prolog constant is then represented by a multifield structure, one field storing the name string and the subsequent fields storing other information. This particular implementation scheme leaves the problem of garbage collection of constants unresolved, which may be an issue in some applications.

The code for the Prolog programs themselves may be accessed indirectly through the constant structures. For example, indexing of clauses in a particular procedure can be done through the main functor of the procedure. One simple way to do this is to chain procedures by arity, with the pointer to the head of the chain stored in a field of the constant structure for the main functor word. Clause records can then be chained together in a similar fashion off the procedure records. With this approach, procedure invocation begins with a search down the procedure links and backtracking resumes a search down the clause links.

Garbage collection of procedures may be necessary if there is significant database manipulation in a Prolog program. This could be accommodated within this approach by allocating space for the procedures from a heap. The space taken up by the garbage collected procedures is reclaimed by unlinking the procedure and then releasing the procedure memory from the heap.

In summary, the representation of Prolog terms in the PVM uses four kinds of record structures:

1. *Constant record* (2 fields).   The first field in this record is the name string of the constant, and the second field is a pointer to a chain of procedure records.

2. *Structure record* (3 fields).   The first field is a pointer to the constant naming the functor, the second field holds the number of arguments of the structure, and the third is a variable-length field containing the references to the formal arguments of the structure. In the PVM, Prolog structure records are built by *functor* descriptions in space allocated from the structure stack. The WAM uses a similar approach.

3. *Procedure record* (3 fields).   The first field is a pointer to the next procedure in the chain having the same functor but different arity, the second field holds the arity of the procedure, and the third field contains a pointer to a chain of clause records. Space for procedure records can be allocated from a heap.

4. *Clause record* (3 fields).   The first field is a pointer to the next clause record, the second field holds a number indicating how many variables are in the clause, and the third is a variable-length field that contains the code itself. Space for clause records can be allocated from a heap.

Stack Structure

A Prolog machine uses two main stacks. The first is the structure stack, which holds any temporary structures created during the computation. This is a straightforward stack requiring only a pointer to its top.

The second Prolog stack, the control stack, holds state information, the arguments passed to procedures, and procedure variables. This stack is essentially a linear version of the proof tree traced out during a Prolog computation (Figure 4.6).

The Prolog stacks must generally be large relative to the usual C stacks since, in the case of the structure stack, the stack is the mechanism for dynamic memory allocation, and, in the case of the control stack, nondeterminism requires that all state information be saved in case backtracking is necessary. Thus a procedure return does not necessarily pop the control stack, and the stack can grow quite deep.

Implementation of PVM Instructions

The first issue to consider in the software simulation of the PVM is the execution modes of the PVM instructions. As stated earlier, the PVM instructions *const, var,* and *functor* operate in modes, the two main modes being *match* and *arg*. There is a third mode called *copy,* which is a variant of *arg* mode.

The instructions operate in *match* mode when they appear in the head of a clause, matching the parameters of the clause with the arguments passed to the procedure on the control stack. Instructions operate in *arg* mode when they appear in the body of a clause, placing arguments on the control stack prior to a procedure call. Modes are switched by the *call, enter,* and *return* instructions (Figure 4.7).

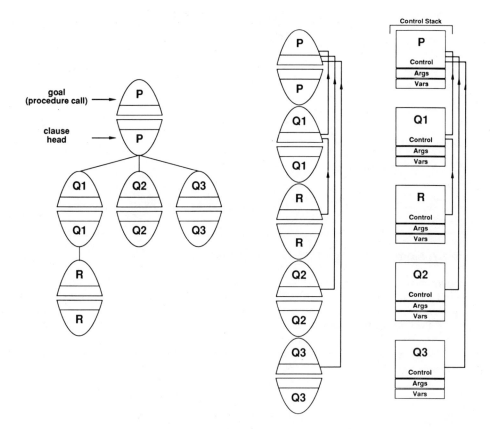

Figure 4.6. Structure of the Control Stack.

The control stack (right-hand side) constitutes a trace of the procedure calls during a Prolog computation and therefore is a representation of the Prolog proof tree (left-hand side), with each stack frame corresponding to a procedure call. The stack frame holds control information, procedure arguments, and the clause variables. In practice, it is possible to reclaim space on the control stack during a computation.

const, *var*, and *functor* in *Arg* Mode

The following discussion considers the operation of PVM instructions in each mode in order according to the mode sequence pictured in Figure 4.7, that is, first *arg* mode, then *match* mode, and finally *copy* mode. To begin, we look again at how a procedure call (goal) compiles, focusing now on what the code does. For example, the goal "fault(device-1,X)" compiles to the PVM instructions

```
const(device-1)      % push reference to device-1
var(n)               % push reference to variable X
call(fault,2)        % call fault/2
```

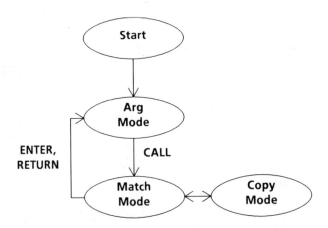

Figure 4.7. Mode Switching in the Prolog Machine

A procedure invoked from top level would begin executing in *arg* mode, placing arguments on the control stack prior to a call. The call (PVM instruction *call*) switches the mode to *match,* and the arguments are matched with the parameters in the head of the clause. If the match is successful, the body of the clause is entered (PVM instruction *enter*), the mode is switched to *arg,* and arguments are placed on the control stack prior to the first call in the body. The mode is also switched to *arg* on a procedure return (PVM instruction *return*). This is only strictly necessary when returning from unit clauses.

and, if this procedure call is successful, the variable X is bound to the device type of "device-1."

At this stage of execution, the PVM is in *arg* mode, and the effect of PVM instructions is to place references to arguments on the control stack. An argument pointer is maintained to indicate where the arguments are to go. The actions of PVM instructions in *arg* mode are described in the Table 4.2.

Table 4.2 PVM Instructions in arg mode

Instruction	Parameter(s)	Description (arg mode)
const	C: pointer to an atom	Push reference to C on control stack; advance arg atom pointer; continue.
var	I: index into environment	Dereference Ith variable; push result on control stack; advance arg pointer; continue.
functor	F: pointer to an atom	Build F/N on structure stack; push reference to it on control stack; push copy of arg pointer;
	N: integer	reset arg pointer to 1st parameter of F/N; continue.
pop	None	Pop arg pointer; continue.

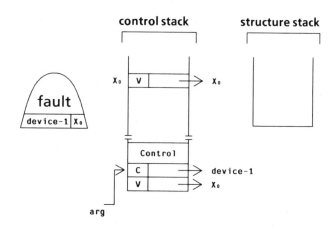

Figure 4.8. Stacks Before *call*

References to the arguments have been loaded on the control stack, and an argument pointer is set to the first argument reference. The C in the tag field of the first argument indicates that it references a constant; its val field points to the constant. The V in the tag field of the second argument indicates that it references a variable; its val field points up earlier in the control stack to the original variable reference. The fact that the val field of this earlier variable reference points to itself denotes that the variable is unbound.

Thus, in executing the "fault(device-1,X)" goal, just before the procedure call is made, the control stack has two argument references on it, the argument pointer indicating the first of these (Figure 4.8).

The PVM instruction sequence "call(fault,2)" results in a search through the procedure records from the constant record for "fault", looking for procedures whose arity is 2. If one is found, the execution mode is switched to *match*, control is transferred to the procedure code, and the pattern-matching process begins. The operation of transfer of control instructions is detailed later.

A more complicated example, one that involves the structure stack, is the code for the "derivative(sin(a),a,Y)" goal. If this procedure is successful, it results in the binding of the variable Y to the derivative of sin(a) with respect to a.

```
functor(sin,1)    % create sin/1, push reference, reset arg pointer
const(a)          % push reference to "a"
pop()             % restore arg pointer to derivative/3 from sin/1
const(a)          % push reference to "a"
var(n)            % dereference var, push reference
call(derivative,3)
```

When the derivative(sin(a),a,Y)) goal executes, the control stack has three argument references on it just before the procedure call is made, and the argument pointer is pointing to the first of these (Figure 4.9). The first argument in this call references a structure on the structure stack.

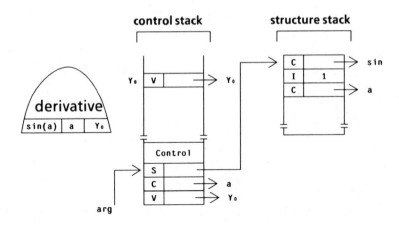

Figure 4.9. Stacks Before *call*.

References to the arguments have been loaded on the control stack and an argument pointer is set to the first argument reference. The S in the tag field of the first argument indicates that it references a structure; its val field points to the structure, which is located in the structure stack. The structure was built by the instruction sequence functor(sin,1)const(a)pop() operating in *arg* mode.

As before, the PVM instruction sequence "call(derivative,3)" results in a search through the procedure records from the constant record for the constant "derivative," looking for any procedures whose arity is 3. If one is found, the execution mode is switched to *match*, control is transferred to the procedure code, and the pattern-matching process begins.

const, var, and *functor* in *Match* Mode

The *call* instruction switches the execution mode of the PVM to *match* before transferring control. In this mode, the PVM instructions of the compiled procedure effect the matching between the argument and the parameters of the clause. For any instruction, if the argument is an unbound variable, the instructions immediately bind that variable to the appropriate term. For arguments that are other than unbound variables, the actions of PVM instructions in *match* mode are described in the following table.

As an example of *match* mode operation, consider the compiled forms of the unit clauses "connected(device-1,device-2)" and "connected(device-2,device-3)."

```
const(device-1)     % match 1st arg with "device-1"
const(device-2)     % match 2nd arg with "device-2"
return()

const(device-2)     % match 1st arg with "device-2"
const(device-3)     % match 2nd arg with "device-3"
return()
```

Table 4.3 PVM Instruction in match mode

Instruction	Parameter(s)	Description (*match* mode)
const	C: pointer to an atom	If arg is not a constant, then fail; else if arg is not = C, then fail; else advance arg pointer, and continue.
var	I: index into environment	Dereference the Ith variable; if the result is an unbound variable, bind to arg, advance arg pointer and continue; else if result type is not = arg type, fail; else unify result and argument; if unificiation not successful, then fail; else advance arg pointer, and continue.
functor	F: pointer to an atom	if arg is not a structure, then fail; else if the functor of ar is not = F or the arity of arg is not = N, fail;
	N: integer	else push a copy of arg pointer; reset arg pointer to the 1st parameter of arg; continue.
pop	none	Pop arg pointer; continue.

The way this code operates to perform the unification is straightforward (Figure 4.10). If any of the matches fails, backtracking is invoked. The following figures show stack pictures illustrating the execution of a PVM unit clause.

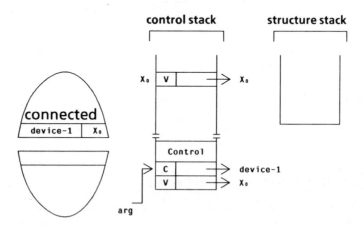

Figure 4-10(a). After *call*, Before const(device-1)

Before the beginning of the execution of the PVM code for the procedure, the control stack contains the arguments, and an argument pointer indicates the first of them. The PVM code const(device-1) checks whether the first argument references the constant device-1. In the case illustrated, the first argument does reference device-1, so the match succeeds, the argument pointer is advanced, and execution continues.

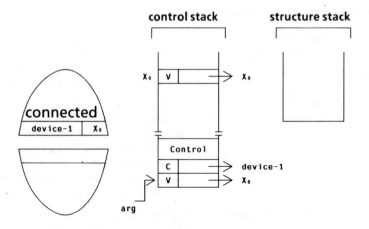

Figure 4.10(b). After const(device-1), Before const(device-2)

The argument pointer now points to the second argument, which references an unbound variable. The PVM code const(device-2) notes that the argument is an unbound variable and therefore binds it by making it a reference to the constant device-2.

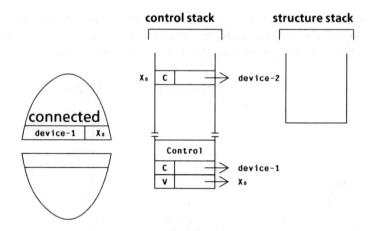

Figure 4.10(c). After const(device-2), Before *return*

Note that the variable referenced by the second argument has been replaced by a reference to the constant device-2. At this point the stack frame for the procedure could be reclaimed if no more alternatives remained. Otherwise, argument and control information must be maintained for this procedure, in the event that the computation backtracks to this point.

Two additional illustrations of unit clause PVM code follow.
The first example is the code for the clause

```
derivative(sin(X),X,cos(X)).
```

This clause states that the derivative of the sine of any argument with respect to that argument is the cosine of that argument. This clause compiles to

```
functor(sin,1)     % match 1st arg with sin/1, reset arg pointer
var(1)             % match 1st parameter of sin/1 with first var
pop()              % restore arg pointer to derivative/3 from sin/1
var(1)             % match 2nd arg with first var
functor(cos,1)     % match 3rd arg with cos/1, reset arg pointer
var(1)             % match 1st parameter of cos/1 with first var
pop()              % restore arg pointer to derivative/3 from cos/1
return()           % .
```

The second example, which contains nested structures, is the clause

```
derivative(**(sin(X),2),X,*(2,*(sin(X),cos(X)))).
```

This clause states that the derivative of the square of the sine of some argument is twice the product of the sine and the cosine. Using infix notation, the clause would read

```
derivative(sin(X)**2,X,2*sin(X)cos(X)).
```

The clause compiles to

```
functor(**,2)      % match 1st arg with **/2, reset arg pointer
functor(sin,1)     % match 1st parameter of **/2 with sin/1, reset
                   % arg pntr
var(1)             % match 1st parameter of sin/1 with first var
pop()              % restore arg pointer to **/2 from sin/1
const(2)           % match 2nd parameter of **/2 with "2"
pop()              % restore arg pointer to derivative/3 from **/2
var(1)             % match 2nd arg with first var
functor(*,2)       % match 3rd arg with */2, reset arg pointer
const(2)           % match 1st parameter of */2 with "2"
functor(*,2)       % match 2nd parameter of */2 with */2, reset arg
                   % pntr
functor(sin,1)     % match 1st parameter of */2 with sin/1, reset
                   % arg pntr
var(1)             % match 1st parameter of sin/1 with first var
pop()              % restore arg pointer to **/2 from sin/1
functor(cos,1)     % match 2nd parameter of */2 with cos/1,
                   % reset arg pntr
var(1)             % match 1st parameter of cos/1 with first var
pop()              % restore arg pointer to **/2 from cos/1
pop()              % restore arg pointer to **/2 from **/2
pop()              % restore arg pointer to derivative/3 from **/2 —
return()           % .
```

const, var, and *functor* in *Copy* Mode

The remaining complication that must be dealt with to understand the operation of the PVM instructions *const, var,* and *functor* is operation in *copy* mode. *Copy* mode is entered when an argument is an unbound variable and the corresponding parameter is a structure. In this case, the structure must be built and placed on the structure stack and the variable reference must be replaced by a reference to the structure. The process of building the structure is similar to what takes place in the body of a clause, except that in this case the structure building code is in the clause head, which causes the need for a different mode. The operation of the PVM instructions in this mode is described in the following table.

Table 4.4 PVM Instructions in copy mode

Instruction	Parameter(s)	Description (copy mode)
const	C: pointer to an atom	Copy C reference to structure stack; advance arg pointer; continue.
var	I: index into environment	Dereference Ith variable: if result is an unbound variable, create new unbound var on struct. stack bind referenced var to new var; else copy reference to structure stack; then advance arg pointer; continue.
functor	F: pointer to an atom N: integer	Build F/N on structure stack; push copy of arg pointer; reset arg pointer to 1st parameter of struct; continue.
pop	None	Pop arg pointer; continue.

As an example of *copy* mode operation, consider the clause

```
derivative(sin(X),X,cos(X)).
```

as called by

```
derivative(sin(a),a,Y)
```

Pictures of the stacks through the various steps of execution are given in Figure 4.11.

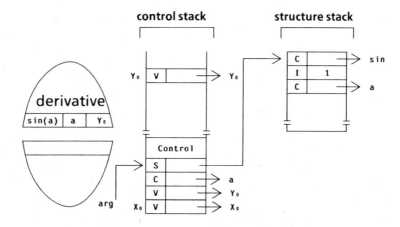

Figure 4.11(a). After call(derivative,3), Before functor(sin,1)

Before the beginning of the execution of the PVM code for this procedure, the control stack contains the arguments, and an argument pointer indicates the first of them. Since the clause contains one variable, space has been allocated on the control stack following the procedure arguments, and the variable has been initialized as unbound. The PVM code functor(sin,1) checks whether the first argument references a structure with functor = sin and arity = 1. In the case illustrated, the first argument does reference such a structure, so the match succeeds, a copy of the argument pointer is saved, and the argument pointer is set to point to the first parameter of the structure.

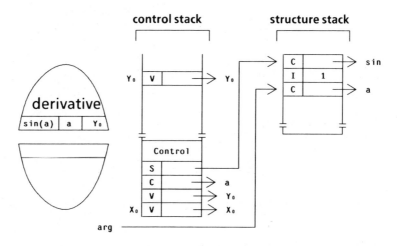

Figure 4.11(b). After functor(sin,1), Before var(1)

The PVM code var(1) dereferences the procedures' first variable and compares the result with the reference pointed to by the argument pointer. At this stage of the computation, the variable is unbound and the argument reference is to the constant a, so the variable is bound to a (its reference is changed to a). The argument pointer is advanced.

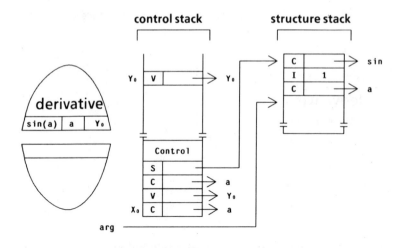

Figure 4.11(c). After var(1), Before pop()

The PVM code *pop* restores the argument pointer to the value it had before *functor* was executed. Note that the cell allocated for the first variable of the procedure now references the constant *a*.

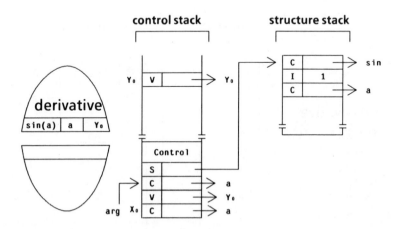

Figure 4.11(d). After pop(), Before var(1)

The PVM code var(1) consults the term referenced at the memory location of the first procedure variable and compares the result with the reference pointed to by the argument pointer. At this stage of the computation, the variable is bound to the constant *a* and the argument reference is to the constant *a*, so the variable and the argument will match. The argument pointer is advanced.

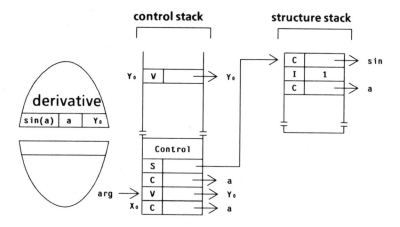

Figure 4.11(e). After var(1), Before functor(cos,1)

The PVM *functor* instruction notices that the next argument references an unbound variable, so the mode is switched to *copy* and a structure is constructed on the structure stack. The structure is known to have functor = cos and arity = 1, so space for the structure can be allocated, and the corresponding structure reference can replace the unbound variable reference.

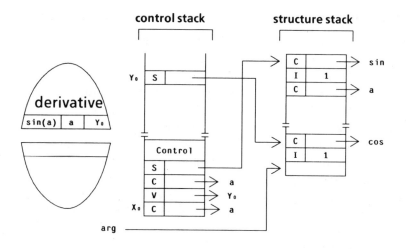

Figure 4.11(f). After functor(cos,1), Before var(1)

Once space for the structure has been allocated and the variable bound, a copy of the argument pointer is saved and the pointer is reset to the first parameter position of the new structure. The following PVM code causes references to Prolog terms to be placed at the positions indicated by the argument pointer.

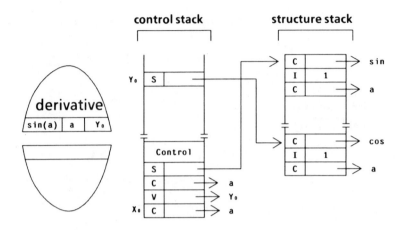

Figure 4.11(g). After var(1) pop()

The first variable is again dereferenced and copied to the position indicated by the argument pointer. Execution of *pop* restores the argument pointer to its value before execution of *functor* and changes the execution mode back to *match*.

In closing this section, some final comments on references to Prolog terms and the binding of Prolog variables are in order.

- The only Prolog terms that reside in the control stack are variables.

- Structures reside only in the structure stack. No subterm of a structure exists in the control stack.
- Variables in the control stack can be bound only to constants, terms in the structure stack, or variables occurring earlier in the control stack.

Maintaining this discipline makes it easier to restore the state of the Prolog computation in case backtracking is required. The fact that structures live completely and only in the structure stack means that they can be readily disposed of on backtracking simply by changing the pointer to the top of the structure stack. Similarly, variable-variable binding is required to be from the most recent variable to the least recent variable, both in the control and the structure stacks. This binding discipline simplifies backtracking and means as well that the control stack frame for deterministic procedures may be reclaimed without creating dangling pointers.

There must also be a mechanism that will note the binding of variables that have been created before the most recent backtrack point, since, on backtracking, the bindings of these variables must be undone. The mechanism is a special stack called the *trail*. On binding a variable that was created prior to the most recent backtrack point, a pointer to the variable is pushed on the trail. The trail stack pointer is part of the control information saved with a control frame, thereby providing the necessary information to reset variables on backtracking.

Transfer of Control Instructions *call, enter,* and *return*

The instructions of the PVM that remain to be described are the flow of control instructions *call, enter,* and *return.* Most of what these instructions do was described earlier, as summarized in the following table:

Table 4.5 Transfer of Control Instructions

Instruction	Parameter(s)	Description
call	F: pointer to an atom	Find first clause with functor F arity N; if found, allocate space for variables, copy control information to control stack;
	N: integer	if current clause has remaining alternatives, update backtrack pointer, copy backtrack info to control stack
		set execution mode to *match*;
		transfer control to clause;
		else fail
enter	None	Set execution mode to arg; adjust stack frame pointers
return	None	if deterministic, reclaim control stack frame set execution mode to *arg* transfer control back to caller

As an example of the compilation of a full clause, consider

```
fault(X,inverter) :- inverter(X),input(X,Y),output(X,Y).
```

which compiles to

```
var(1)              % match 1st arg with first var
const(inverter)     % match 2nd arg with the constant inverter
enter()             % set execution mode to "arg"
var(1)              % dereference then copy 1st var to control stack
call(inverter,1)    % transfer control to inverter/1 or backtrack
var(1)              % dereference then copy 1st var to control stack
var(2)              % dereference then copy 2nd var to control stack
call(input,2)       % transfer control to input/2 or backtrack
var(1)              % dereference then copy 2st var to control stack
var(2)              % dereference then copy 2nd var to control stack
call(output,2)      % transfer control to output/2 or backtrack
return()            % reclaim stack area, return control to caller
```

Several Prolog machine implementation registers are needed to support the computation (Table 4.6). These registers contain pointers into the code; pointers to the control, structure, and trail stacks; a flag indicating the execution mode; and the argument pointer.

Some of the registers are saved by the instructions *call* and *enter,* and then restored by *return* and the backtracking mechanism. *Call* and *return* always save and restore the program counter and a pointer to the control stack frame of the current procedure. These are the first two registers in Table 4.6. If the procedure is deterministic, these are the only two registers saved. If a procedure is nondeterministic, that is, there are remaining alternative procedures (as indicated by the link on the code record), *call* saves the contents of all six registers in the table. (see Figure 4.12.) These six constitute sufficient information to restore the execution state on backtracking.

Table 4.6 Prolog State Registers

Register	Description
RC	Pointer to code; the return point in the calling procedure.
RF	Pointer to the control stack; stack frame of the calling procedure.
BC	Pointer to a procedure; next procedure on backtracking.
BF	Pointer to the control stack; last choice point.
SS	Pointer to structure stack; reset to this value on backtracking.
TS	Pointer to trail stack; reset variables on here on backtracking.

Backtracking

Backtracking occurs on the failure to find a procedure with the correct functor and arity (*call*), on the failure to match the arguments of a call and the parameters of a procedure (*const, var,* or *functor*), or on explicit invocation via the predicate "fail". The following events are triggered by backtracking:

- Go back to most recent choice point (set current frame pointer to contents of BF register).

- If there is only one remaining alternative clause, update the choice point (restore BF from (new) current frame pointer if necessary).

- Garbage collect the structure stack (restore SS from (new) current frame).

- Reinitialize variables where necessary (restore TS from (new) current frame; unbind any trailed variables).

- Transfer control to the next alternative clause (reset program counter from BC in (new) current frame).

A set of C procedures that sketches an implementation of the PVM instructions described here is given in Appendix A. This code indicates most of the functionality required by the Prolog machine.

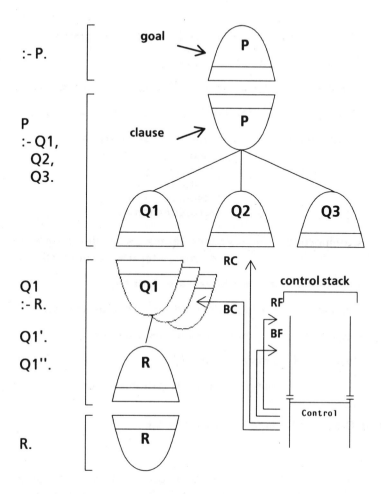

Figure 4.12. Control Information Saved by *call*.

This figure indicates the main registers saved by *call* in the case of a call to a procedure that has more than one clause. Also saved are the trail and structure stack pointers.

The Compiler

Basics

The Prolog compiler whose (Prolog) code appears in Appendix B accepts a restricted Prolog syntax (Figure 4.13). The most important restriction of the syntax is that all predicates be expressed in functional form. Extension of this compiler to accept other operator positions does require a significant effort, although a straightforward path to the

<horn←clause> :: = <atmf>. | <atmf> :- <atmfs>.

<atmfs> :: = <atmf> {,<atmf>}

<atmf> :: = <atom←name> | <atom←name> (<args>)

<args> :: = <simple←term> | <simple←term> , <args>

<simple←term> :: = <atom←name> (<args>) |
                    <variable> |
                    <constant> |
                    <list> |
                    (<simple←term>) |
                    (<conjunction>)

<conjunction> :: = <simple←term> , <simple←term>
                    <simple←term> , <conjunction>

<atom←name> :: = <lower case identifier>

<variable> :: = <identifier starting with uppercase or "←">

<constant> :: = <atom←name> | <integer>

<list> :: = [<simple←term>] |

           [<simple←term> {, <simple←term> } | <list>]

Figure 4.13. Grammar Accepted by the Compiler

more general syntax would be to build a preprocessor that transforms all predicates into functional form. The output of this program could then be used as the compiler input, and the compiler per se would not have to be modified. There are other parts of the usual grammar that are not recognized by the grammar used here (for example, strings), but adding them requires only simple modifications.

The input to this compiler is a list of tokens for a single clause, terminated by the token '.'. The tokens are the names of each constant, variable, and functor, along with parentheses, quotes, punctuation, and the clause neck (":-"). The tokenizer is not described here, but it is relatively easy to construct (see Clocksin and Mellish 1981, p. 86). Note that the grammar accepted by the compiler recognizes structured terms with spaces between the functor name and the left parenthesis bracketing the functor arguments. One approach to improving on this is to annotate the identifiers produced by the tokenizer, thereby indicating to the compiler that an atom followed immediately by a left parenthesis is a functor name.

The compiler is implemented as a grammar, using the grammar rule facility provided in most Prologs. The grammar consists of a collection of rules that define the strings of symbols that are valid sentences of the language. Grammar rules may also provide for some analysis of the sentence, often transforming it into a structure that is meant to clarify its meaning. The grammar presented here analyzes the input string in this manner, transforming it into code for the Prolog machine.

Optimizations

The compiler and PVM have been simplified as much as possible for the purpose of exposition. However, a number of modifications will increase execution efficiency, at the expense of increasing the complexity of the compiler and adding to the C code.

For example, the density of the compiled code could be reduced by putting all object references for each clause into a table. Then, instead of each type word taking an object reference as its argument, it could just take an index into the reference table. Type words could then be specialized by index, for example, constant_1() and constant_2(). The result would be that only one cell is required in that code for most primitive object descriptions. The cost is the time required to extract the references from the table.

The PVM instructions may be specialized in other ways. For example, the constant nil (as in const(nil)) could be described by a special procedure, say, const_nil(), thereby saving both time and space in the reference table. A special functor description word for "cons/2" is also desirable since lists are a very common structure. Similarly, unnamed variables could be described by a special PVM instruction, say, void().

Specialization of variable descriptions also provides a number of opportunities to increase efficiency. Instead of initializing variables on entry into a procedure, variables could be initialized on first appearance there in the clause and compiled to a PVM instruction called, say first_var(). In *match* mode, such a special description would also save the check to determine the binding of a variable. Consecutive unnamed variables might also be compiled to a single procedure of one argument.

Finally, one might consider combining *call-return* pairs into a single description and compiling the code address of special-purpose functions directly. Directions for further extensions to the word set are suggested in Clocksin's 1985 paper and Warren's 1983 technical note describing his abstract Prolog machine.

Mixing Prolog and C

With the design described here, C and Prolog can be mixed freely since the Prolog machine is simulated directly in C. Prolog computations can be launched from C and C computations launched from Prolog. One way to mix the two would be to have the Prolog compiler recognize directives that would cause the enclosed C code to be included in-line in the compiled Prolog code. For example, the definition of a Prolog procedure that takes a list L and, as a side effect, prints the time taken for a naive reverse of the list, might look like

```
test(L) :-
    $$start_code
    start_timer(0)
    $$end_code
```

```
nrev(L,L1)
$$start_code
stop_timer()
$$end_code.
```

This would compile to the equivalent C procedure calls

```
start_timer(0)
var(1) var(2) call(nrev,2)
stop_timer()
```

With this approach, no overhead is involved in mixed language programming. However, there is some ugliness in the interface.

Another reasonable approach is to provide a facility for the declaration of a Prolog interface to C. The syntax of such a declaration could be

```
c_predicate(<C procedure>,<Prolog predicate>)
```

where the predicate has +'s and −'s in its argument positions to indicate input and output arguments, respectively. For example, the declaration

```
c_predicate('test',test(+,+,-))
```

would specify that a call to the Prolog procedure "test/3" would compile to code that would place the first two arguments on the C data stack, execute the C procedure "test()", bind/compare the result of the C procedure with the third argument of the call, and then either fail or succeed on the basis of the comparison. The cost of this approach is the overhead involved in transferring values between the Prolog control stack and the C data stack.

PLM Instruction Set

The Prolog Virtual Machine described in this chapter is a quite workable solution to the problem of embedding the functionality of Prolog in some larger system. In this section, we'll look at the Programmed Logic Machine (PLM), a more conventional virtual machine architecture designed to support the execution of Prolog.

The instruction set and the architecture of the PLM are a refinement of the original abstract Prolog machine developed by Warren and published in 1983. The PLM differs from the PVM in a number of areas. Architecturally, the major difference is that the PLM uses machine registers instead of the control stack to pass arguments between procedures. The net result of using registers can be increased speed, particularly if the registers of the virtual machine can be mapped to registers in the underlying implementation machine. Register allocation, however, makes the Prolog compiler more complex.

A second difference between the PLM and the PVM is the indexing method. The PLM instruction set includes an indexing instruction, which transfers control to the appropriate clauses of the procedure, based on the type of the first argument to the procedure. For example, if the first argument is a constant, the indexing causes the transfer of control to a set of clauses whose first elements are constants. It is the job of the compiler to analyze all the source code for a procedure and then group clauses with the same initial argument type into code blocks. By contrast, the PVM compiles a procedure on a clause-by-clause basis and does not analyze the overall procedure structure.

Since the basic instructions of the Prolog machine are familiar from the PVM, only an outline of the instruction set of the PLM is given here. Examples illustrate how clauses are compiled into the PLM instructions. The examples should make clear the very strong similarities between the two instruction sets, and the efficiencies that the PLM architecture may enable.

Code for a compiler for the PLM is given in Appendix C

Indexing Instructions
switch_on_term
switch_on_constant
switch_on_structure

Get instructions
get_variable
get_value
get_constant
get_structure
get_nil
get_list

Procedure Control Instructions
try
retry
trust
try_me_else
retry_me_else
trust_me_else
fail
cut
cutd

Put Instructions
put_variable
put_value
put_unsafe value
put_constant
put_nil
put_structure
put_list

Clause Control Instructions
proceed
execute
call
allocate
deallocate

Unify Instructions
unify_void
unify_value
unify_variable
unify_constant
unify_cdr
unify_nil

Indexing Instructions

Indexing instructions are designed to reduce the search space by eliminating clauses that cannot match with the procedure call. This is accomplished by a straightforward strategy in the WAM. The first argument of the caller is examined and the procedure branches to a set of candidate clauses that have first arguments of the same type. The syntax of the WAM switch instruction is

```
switch_on_term Constant_label, List_label, Structure_label
```

where the *switch_on_term* instruction takes three arguments, the labels of the code blocks for the clauses having first argument constant, list, and structure, respectively. For an example of the instructions' usage in the object code, consider the procedure func/2 having the following three clauses

```
func(c,X) :- ...
func([a,b],X) :- ...
func(s(1,2),X) :- ...
```

The clause would be compiled into the following WAM code:

```
func: switch-on-term L1,L2,L3

      L1   code for first clause
      L2   code for second clause
      L3   code for third clause
```

If the first argument in a call to this procedure is an unbound variable, the *switch_on_term* instruction just falls through to the next instruction. Otherwise, control transfers to the code at the indicated labels. Between the clauses for the code in these blocks, the procedure control instructions *try* and *try_else* are used to specify that at run-time the second clause is to be tried if the first fails, and that the third clause is to be executed if the second fails, and so on.

Before discussing transfer of control instructions in more detail, first look at the two remaining indexing instructions. These are auxiliary instructions that specify a second-level branch if there is more than one clause with first argument of a particular type.

```
switch_on_constant Number_of_clauses, Table_address
```

The *switch_on_constant* instruction takes two arguments, the size of a table of addresses and the address of the table. For very large numbers of clauses in a procedure, the table should be a hash table that uses the constant as a key to access the address of the clauses whose first argument is the constant. For small numbers of clauses, the table can be searched linearly for the matching clause address. For example, the procedure

```
func(a) :- ...
func(b) :- ...
func(c) :- ...
func(d) :- ...
```

compiles to the block of code

```
switch_on_constant 4, table address
    L1          code for first clause
    L2          code for second clause
    L3          code for third clause
    L4          code for fourth clause
```

In this case, the number of clauses is small, so the table is organized as follows

```
    a           L1
    b           L2
    c           L3
    d           L4
```

and a simple linear search is performed at run time. The syntax for the *switch_on_ structure* instruction is

```
switch_on_structure Number_of_clause, Table_address
```

The *switch_on_structure* instruction is similar to the *switch_on_constant* instruction. For its key the table uses the principle functor of the structure pointed to by the index argument.

Procedure Control Instructions

Procedure control instructions are responsible in the WAM for manipulating choice points on the control stack. There are two classes of procedure control instructions, the *try* instructions and the *try else* instructions. The *try* instructions are used when more than one clause can be executed. The *try* instruction is used for the first clause, the *trust* instruction is used for the last clause, and the *retry* instruction is used for intervening clauses.

try *Label*   Label is the address of the code for the first clause of the code block. The *try* instruction creates the choice point and saves a pointer to the code that follows, where execution resumes should the clause at *Label* fail.

retry *Label*   The *retry* instruction saves a pointer in the choice point to the code that follows and branches to the address *Label*.

trust *Label*   At run-time, the trust instruction removes the current choice point since there aren't any remaining clauses to try should the last clauses at *Label* fail.

try_me_else *Label*   This instruction sets up a choice point on the control stack and saves *Label* as the address to return to should the code following this instruction fail. The "try else" instructions are variants on the "try" instructions. The difference is that for "try" instructions, the label indicates the next code to execute. For "try else" instructions the label indicates the alternative code to execute should the code following the "try else" instructions fail.

retry_me_else *Label*   Like retry, this instruction just saves *Label* as the point to return, should the code following the *retry* instruction fail.

trust_me_else fail   This instruction discards the current choice point and continues execution. The parent goal fails if the clause following this instruction fails.

cut   This instruction implements the Prolog *cut* operator. The choice points above the B register value are discarded.

cutd label   The "cutd" instruction is a variant of "cut" that is used to correctly handle disjunctions.

fail   The *fail* instruction invokes the *fail* routine directly.

Clause Control Instructions

The clause control instructions are responsible for transfer of control and the environment allocation associated with procedure calling. Of the five instructions in this group, three deal with transfer of control (*call, execute,* and *proceed*) and the remaining two treat allocation and deallocation of environments.

proceed   The proceed instruction is used at the end of a unit clause to return control to the point following the parent goal.

execute *Procedure*   In the body of a clause, the final goal needs no return. The execute instruction just transfers control to the procedure referenced by its argument. The "execute" instruction is equivalent to "go to."

call *Procedure, Num_Vars*   When more than one goal remains in the body of a clause, the call instruction is used to transfer control. The return pointer is set to the code that follows, and control is transferred to procedure.

allocate   The allocate instruction is used in a clause with more than one goal in the body. It saves the contents of the registers in the current environment and then allocates space for the new environment of the current clause.

deallocate   This instruction is used to remove the environment from the control stack when it is no longer needed. This environment structure can be discarded as soon as the next to last goal in the clause has completed.

Get Instructions

The get instructions are used to unify the contents of the argument registers with the appropriate elements of the head of the clause being executed. All get instructions are of the form

```
get destination,source
```

where the source is always an argument register and the destination is either unified with the contents of the argument register or the contents are stored there.

get_constant `Constant, Argument`   The *get_constant* instruction dereferences the argument and then attempts to unify the result with the constant.
If unification fails, the goal fails and backtracking is invoked.

get_nil `Argument`   This is a special case of the *get_constant* instruction, where
the destination is implicitly the constant nil.

get_variable `Register,Argument`   This instruction transfers the contents
of the argument register into the register specified as the destination. If
necessary, permanent variables are allocated in the current environment.

get_value `Register,Argument`   This instruction dereferences the argument
register and then attempts to unify the result with the contents of the destination register.

get_list `Argument`   This instruction dereferences the argument and checks
that the result is a list. In this case, the arg pointer is set to point to the first
element of the list. If the argument dereferences to a variable, the mode is
switched to *copy,* and a new list is allocated on the structure stack and bound
to the variable. The arg pointer is then set to point to the first element.

get_structure `Argument`   This instruction operates like *get_list,* but for
structures. It is used whenever an argument in the head of a clause is a
structure. If execution switches into *copy* mode, the new structure is built on
the structure stack.

Put Instructions

The put instructions are used to move data into the argument registers. All instructions
in this group are of the form

```
put source,destination
```

where the destination is the argument register and the source is an argument register, a _
permanent variable or a constant.

`put_constant` *Constant, Argument*   This instruction puts the constant into the argument register.

`put_nil` *Argument*   This is a special form of put_constant, where the constant is implicitly the constant nil.

`put_value` *Source, Argument*   This instruction simply puts the contents of the source into the argument register.

`put_variable` *Source, Argument*   This instruction is used for arguments that are unbound variables. Its chief side effect is the initialization and/or creation of the unbound variable, before a reference to it is placed in the argument register.

`put_list` *Argument*   This instruction puts a list reference in the argument register (the list is built on the top of the structure stack) and sets the mode to write.

`put_structure` *Functor, Argument*   Like the put_list instruction, put_structure creates a structure reference in the argument register and then sets the unification mode to write so that the structure is built on the structure stack.

`put_unsafe_value` *Variable, Argument*   This instruction creates a variable in the structure stack and sets the argument register to reference it, if the source variable is within the current environment. This instruction is used before the last goal, at the time the current environment is deallocated.

Unify Instructions

The unify instructions are used to unify against elements of existing structures and to build new structures.

`unify_constant` *Constant*   This instruction is used for elements of lists or structures that are constants. The instruction uses the arg pointer to locate the element to be matched with the constant (if in *read* mode) or the location where the constant is to be written (if in *write* mode).

`unify_value` *Source*   In *read* mode, the element pointed to by the arg pointer is unified by the dereferenced contents of the source. In *write* mode, the contents of the source are pushed onto the structure stack.

`unify_variable` *Source*   This instruction is used for structure elements that are unbound variables and that occur more than once in the clause. In *read* mode, the contents of the location pointed to by the arg pointer are moved to the source. In *write* mode, an unbound variable is created on the structure stack, and a reference to it is stored in the source.

unify_void *Num*   This instruction handles single occurrence variables. In *read* mode, Num elements of the structure referenced by the arg pointer are skipped. In *write* mode, Num new unbound variables are pushed on the structure stack.

unify_cdr *Source*   The *unify_cdr* instruction handles unification and binding of the end of a list.

unify_nil   The *unify_nil* instruction is similar to the *get_nil* and *put_nil* instructions. It is used to unify elements of a structure with the constant nil.

PLM Compiler

Procedure Compiler

The compiler for the PLM instruction set uses the type of the first argument of each clause in a procedure to group clauses into blocks. The first instruction of the procedure then jumps to the appropriate block, depending on the type of the first argument. Thus, at the highest level, the compiled code for a procedure looks like:

```
procedure Name/Arity
     switch_on_term Constant_Label, List_Label, Structure_Label

     Variable_Label
          <Variable Block: Code to execute if the first argument is a
               variable>

     Constant_Label
          <Constant Block: Code to execute if the first argument is a
               constant>

     List_Label
          <List Block: Code to execute if the first argument is a
               list>

     Structure_Label
          <Structure Block: Code to execute if the first argument is
               a structure>
```

The only code block in a procedure that contains the code for the clauses is the variable block. The other code blocks transfer control into the variable block. Within the variable block, the code for each clause is linked together with *try_me_else* instructions. In this way, choice points are created and control is transferred appropriately during backtracking. With the *try_me_else* instructions, the code in the variable block looks like:

```
                try_me_else Choice 2
C1:             <code for clause #1>

Choice 2:       retry_me_else Choice 3
C2:             <code for clause #2>

Choice 3:       retry_me_else Choice 4
C3:             <code for clause #3>
                    •
                    •
                    •
Choice N-1:     retry_me_else Choice N
CN-1:           <code for clause #N-1>

Choice N:       trust_me_else fail
CN:             <code for last clause>
```

Note that the first clause always has a *try_me_else* instruction to set up the choice point, and the last clause always has a *trust_me_else* clause to remove the choice point. The labels $C_1 \ldots C_n$ refer to the code for the individual clauses and are used as references in the other code blocks.

Each of the other code blocks are structured to transfer control within the variable block. For example, the *List_block* code looks like:

```
List_Label:
    try C1
    retry C2
    •
    •
    •
    retry Cn-1
    trust Cn
```

Each label points to clause code within the variable block. All clauses with either a list or a variable in the first argument position are tried.

The list block is the simplest to compile because the first argument position is not used for indexing of the clauses. The constant block and the structure block are compiled in a similar fashion, but their compilation is more complex than compilation of the list block. The complexity is related to the need to generate hash tables that enable the procedure to quickly find constants and the main functor of structures at run-time. There are degenerate cases that are nevertheless valid Prolog programs. For example, the compiler should generate a single entry for multiple clauses in the same procedure that had the same constant as the first argument. This sort of degenerate clause may be unlikely to occur though, because data elements put in a table for fast access are usually distinct.

Most of the optimizations the compiler applies to code block generation are straightforward. For example, empty code blocks are not generated. Instead the label in the *switch_on_term* instruction is set to *fail*. Similarly, if the code block has only one clause, that is, would branch to only one label, that label is used in the *switch_on_term* instruction. If the procedure contains only one clause, no selection code is generated. Similarly, if the arity of the procedure is zero, only the variable block is generated.

By virtue of the selection code, (that is, indexing procedures) procedure compilation in the PLM is therefore quite distinct from the compilation procedures illustrated in the PVM compiler. PLM procedure compilation is illustrated in the following examples.

Example 1 is a simple data base lookup table using constants as the search index. The constants are in the first argument position in the Prolog clauses. The code that is generated by the compiler consists of three instructions for each clause, linked together with the instruction *(re)try_me_else*.

```
example1(f,x).
example1(s,l).
example1(i,a).
example1(m,g).
```

procedure example1 / 2

Label	Instruction
	switch_on_term L9, fail, fail
L1:	try_me_else L3
L2:	get_constant f, X1
	get_constant x, X2
	proceed
L3:	retry_me_else L5
L4:	get_constant s, X1
	get_constant I, X2
	proceed
L5:	retry_me_else L7
L6:	get_constant i, X1
	get_constant a, X2
	proceed
L7:	trust_me_else fail
L8:	get_constant m, X1
	get_constant g, X2
	proceed
L9:	switch_on_constant 4
	m
	i
	s
	f

Example 2 has constant, list, structure, and variable clauses. Constant, list and structure clauses must try the variable clause if they fail.

```
example2(f,f).
example2([a|b],g).
example2(s(x),h).
example2(X,i).
```

procedure example2 / 2

Label	Instruction
	switch_on_term L10,L9,L11
L1:	try_me_else L3
L2:	get_constant f,X1
	get_constant f,X2
	proceed
L3:	retry_me_else L5
L4:	get_constant g,X2
	get_list X1
	unify_constant a
	unify_cdr X1
	get_constant b,X1
	proceed
L5:	retry_me_else L7
L6:	get_structure s/1,X1
	unify_constant x
	unify_nil
	get_constant h,X2
	proceed
L7:	trust_me_else fail
L8:	get_constant i,X2
	proceed
L9:	try L4
	trust L8
L10:	try L2
	trust L8
L11:	try L6
	trust L8

Clause Compiler

Individual clauses are compiled separately and then linked into the code blocks in the clause structure. The basic structure and processing flow between the modules in the compiler is given in Figure 4.14.

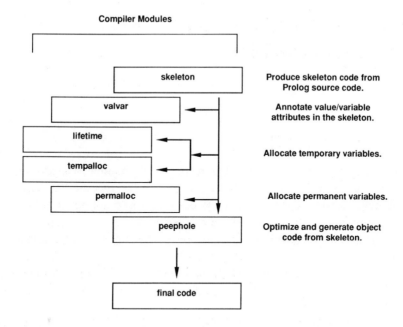

Figure 4.14. Program Modules and Flow for Simple Clause Compilation

Many of the elements in a full Prolog implementation that are not found in the simple PVM syntax make optimal compilation difficult. For example, disjunctions represent parallel and independent execution paths and therefore make register allocation difficult. Compiling the cut instruction, built-in predicates, and special predicates like *if-then-else, assert,* and *retract,* introduce other complexities.

Looking for the moment at just those clauses that do not have disjunctions, cuts, or built-ins (*simple* clauses), the compilation procedure can be divided into six steps, each with a corresponding program module. Compilation of the complete clause requires six more modules to handle the complexities that disjunctions, cuts, and built-ins can introduce.

The first module used for simple clause compilation is the skeleton module, which compiles the clause into a sequence of *get, put, unify,* and *call* instructions. These instructions have the following format:

```
get(_,X,Y)
put(_,X,Y)
unify(_,X)
call(name/arity,N)
```

Most of the arguments in these skeletal instructions are unknown initially. The X and Y variables will be assigned registers in a later step. The underscore variables will be assigned the type of the instruction, for example, variable, value, or unsafe_value. The environment size N is determined later when permanent variables are allocated.

Appendix A: C Implementation of Prolog Virtual Machine

Glossary

The C procedures used to simulate the Prolog machine are described here.

call (atom, arity)   Takes an integer(arity) and a pointer to an atom record and searches the clause records for a clause with the specified arity. Backtracks if unsuccessful. Otherwise, if there are multiple applicable clauses, backtracking information is saved—a pointer to the next code record, a pointer to the next most recent choice-point frame in the control stack, and the trail and global stack-pointers. Sets the execution mode to *match*. Also saves the top of the return stack in the next Prolog control stack frame and initializes the argument pointer to the first argument position in the next control frame.

enter ( )   Commits to execution of the body of a procedure. Sets execution mode to *copy* and adjusts control stack pointers.

return ( )   Indicates successful exit. Gets the return pointer saved by *call* and pushes it on the return stack. Sets execution mode to *arg* and adjusts control stack pointers, reclaiming control stack frames where possible.

const (atom)   *Match* mode: tests whether the next argument is a constant whose name is given by atom. Backtracks if they do not match; continues with execution otherwise. *Copy* mode: builds an argument with tag = 2 and val = a pointer to the atom.

var (n)   *Match* mode: dereferences the variable specified by the input index, and then, if the variable is unbound, it is bound to the argument; otherwise, *var* tests whether the next argument matches the binding. Backtracks if they do not match; otherwise, continues with execution. *Copy* mode: copies the variable binding to the next argument position.

functor (atom, arity)   *Match* mode: tests whether the next argument is a structured term with the specified arity, whose functor is given by atom. Backtracks if they do not match; otherwise, saves the argument pointer and resets it to point to the first argument of the structured term, that is, to point to the first cell of the argument field of the structure record pointed to by the structure pointer. Execution continues from this point. *Copy* mode: allocates space for a structure record from the structure stack and then sets the first two fields of the record (that is, functor name and arity). Builds an argument with tag $= 3$ and val $=$ a pointer to the structure. Saves the argument pointer and resets it to point to the first cell of the argument field of the structure record. Execution continues from this point.

pop ( )   Restores the argument pointer in both execution modes.

C Code

```
#define  var_type            1
#define  const_type          2
#define  structure_type      3
#define  bytes_per_cell      4
#define  bytes_per_frame     12
#define  match_mode          0
#define  arg_mode            1
#define  OFF                 0

extern struct reference *pop_arg();      /* pops an argument off a control stack frame  */
extern struct reference *push_arg();     /* pushes an argument onto a control stack frame */
extern int unify_var();                  /* unify variable and an argument              */
extern int unify_constant();             /* unify constant and an argument              */
extern int unify_structure();            /* unify structure and an argument             */
extern int match_var();                  /* match a structure and an argument variable  */
extern int match_structure();            /* match a structure and an argument structure */
extern int push_struct();                /* allocates structure on strcture stack       */
extern int backtrack();                  /* fail                                        */
extern struct clause *find_proc();       /* find procedure given functor,arity          */
extern struct reference
       *dereference();                   /* dereference a variable                      */
extern struct stack_frame
       *make_control_frame();            /* make a control stack frame                  */



/* ********************************** */
/* Some PVM machine registers        */
/* ********************************** */

struct stack_frame *current_frame;       /* current_frame pointer                       */
struct stack_frame *next_frame;          /* next_frame pointer                          */
int structure_stack;                     /* structure_stack pointer                     */


/* ********************************** */
/* Temporary Storage                 */
/* ********************************** */

int mode_flag;                           /* match-arg mode flag                         */
int copy_flag;                           /* copy mode flag                              */
```

```
/* ********************************** */
/* Stack Frame Structure             */
/* ********************************** */

struct stack_frame
    {
    struct list *RC;
    struct stack_frame *RF;
    struct clause *BC;
    struct stack_frame *BF;
    int SS;
    int TS;
    int args;
    int vars;
    };

/* ********************************** */
/* Constant Structure                */
/* ********************************** */

struct constant
    {
    char name;
    struct constant *next;
    };

/* ********************************** */
/* Procedure Structure               */
/* ********************************** */

struct procedure
    {
    struct procedure *next;
    int arity;
    struct clause *code;
    };


/* ********************************** */
/* Clause Structure                  */
/* ********************************** */

struct clause
    {
    struct clause *next;
    int num_vars;
    struct list *code;
    };


/* ********************************** */
/* Reference Structure               */
/* ********************************** */

struct reference
    {
    int type;
```

```
        int *ref;
        };


/* *********************************** */
/* PVM Instructions                 */
/* *********************************** */


/* **** pop() **** */

int pop()
    {
    restore_arg_pointer();
    }


/* **** functor(arity,atom) **** */

int functor(name,arity)
    int arity;
    struct constant *name;
    {
    struct reference *arg;
    int unify_result;

    if (mode_flag = arg_mode)
        {
        push_arg(structure_type,structure_stack);
        push_structure(name,arity);
        }
    else
    unify_result = 0;
    arg = pop_arg();
    switch (arg->type)
        {
        case var_type:
        unify_result = match_var(arity,name,arg);
        break;

        case structure_type:
        unify_result = match_funct(arity,name,arg);
        }
    if (unify_result == 0) backtrack();
    }


/* **** var(index) **** */

int var(index)
    int index;
    {
    struct reference *arg;
    struct reference *var;
    int unify_result;

/* build argument from the variable reference */
```

```
    if (mode_flag = arg_mode)
        {
        make_arg(var_type,index);
        }
    else
    unify_result = 0;
    var = get_variable(next_frame,index);
    arg = dereference(var);
    switch (arg->type)
        {
        case var_type:
        unify_result = unify_var(arg);
        break;

        case structure_type:
        unify_result = unify_structure(arg);
        break;

        case const_type:
        unify_result = unify_constant(arg);
        }
    if (unify_result == 0) backtrack();
    }


/* **** constant(char) **** */

int const_(atom)
    struct constant *atom;
    {
    struct reference *arg;
/* build argument from the constant reference */
    if (mode_flag != match_mode)
        make_arg(const_type,atom);
    else
    arg = pop_arg();
    if (arg->type == var_type)
        bind(arg,const_type,atom);
    else
    if(arg->ref != (int)atom)
        backtrack();
    }


/* **** return() **** */

int return_()
    {
    if (mode_flag = match_mode)
            return_unit_clause();
    else    return_procedure();
    mode_flag = arg_mode;
    }


/* **** enter() **** */

int enter()
    {
```

```
    mode_flag = arg_mode;
    copy_flag = OFF;
    next_frame->RF = current_frame;
    current_frame = next_frame;
    next_frame = make_control_frame();
    }


/* **** call(proc,arity) **** */

int call(proc,arity)
    int arity;
    struct constant *proc;
    {
    struct clause *function;
    int num_vars;
    if(function= find_proc(proc,arity))
        {
        mode_flag = match_mode;
        eval(function);
        }
    else    backtrack();
    }
```

Appendix B: Prolog-PVM Compiler

```
/* =====  =====  =====  =====  ===== */
% COMPILER
% All args are output
% NVars is the number of vars in the clause
% Code is the object code
% Sent is a list of tokens, terminated by the token '.'
% the variable Sent is bound by the procedure "read_in"

compile_clause(Pred/Arity,Nvars,Code) :-
    read_in(Sent), horn_clause(Pred/Arity,Vars,[],Cd,Sent,_),
    nrev(Cd,Code),memberchkN(-1,Vars,-1,Nvars).


/* =====  =====  =====  =====  ===== */
% Old is the input code sequence ([] here)

horn_clause(Pred/Arity,Vars,Old,['RETURN'|New]) -->
    atmf(Vars,Old,[_,_,_|Nl],Pred/Arity),
    (["."],{New=Nl} | [":-"],atmfs(Vars,['ENTER'|Nl],New ) ).
```

```
/* =====   =====   =====   =====   ===== */
% atmfs are terms that aren't numbers or variables
%    Arg1: list of vars in the clause
%    Arg2: input code sequence
%    Arg3: output code sequence
atmfs(Vars,Old,New ) -->
    atmf(Vars,Old,N1,_),
    (['.'],{NewN1}|[','],atmfs(Vars,N1,New)).

atmf(Vars,Old,['CALL',Pred,0|Old],Pred/0) -->
    atom_name(Pred).

atmf(Vars,Old,['CALL',Pred,Arity|N1],Pred/Arity) -->
    atom_name(Pred),['('],args(Vars,Old,N1,0,Arity),[')'].

/* =====   =====   =====   =====   ===== */

% simple_term parses terms, lists and structured terms in
%          functional form
% This is basically a case analysis and is meant to be
%          deterministic, thus the cut
%    Arg1: Variable symbol list (difference list - built
%          during compilation)
%    Arg2: Input Code list (input)
%    Arg3: Output Code list (output)

simple_term(_,_,_) -->
    ['.'],!,fail.

simple_term(Vars,Old,['POP'|N1]) -->
    atom_name(Pred),['('],
    args(Vars,['FUNCTOR',Pred,Arity|Old],N1,0,Arity),[')'],!.

simple_term(Vars,Old,New ) -->
    variable(Vars,Old,New),!.

simple_term(_,Old,New ) -->
    constant(Old,New),!.

simple_term(Vars,Old,New ) -->
    ['('],(simple_term(Vars,Old,New ) ;
    conjunction(Vars,Old,New )),[')'],!.

simple_term(Vars,Old,New ) -->
    list(Vars,Old,New ),!.
```

```
conjunction(Vars,Old,New ) -->
    simple_term(Vars,Old,Nl ),[','],
    (simple_term(Vars,Nl,New ) | conjunction(Vars,Nl,New )).


/* =====   =====   =====   =====   ===== */
% args parses arguments
%   Argl: - Arg3:   see arguments for simple_term
%   Arg4: arg count (input)
%   Arg5: arg count (output)

args(Vars,Old,New,NumO,Numl ) -->
    simple_term(Vars,Old,Nl),
    ([','],{Num is NumO+l},args(Vars,Nl,New,Num,Numl) |
      {New = Nl,Numl is NumO+l}).


/* =====   =====   =====   =====   ===== */
% char(N,Atom,M)- M is the N-th character of Atom
% ascii(M,N)      - the ascii code for M is N

atom_name(Name) -->
  [Name],{char(1,Name,M),
  ascii(M,N),ascii(a,_a),ascii(z,_z),_a =< N,N =< _z},!.


variable(Vars,Old,['VAR',Num |Old]) -->
  [Var],{char(1,Var,L),ascii(L,M),
  (ascii('_',M) ; ascii('A',_a),ascii('Z',_z),_a =< M,M =< _z),
  memberchkN(Var,Vars,0,Num)},!.


constant(Old,[Inst,X |Old]) -->
  atom_name(X),{Inst = 'CONST'}|
  [X],{integer(X),Inst = 'INTEGER'}.


list(Vars,Old,New) -->
  ['[',']'],{New=['CONST',nil|Old]}|
  ['['],simple_term(Vars,['FUNCTOR',cons,2|Old],Nl),
  list_tail(Vars,Nl,New ) .


/* =====   =====   =====   =====   ===== */
/* Auxiliary relations */

list_tail(Vars,Old,['POP','CONST',nil|Old]) -->
  [']'].
```

```
list_tail(Vars,Old,['POP'|New]) -->
  ['|'],simple_term(Vars,Old,New),[']'].

list_tail(Vars,Old,New) -->
  [','], simple_term(Vars,['FUNCTOR',cons,2|Old],N1).
list_tail(Vars,N1,New) .

% memberchkN
memberchkN(X,[X|_],M,N) :-
  N is M+1,!.
memberchkN(X,[_|T],L,N) :-
  M is L+1,memberchkN(X,T,M,N).

% naive reverse

nrev([X|L0],L) :-
  nrev(L0,L1),concatenate(L1,[X],L).
nrev([],[]).

% concatenate

concatenate([],L,L).
concatenate([X|L1],L2,[X|L3]) :- concatenate(L1,L2,L3).
```

Appendix C: Prolog-PLM Compiler

```
Main Program Module (modified from Van Roy 1984)

% WAM.ARI (Arity Prolog)
% Compile all procedures on a file:
% Uses procedure 'compileclause' from lower level.

% Top Level Procedures

% Compile 'FileName' and put results to screen:

plm_screen(FileName) :-
    open(H,FileName,r),
    read_clauses(H,CI),
    close(H),
    write('Finished reading file'), nl,
```

```
    time(time(0,0,0,0)),
    compileallprocs(CI),
    time(time(Hour,Min,Sec,Hun)),
    write('Total cputime is '),
    write(Hour),write(':'),write(Min),write(':'),
    write(Sec),write(':'),write(Hun),write(':'),nl,nl,!.

% Compile 'FileName' and
% put WAM code in 'FileName.plm'
% put Intermediate Code in 'FileName.for'

plm(Infile,Type) :-
    open(H,Infile,r),
    read_clauses(H,CI),
    close(H),
    write('Finished reading file'), nl,
    convert_name(Infile,Outfile,Type),
    time(time(0,0,0,0)),
    ifthenelse(Type = wam,
        (tell(Outfile),
         compileallprocs(CI)),
        (tell('temp.obj'),
         compileforthprocs(CI,Procedures,Atoms)) ),
    time(time(Hour,Min,Sec,Hun)),
    told,
    ifthen(Type = forth,
        (create(H2,Outfile),
         write(H2,Procedures),write(H2,'.'),nl(H2),
         write(H2,Atoms),write(H2,'.'),nl(H2),
         move_clauses(H2),
         close(H2)) ),
    write('Total cputime is '),
    write(Hour),write(':'),write(Min),write(':'),
    write(Sec),write(':'),write(Hun),write(':'),nl.

% Start of Compiler

read_clauses(H,ClauseInfo) :-
    read(H,Clause),
    ifthenelse(Clause=end_of_file,
        ClauseInfo=[],
        (getname(Clause, NameAr),
         ClauseInfo=[source(NameAr,Clause)|Rest],
         read_clauses(H,Rest)) ).
```

```
getname(Clause, Name/Arity) :- !,
    (Clause = (Head :- _); Clause = Head),
    Head =.. [Name|Args],
    length(Args, Arity).


% Generate and write code for all
% procedures in ClauseInfo:
compileallprocs([]) :- write(end), nl, nl.
compileallprocs(ClauseInfo) :-
    filteroneproc(ClauseInfo, NextCI, NameAr, OneProc),
    compileproc(NameAr, OneProc, Code-[]),
%    g_c(compileproc(NameAr, OneProc, Code-[])),
    write_plm(NameAr, Code),
    compileallprocs(NextCI).


/* ************************************************************** */


% Compile one procedure.
% Input is a list of clauses in unaltered form.
% Output is complete code for the procedure.
% The labels remain uninstantiated.
% The separate blocks for lists, constants, or structures
% are not needed if:
%    1. Arity=0, no first arguments.
%    2. procedure consists of just one clause.
%    3. all first arguments are variables.
% Also recognized are the cases where all first arguments are either
% variables or one other kind.

compileproc(_/Arity, Clauses, Code-Link) :-
    compileclauses(Clauses, CompC),
    var_block(CompC, VarLbl, VCode-VLink),

    % Easy optimizations first:
    ifthenelse(
        (Arity = 0; length(Clauses, 1); all_var(CompC)),
            (Code=VCode, Link=VLink),

    % Optimizations if only variables and one other kind
    %          are present:
    ifthenelse(same_or_var(CompC, Kind),
        (filterv(CompC, VarC),
        try_block(VarC, TryLbl, VLink-TLink),
            ifthenelse(Kind=list,
                (TLink=Link,
```

```
                    CLS=[TryLbl, VarLbl, TryLbl]),
                 (cs_block(CompC, BlkLbl, BlkCode-BlkLink, Hashed),
             % if no hashing then no separate try-block:
                    ifthenelse(Hashed = no_hash,
                       (CSLbl=VarLbl, TLink=Link),
                       (CSLbl=BlkLbl, TLink=BlkCode, Link=BlkLink)),
                    ifthenelse(Kind = constant,
                       CLS=[CSLbl, TryLbl, TryLbl],
                       CLS=[TryLbl, TryLbl, CSLbl])) ),
                 Switch=..[switch_on_term|CLS],
                 Code=[Switch|VCode]
                 ),
           % General case: generate code for list, constant, and structure
           % blocks. (This would generate nonoptimal code for
                    above cases).
              (filterlcs(CompC, ListC, ConstC, StrucC),
               try_block(ListC, ListLbl, VLink-LLink),
               cs_block(ConstC, ConstLbl, LLink-CLink, _),
               cs_block(StrucC, StrucLbl, CLink-Link, _),
               Code=[switch_on_term(ConstLbl,ListLbl,StrucLbl)|VCode]
               )
        ) ), !.



% Succeeds if first arguments are all variable and one other kind:
same_or_var([clause(FArg,_,_)|Rest], Kind) :-
    kind(FArg, K),
    (K=variable; K=Kind),
    same_or_var(Rest,Kind).
same_or_var([], _).



%Succeeds if first arguments are all variables:
all_var(CompC) :- same_or_var(CompC, variable).


compileclauses([C|Clauses],
[clause(FArg,Lbl,[label(Lbl)|Code]-Link)|Rest]) :-
    % !! getfirstarg must come before compileclause, since
    % compileclause instantiates variables in the head
        to registers.
    getfirstarg(C, FArg),
    compileclause(C, Code-Link),
    compileclauses(Clauses, Rest).
compileclauses([], []).
```

```
getfirstarg(Clause, FArg) :-
    (Clause = (Head :- _); Clause = Head),
    Head =.. [ _ | HArgs],
    (HArgs=[Arg1|_]; true),
    ifthenelse(var(Arg1),
        true,
        ifthenelse(atomic(Arg1),
            FArg=Arg1,
            (Arg1 =.. [Struc|Args],
            length(Args, Arity),
            FArg = Struc/Arity )) ).
```

```
/* ********************************************************** */
```

```
% LABELS.ARI
% April, 1988
```

```
% Resolve Labels in the code to addresses
% Return the length of the procedure and list of atoms
```

```
resolve_labels(Code,NewCode,End,Atoms) :-
    x_resolve_labels(Code,NewCode,0,End,Atoms).
```

```
x_resolve_labels([label(l(Start))|List],
        List1,Start,End,Atoms) :-
    x_resolve_labels(List,List1,Start,End,Atoms),!.
x_resolve_labels([X|List],[X|List1],Start,End,Atoms) :-
    code_length(X,Start,End1,Atoms),
    x_resolve_labels(List,List1,End1,End,Atoms),!.
x_resolve_labels([],[],End,End,_).
```

```
/* ********************************************************** */
```

```
% Some Utilities
```

```
convert_name(Infile,Outfile,Type) :-
    string_search($pro$,Infile,Pos),
    substring(Infile,0,Pos,Out1),
    ifthenelse(Type = wam,
        concat(Out1,$wam$,Outfile),
        concat(Out1,$for$,Outfile) ).
```

```
move_clauses(HO) :-
    open(H1,'temp.obj',r),
    repeat,
```

```
        read(H1,Clause),
        (Clause = end_of_file;
         write(HO,Clause),write(HO,'.'),nl(HO),fail),
        close(H1).


% Used to open all the link files
open_files([],[]).
open_files([InFile|Names],[H|Handles]) :-
    open(H,InFile,r),
    open_files(Names,Handles).
```

Skeleton Program Module (unravel, partobj, objcode)

```
% UNRAVEL.ARI
% June, 1988

:- public
   unravel/3.

:- extrn
   list/1,nonlist/1,in_list/2,notin/2.

:-op(700, xfx, [in_list, notin]).


% All structures are unraveled into unify goals.
% All unify goals are of the form Var1=(Var2 or Atom or Struc),
% where Var1 is temporary or permanent and
% where Struc has only variables and atoms as arguments.
% If Var1 is permanent then so is Var2.
% Preexisting unify goals are transformed into this type.
% The structure of disjunctions remains the same (i.e.
% the operator ';' remains). Only the content is unraveled.


unravel(X, [NewHead|Ravel], Perms) :-
    (X = (Head :- Body); X = Head),
    spread(Head, NewHead, Ravel - L),
    ifthenelse(nonvar(Body),
        xunravel(Body, L - [], Perms), L = []), !.

xunravel(X, [DRavel|Ravel]-Link, Perms) :-
    Dis = ((_;_)),
    (X = (Dis,Rest); X = Dis),
    disunravel(Dis, DRavel, Perms),
```

```
        ifthenelse(nonvar(Rest),
            xunravel(Rest, Ravel-Link, Perms), Ravel = Link).

    xunravel(X, Ravel-Link, Perms) :-
        Goal = ((_ = _)),
        (X = (Goal,Rest); X = Goal),
        varunify(Goal, Ravel-L, Perms),
        ifthenelse(nonvar(Rest),
            xunravel(Rest, L-Link, Perms),
            L = Link).

    xunravel(X, Ravel-Link, Perms) :-
        (X = ((Goal,Rest)); X = Goal),
        spread(Goal, NewGoal, Ravel-L),
        L=[NewGoal|L2],
        ifthenelse(nonvar(Rest),
            xunravel(Rest, L2-Link, Perms),
            (L2 = Link)).

    disunravel((A;B), (ARavel;BRavel), Perms) :-
        xunravel(A, ARavel-[], Perms),
        disunravel(B, BRavel, Perms).
    disunravel(A, ARavel, Perms) :-
        xunravel(A, ARavel-[], Perms).


    % Unification optimization.
    % Turn the general goal 'X=Y' into a sequence
    % of simpler unifications of the form
    % Var1=(Var2 or Atom or Struc),
    % where Var1 is a temporary or permanent variable, and
    % where Struc has only atoms and variables as arguments.
    varunify(X=Y, Code-Link, Perms) :-
        (xvarunify(X=Y, Code-Link, Perms); Code=[fail|Link]).


    % One argument is a temporary variable:
    xvarunify(A=B, [A=NewB|L]-Link, Perms) :-
        var(A), A notin Perms, !,
        spread(B, NewB, L-Link).
    xvarunify(A=B, [B=NewA|L]-Link, Perms) :-
        var(B), B notin Perms, !,
        spread(A, NewA, L-Link).

    % One argument is a permanent variable:
    xvarunify(A=B, [A=NewB|L]-Link, Perms) :-
        A in_list Perms, !,
        spread(B, NewB, L-Link).
```

```
xvarunify(A=B, [B=NewA|L]-Link, Perms) :-
    B in_list Perms, !,
    spread(A, NewA, L-Link).
% Both arguments are nonvariables:
xvarunify(A=B, Code-link, Perms) :-
    ifthenelse(atomic(A),
        ifthen(atomic(B),
                ifthen(A = B, Code = Link)),
        ifthenelse(atomic(B), fail,
            % A & B are strucs:
            (A=..[Func|ArgsA],
             B=..[Func|ArgsB], % must have same functors
             lvarunify(ArgsA, ArgsB, Code-Link, Perms)) ) ).
lvarunify([A|ArgsA], [B|ArgsB], Code-Link, Perms) :-
    xvarunify(A=B, Code-L, Perms), !,
    lvarunify(ArgsA, ArgsB, L-Link, Perms).

lvarunify([], [], Link-Link, Perms).


% Take a (possibly nested) structure apart into
% (1) a simple structure, and (2) a series of unify goals.
% A list is considered as a structure with variable arity.
% Its cdr field is given a separate unify goal to
% accommodate the unify_cdr instruction.
spread(List, SimpleList, Rest-Link) :-
    list(List), !,
    argspread(CdrUnify, List, SimpleList, Ravel-Link),
    ifthenelse(CdrUnify=none, Rest = Ravel,
                Rest=[CdrUnify|Ravel]).

spread(Struc, SimpleStruc, Rest-Link) :-
    Struc=..[Name|Args],
    argspread(_, Args, VArgs, Rest-Link),
    SimpleStruc=..[Name|VArgs].

spread(Other, Other, Link-Link).


argspread(CdrUnify, Cdr, T, Ravel-Link) :-
    nonlist(Cdr), !,
    ifthenelse((var(Cdr); (Cdr==[])),
        (CdrUnify = none, T = Cdr, Ravel = Link),
        (spread(Cdr, SimpleCdr, Ravel-Link),
        CdrUnify = ((T=SimpleCdr)) ) ).
```

```
argspread(CdrUnify, [A|Args], [A|VArgs], Ravel-Link) :-
    (atomic(A); var(A)), !,
    argspread(CdrUnify, Args, VArgs, Ravel-Link).
argspread(CdrUnify, [S|Args], [T|VArgs], Ravel-Link) :-
    Ravel=[T=V|L],
    spread(S, V, L-L2),
    argspread(CdrUnify, Args, VArgs, L2-Link).


% PARTOBJ.ARI
% June, 1988

:-op(700, xfx, [in_list, notin]).
% Convert unraveled code into partial object code:

partobj([Head|BodyGoals], [HeadObj|BodyObj], Perms) :-
    Head=..[_|Args],
    gp_block(get, Args, HeadObj, 1),
    xpartobj(BodyGoals, Perms, BodyObj, yes), !.


xpartobj([], _, [], _).
xpartobj([Dis|Rest], Perms, Result, Flag) :-
    Dis = ((_;_)), !,
    % Initialize permanent variables just before
                first disjunction:
    ifthenelse(Flag=yes,
        (initblock(Perms, PermInit),
         Result=[PermInit,DisCode|RestCode]),
        Result=[DisCode|RestCode]),
    dispartobj(Dis, Perms, DisCode),
    xpartobj(Rest, Perms, RestCode, no).

xpartobj([Goal|Rest], Perms, [GoalCode|RestCode], Flag) :-
    goalpartobj(Goal, Perms, GoalCode),
    xpartobj(Rest, Perms, RestCode, Flag).


dispartobj((A;B), Perms, (ACode;BCode)) :-
    xpartobj(A, Perms, ACode, no),
    dispartobj(B, Perms, BCode).

dispartobj(A, Perms, ACode) :-
    xpartobj(A, Perms, ACode, no).
```

```
% Convert goals into their object code:
% Recognizes !, true, unify goals, and calls with simple arguments:

% cut is simple:
goalpartobj(!, _, cut).
% 'true' needs no code:
goalpartobj(true, _, Link-Link).
% translation of unify goals:
goalpartobj(V=W, Perms, [put(_,V,Temp)|Code]-Link) :-
    ifthenelse(V in_list Perms, Temp = x(8), Temp = V),

% Use register 8 for permanents
    ifthenelse(var(W),
        Code=[get(_,W,Temp)|Link],
        ifthenelse(atomic(W),
            Code=[get(constant,W,Temp)|Link],
            (
            ifthenelse(list(W),
                (W=Args,
                Name/Arity = ('.'/2),
                Type=list),
                (W=..[Name|Args],
                length(Args, Arity),
                Type=nonlist) ),
            Code=[get(structure, Name/Arity, Temp)|L],
            unifyblock(Type, Args, L-Link)
            ) )).

% translation of other goals:
goalpartobj(Goal, _, Code-Link) :-
    Goal=..[Name|Args],
    length(Args, Arity),
    gp_block(put, Args, Code-L, 1),
    ifthenelse(builtin(Name,Arity),
        L=[Name/Arity|Link],
        L=[call(Name/Arity,_)|Link]).

% Initialization of variables:
% Uses register 8 as a holder.
initblock([], Link-Link).
initblock([V|Vars], [put(_,V,x(8))|Rest]-Link) :-
    initblock(Vars, Rest-Link).

% Get or put of all head arguments:
% (If Type is get or put).
gp_block(Type, [A|Args], [X|Rest]-Link, N) :-
```

```
        X=..[Type,T,A,x(N)],
        ifthenelse(atomic(A),T=constant,true),
        N1 is N+1,
        gp_block(Type, Args, Rest-Link, N1).
gp_block(_, [], Link-Link, _).

% Block of unify instructions to unify structures or lists:
unifyblock(nonlist, [], [unify_nil|Link]-Link).
unifyblock(list, V, Rest-Link) :-
        (var(V), Rest=[unify(cdr,x(8)),get(_,V,x(8))|Link];
        V=[], Rest=[unify_nil|Link]).
unifyblock(Type, [A|Args], [unify(T,A)|Rest]-Link) :-
        ifthenelse(atomic(A),T=constant,true),
%          (atomic(A) -> T=constant; true),
        unifyblock(Type, Args, Rest-Link).

% Adding initialization instructions
% in disjunctions to variables which need it.
% Result is a modified PartObj.
% Traverses code once; passes over everything without
% a passing glance except disjunctions.

% Must be used before tempalloc.

varinit(Forward, Backward, Partobj, Newobj) :-
        xvarinit(Forward, Backward, Partobj, Newobj-[]), !.

xvarinit([_], _, X, R-L) :- linkify(X, R-L), !.

% The first two clauses traverse Forward, Backward, and PartObj
% until a disjunction is found:
xvarinit([_,FIn|Forward], [_,BIn|Backward], PartObj, NewObj) :-
        +FIn = ((_;_)), !,
    % Note: since Forward and Backward have identical
    % structure, only one must be tested
        xvarinit([FIn|Forward], [BIn|Backward], PartObj, NewObj), !.
xvarinit(Forward, Backward, [G|PartObj], [G|NewObj]-Link) :-
        + G = ((_;_)), !,
        xvarinit(Forward, Backward, PartObj, NewObj-Link), !.

% At this stage all three arguments have disjunctions:
xvarinit([FLeft, (FA;FB),FRight|Forward],
        [BLeft, (BA;BB),BRight|Backward],
        [(A;B)|PartObj], [(NA;NB)|NewObj]-Link) :- !,
        diffv(FRight, FLeft, T),
        intersectv(T, BRight, V),
```

```
    dis_varinit(V, (FA;FB), (BA;BB), (A;B), (NA;NB)),
    xvarinit([FRight|Forward],
        [BRight|Backward], PartObj, NewObj-Link),!.

dis_varinit(V, ((FA;FB)), ((BA;BB)), ((A;B)), ((NA;NB)) ) :-
    one_choice(V, FA, BA, A, NA),
    dis_varinit(V, FB, BB, B, NB).
dis_varinit(V, FA, BA, A, NA) :-
    one_choice(V, FA, BA, A, NA).


one_choice(V, FA, BA, A, NA) :-
    xvarinit(FA, BA, A, NA-Link),
    last(FA, FLast),
    diffv(V, FLast, InitVars),
    ifthenelse(InitVars=[],
        Link=[],
        (init_list(InitVars, InitInstr),
        Link=[InitInstr]) ).


init_list([V|Vars], [put(variable,V,V)|Rest]-Link) :-
    init_list(Vars, Rest-Link).
init_list([], Link-Link).


% OBJCODE.ARI
% January, 1988


% Turn partial object code, which still contains the
% hierarchy of goals and disjunctions, into a uniform list.
% The control instructions for disjunctions are compiled and
% the labels for the cut instructions are instantiated.
objcode(PartObj, ObjCode) :-
    xobjcode(PartObj, ObjCode-[], proc, _), !.


xobjcode([], Link-Link, _, _).
xobjcode([cut|RestCode], Code-Link, CutLbl, yes) :-
    % Distinguish between the two kinds of cut instructions:
    ifthenelse((CutLbl == proc),
        Code = [cut|C], Code = [cutd(CutLbl)|C]),
    xobjcode(RestCode, C-Link, CutLbl, _).
xobjcode([Code-L|RestCode], Code-Link, CutLbl, IsCut) :-
    xobjcode(RestCode, L-Link, CutLbl, IsCut).
xobjcode([((X;Choices))|RestCode],
    [try(else,L1)|ChCode]-Link, CutLbl,IsCut) :-
    xobjcode(X, ChCode-ChLink, L1, _),
    ChLink=[execute(EndLbl),label(L1)|C3],
```

```
        xdiscode(Choices, C3-L, EndLbl),
        xobjcode(RestCode, L-Link, CutLbl, IsCut).

    xdiscode((X;Choices), [retry(else,L2)|ChCode]-Link, EndLbl) :-
        xobjcode(X, ChCode-ChLink, L2, _),
        ChLink=[execute(EndLbl),label(L2)|C3],
        xdiscode(Choices, C3-Link, EndLbl).
    xdiscode(LastChoice, Code-Link, EndLbl) :-
        xobjcode(LastChoice, ChCode-ChLink, CutLbl, IsCut),
        ifthenelse( (IsCut == yes),
            (Code = [retry(else,CutLbl)|ChCode],
             ChLink = [execute(EndLbl),
             label(CutLbl),trust(else,fail),(fail/0)|L]),
             (Code = [trust(else,fail)|ChCode],
%       ChLink=L),
        L=[label(EndLbl)|Link].
```

Lifetime Module (varlist, lifetime)

```
% VARLIST.ARI
% June, 1988

% Calculate from the unraveled source code
% the varlist used for calculating lifetimes.
% All goal arguments (variables & atoms) are simply listed.
% For unify goals only the variables are listed.
% Goal arguments are delimited by one or both
% of arity(Arity) and fence(Name)
% This is determined as follows:
%    1.   arity(Arity) allows tempalloc to do more
%              optimal allocation.
%         It comes before the arguments.
%         It is generated for all goals, even built-ins (except unify,
%         or goals with arity zero, or if all arguments are
%              nonvariable).
%    2.   fence(Name) is used in lifetime to kill temporaries.
%         It comes after the arguments.
%         It is not generated for built-ins or the head of the clause.

varlist([Head|RestCode], [arity(Arity)|Vars]) :-
    Head=..[Name|Args],
    length(Args, Arity),
    linkify(Args, Vars-L),
    xvarlist(RestCode, L-[]), !.
xvarlist([X|RestCode], [Dis|Vars]-Link) :-
    X = ((_;_)),
```

```
        dislist(X, Dis),
        xvarlist(RestCode, Vars-Link).
xvarlist([Goal|RestCode], Vars-Link) :-
        goalsvars(Goal, Vars-L),
        xvarlist(RestCode, L-Link).
xvarlist([], Link-Link).

dislist( ((A;B)), ((AVars;BVars)) ) :-
        xvarlist(A, AVars-[]),
        dislist(B, BVars).
dislist(B, BVars) :-
        xvarlist(B, BVars-[]).
goalsvars(A=S, Vars-Link) :-
        ifthenelse(var(S), SVars = [S],
            ifthenelse(list(S), SVars = S, S =.. [_|SVars])),
        getvars([A|SVars], Vars-Link).

goalsvars(Goal, Vars-Link) :-
        Goal=..[Name|Args],
        length(Args, Arity),
        ifthenelse( ((Arity=0;getvars(Args, []-[])) ),
            Vars = L,
            (Vars = [arity(Arity)|V],
             linkify(Args, V-L)) ),
        ifthenelse(builtin(Name,Arity),
            L = Link,
            L = [fence(Name)|Link]).


% LIFETIME.ARI
% June, 1988

% Calculate lifetimes of all temporary
% variables using the varlist.
% (Permanents must be allocated beforehand)
% Uses fence(_) to forget temporaries.
% Two passes needed: Down & back up.

lifetime(VarList, LifeList, ForwList, BackList) :-
        ForwList=[[]|_],
        forward(VarList, ForwList, _),
        backward(VarList, BackList, []),
        mapclause(intersectv, ForwList, BackList, LifeList), !.

% Forward Pass:
% Watch out for data flow!
```

```
% FLast is an output, FLeft is given.

forward([X|Rest], [FLeft,FRight|FRest], FLast) :-
    var(X), !,
    unionv([X], FLeft, FRight),
    forward(Rest, [FRight|FRest], FLast).
forward([fence(_)|Rest], [_,[]|FRest], FLast) :-
    forward(Rest, [[]|FRest], FLast).
forward([Dis|Rest], [FLeft,FIn,FRight|FRest], FLast) :-
    Dis = ((_;_)),
    forwdis(Dis, [FLeft,FIn], FRight),
    forward(Rest, [FRight|FRest], FLast).
forward([_|Rest], [FLeft,FLeft|FRest], FLast) :-
    forward(Rest, [FLeft|FRest], FLast).
forward([], [FLast], FLast).


% Given: FLeft.
% To be calculated: AIn, BIn, FRight.

forwdis( ((A;B)), [FLeft, ((AIn;BIn)) ], FRight) :-
    AIn=[FLeft|_],
    forward(A, AIn, ARight),
    forwdis(B, [FLeft,BIn], BRight),
    unionv(ARight, BRight, FRight).
forwdis(B, [FLeft,BIn], FRight) :-
    BIn=[FLeft|_],
    forward(B, BIn, FRight).


% Backward Pass:
% Watch out for convoluted data flow!
% Blast is an input, others (BLeft, BRight) are outputs.

backward([X|Rest], [BLeft,BRight|BRest], BLast) :-
    var(X), !,
    backward(Rest, [BRight|BRest], BLast),
    unionv([X], BRight, BLeft).
backward([fence(_)|Rest], [[],L|BRest], BLast) :-
    backward(Rest, [L|BRest], BLast).
backward([Dis|Rest], [BLeft,BIn,BRight|BRest], BLast) :-
    Dis = ((_;_)),
    backward(Rest, [BRight|BRest], BLast),
    backdis(Dis, [BLeft,BIn,BRight]).
backward([_|Rest], [BLeft,BLeft|BRest], BLast) :-
    backward(Rest, [BLeft|BRest], BLast).
backward([], [BLast], BLast).
```

```
% Given: BRight.
% To be calculated: XIn, YIn, BLeft.

backdis( ((X;Y)), [BLeft,((XIn;YIn)),BRight]) :-
    XIn=[XLeft|_],
    backward(X, XIn, BRight),
    backdis(Y, [YLeft,YIn,BRight]),
    unionv(XLeft,YLeft,BLeft).
backdis(Y, [BLeft,YIn,BRight]) :-
    YIn=[BLeft|_],
    backward(Y,YIn, BRight).
```

Chapter 5 **Virtual Machines in Hardware**

Introduction

This chapter is about performance. When performance cannot be sacrificed for money, power consumption, complexity, or for any other resource the designer might otherwise conserve, special-purpose processors are often the solution. The value of embedded intelligence to a particular application may be so great that performance is the highest design priority. Inadequate speed may make an application infeasible, so this chapter looks at specialized processors that have been designed for intelligent applications.

In keeping with the general line of argument that virtual machines are a good design approach for high-level languages, and that threaded code interpreters are good platforms for implementing virtual machines, a good deal of the discussion in this chapter centers on hardware threaded code interpreters. However, there are other important processors developed specifically to execute Prolog and LISP, and these are discussed as well.

The Prolog, LISP, and threaded code languages share an architectural element in that they are all virtual stack machines—they use a stack to pass arguments to subroutines and to return the results of a computation to the caller. Of course, register-oriented implementations of these languages exist, and these implementations are often a good fit with the processing resources of conventional processors.

LISP is also discussed here for the first time. In some respect it is similar to FORTH, an extensible language with a flexible compiler and good support for the construction of virtual machines. However, it is tough to find a commercial LISP that is suitable for embedded systems with severe resource constraints.

On the other hand, LISP machines—processors whose machine instructions constitute a virtual machine for LISP—are commercially important as components of high-powered workstations, and the LISP machine may be either the main processor or a special-purpose coprocessor. LISP is mentioned here mainly for completeness and to point out the architectural similarities between special-purpose, high-performance processors.

Hardware Implementations
of Threaded Code Interpreters

As an implementation tool, threaded code derives its power from the efficiency of the inner interpretive mechanism as well as the expressiveness of the language. Wherever there is overhead though, and there always is, a threaded code implementation will be slower than the equivalent machine code implementation. The same can be said of C. Nevertheless the tradeoffs between machine language coding and coding in higher level languages like C often end up being made in favor of the high-level language exactly because of the expressiveness of the higher level language and the more favorable economics of code development that this implies. Developers count on the upward performance curve of the processors as a fact of life and bet that the speed they need will always come if they wait long enough. It's not unusual for spending on code maintenance to be a large multiple of the spending on code development, so going for speed only through machine code could be counterproductive in the long run.

When a language architecture is perceived as enabling economically important applications that couldn't be built otherwise, there is an economic motivation for implementing the architecture in hardware. The increase in performance that a hardware implementation can bring may be enough to make these important applications not only possible but practical. LISP is a good example of such a language architecture because commercial expert systems were first practical only on LISP machines.

The LISP machine was in part developed because the economic potential of expert systems was perceived to be huge. Practical expert systems could not wait for conventional processor evolution to get to the point where the performance of LISP on conventional machines was adequate for the applications, and it was not clear at the time that it would be economical to develop these applications in languages other than LISP.

Threaded code processors—machines whose basic machine language is a threaded language like FORTH—were developed in response to similar economic forces. Embedded applications were becoming widespread as well as more sophisticated. Conventional processor evolution was reflecting the needs of data processing and workstation applications, not data acquisition and control. Finally, as the embedded applications became larger, the development environments, particularly for programming and debugging, showed the strain.

This chapter introduces some of the threaded code machines that have been developed in the last several years. Since the single most important architectural element of a machine designed to efficiently execute threaded code is likely to be the stack, these machines are commonly called stack machines. Phil Koopman (1989) gives an in-depth treatment of stack machines. Stack machine architectures for LISP and Prolog machines are also discussed here. The following sections describe some general implementation architectures for stack machines. Finally, some specific machines are described along with the performance of some expert systems based on stack machine versions of LISP and Prolog.

Implementations of Stacks

The stack implementation in C illustrated in Chapter 2 and used there as part of the threaded code design in C illustrates how conventional software stacks are built. The stack is simply an array. A variable, referred to as the *stack pointer,* is used to store an index into the array. The index refers to the top stack element. Stacks have two primitive operations, *push* and *pop*. The push operation refers to the procedure for allocating space for a new data element on the stack and then storing data (the procedure argument) in it. The pop operation is a procedure that deallocates a storage space, returning from the procedure with the data element that was in the deallocated location. Both the push and pop operations adjust the stack pointer. The data element that is pushed onto the stack or popped off the stack can be as simple as the contents of a single memory cell, or could be any much more complicated data structure.

In a hardware stack implementation, the logic of the push and pop procedures, the storage for the stack pointer, and the stack structure itself are all implemented in silicon. If in a particular machine the push and pop operations are the only primitive operations permitted on the stack data structure, the only element in the stack that is accessible is the top element. Much of the power of the stack machine, in terms of code compactness, speed, and architectural simplicity derives from this limitation.

A hardware implementation of a stack makes stack accesses faster. The importance of fast stack access increases with the number of machine operations that refer to the stack contents. Hardware stack implementations are, in common practice, made through a bank of contiguous memory locations with a dedicated register used to hold the stack pointer. Another stack implementation option is a shift register.

If the stack and its management mechanisms are the only machine resources available for passing parameters and return values and saving the return address, the speed advantage due to a hardware implementation of the stacks may be significant.

For example, a stack machine may have a performance advantage over a register machine for executing application code that is well structured, meaning that the code is very modular. The performance impact on very modular code is due to the fact that modular code tends to execute many subroutine calls. In addition to speeding up the stack references, the stack machine has advantages due to its very simple architecture—few registers to save and restore on interrupt or context switches, and no instruction cache to manage—so stack machines are often a good choice for embedded applications, particularly where interrupt handling is of paramount importance to the application. No complicated instructions are in the process of being decoded when an interrupt occurs.

The last-in, first-out stack (LIFO) is also one of the simplest mechanisms for achieving dynamic memory management. The ability to allocate and deallocate storage space, even within the limitations of the push and pop primitives, enable powerful software capabilities such as recursion. These capabilities derive from the ability to dynamically store the context of a procedure call independent of and physically separate from the procedure code.

In the broadest sense of the term, the *context* of a procedure call can be interpreted to mean the state of the machine at the time the procedure was invoked. In practice, the information that is usually stored as context is just the control information necessary to return to the caller on completion of the subroutine—conceptually the *return address*— as well as temporary storage for information that might be local to each procedure invocation. For example, both the procedure input parameters and private variables are local to a given procedure call. Language architectures that allocate space for these, along with the procedure code, necessarily make recursion and reentrancy very difficult if not impossible to implement. However, the majority of these languages (FORTRAN is a good example) are not of recent vintage, the advantages of recursion and reentrancy now in general having wide acceptance.

Note that the stack concept should not be limited to a single stack supporting procedure calls. There may well be, as part of the abstract language architecture, several stacks each for input parameters, control information, and local variables. Postscript is a good example of a language whose virtual machine uses a multistack of architecture. Similarly, real machine logic may include support for a number of stacks, several registers being valid stack reference arguments to the push and pop operations.

Coincident with a reexamination of processor instruction set architectures that have framed the CISC/RISC debate, over the past five years there has been a resurgence of interest in the implementations of stack machine architectures. These recent stack machines extend stack support beyond a couple of machine registers set aside as stack pointers and machine logic for push and pop operations. Some feature multiple on-chip stacks, stack buffers, and stack overflow/underflow interrupts. A number of these stack machines have been built, and in one case stack machines constitute a major commercial product line.

Like the RISC machines, the stack processors have been designed for simplicity, on the assumption that in simplicity lies both dependability and performance. By contrast to the RISC machines, the stack machines have been able to achieve high performance with much simpler processor logic and with very low overall system complexity, for example, no pipelines or microcode. The result is a processor that can execute its programs very fast with a low overhead for interrupt response and a low cost for context switching— both critical attributes for embedded systems. As we'll see, programs written for the stack machines are compact, largely as a side effect of the simplicity of the instruction set. Compact programs translate into good use of limited hardware resources.

The remainder of this chapter introduces a taxonomy for categorizing stack machines and discusses the design both of virtual stack machines for AI languages like LISP and Prolog and of commercial stack machine implementations.

Taxonomy of Stack Machines

A taxonomy for stack machine architectures is a useful descriptive device. It facilitates a discussion of the design tradeoffs involved in the architectural elements without delving unnecessarily into the design details of any particular machine. The taxonomy of stack machines presented here has been developed by Phil Koopman and is discussed more fully in his book. Koopman's stack machine design space is illustrated in Figure 5-1.

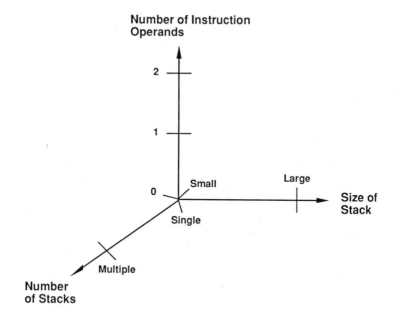

Figure 5.1. Stack Machine Design Space

Stack machine may be characterized by the number of instruction operands that are supported by the stack machine instruction set, the number of stacks supported, and the size of the stacks.

The design space for stack machines has three dimensions: the operand number, stack number, and stack size. For simplicity, the valid values for each design dimension are limited to a small set as follows

Dimension	Values	Notation
Operand Number	0, 1, 2	0, 1, 2
Stack Size	Large, small	L, S
Stack Number	Single, multiple	S,M

The *operand number* refers to the number of operands used by the machine instructions. In a *pure* stack machine, it is understood that operations are applied only to the top element of the stack. Operands are therefore implicit, so the machine is said to have a 0-operand architecture.

For implementing a machine in hardware, the simplicity of the 0-operand architecture has several advantages. The two main advantages are the ability to use a separate single-ported memory for the stack and the need to use only a small number of registers for loading the top stack elements. Moreover, this architecture allows these top-of-stack registers to be loaded in parallel with the process of instruction decoding, thus eliminating any need for instruction pipelining to fetch and store operands. Furthermore, the code for the machine can be extremely compact since the operands of the machine instructions are implicitly the stack elements. One of the reasons that byte-encoded virtual machine designs do not necessarily have very compact code is that the operands for the more complicated opcodes tend to expand the effective length of instructions well beyond a single byte.

These strengths of the 0-operand design bear the seeds of its weakness, however. Simplicity of the opcode design implies that performing a complicated procedure could require multiple simple operations. Similarly, accessing stack elements that are deeply buried in the stack may be time consuming, unless a special provision has been made in the hardware for this sort of operation.

The 1-operand stack machine architecture is sometimes called *stack-accumulator*. The first operand is usually referred to explicitly, and the reference to the operand follows the operator in the source code. The second operand, when there is one, is implicitly the top stack element. This architecture may require a pipeline to prefetch the operands.

The more general architecture is the 2-operand stack machine. This category encompasses some of the existing conventional processors, where the stack, however implemented, is used only to store control information. The two operands are usually interpreted as *source* and *destination* and may refer to registers, memory locations, immediate values, or stack frame offsets (see Figure 2.1). Instruction decoding is correspondingly more difficult than for the 0-operand or 1-operand architectures. Since the operands are not known before an instruction is decoded, the 2-operand machines often employ pipelines to increase efficiency, which can put a burden on the compiler technology if it is expected to generate efficient code.

The remaining two dimensions of the stack machine design space are straightforward to describe. Single-stack machines have exactly one stack supported by the instruction set. This stack is most often intended for context saving. The disadvantage of a single stack is that it is tough to avoid an intermingling of control information and data, which may be a significant disadvantage if there is a need to copy data from one procedure invocation to another. The advantage of the single stack design is its simplicity. Where stacks are built from separate off-chip memories, each additional stack requires a separate set of address pins leading off from the chip. So, in this case, needing one stack is better than needing two.

The multiple stack machines have two or more stacks that can be referenced by the instruction set. The different stacks may be used to separately store control information and data. The great relative advantage of the multiple stack machine is its speed, particularly so when some advantage can be taken of the opportunities to have parallel execution of control and data manipulation operations. The tradeoff made for this speed is the complexity of the instruction set and the implementation hardware.

One relevant example of a multiple stack architecture is the Prolog virtual machine, which employs at least two stacks, a control stack, and a structure stack for storing structures that are constructed during program execution. There may also be hardware support in such a machine for the trail and a push-down list that is used to store pointers during unification.

The final dimension characterizing the stack machines is the size of the stack memory that must be supported by the hardware. This memory size can range from zero in the case where the stack and program memory are identical, to the extreme of large, completely separate stack memory spaces. By contrast to the other design dimensions though, the distinction between small and large stack buffer machines is not always obvious.

The case where memory dedicated to storing stack elements is zero, as in most conventional processors, is representative of the class of small stack buffer machines. These machines have the advantage that memory access operations can be used in the stack space in order to access elements of the stack since the program and stack share the same memory. Hardware support for this architecture consists at most of a buffer to store the first several elements of the stack. The disadvantage of the small stack buffer machine architecture is that the program memory bandwidth can be a performance limiting factor. Control and ALU operations can take place in parallel, providing separate memories are available.

Where main memory bandwidth does not limit performance, the machine is by definition categorized as large stack buffer; that is, the buffer is "large enough." A rule of thumb for the appropriateness of this characterization might be whether or not several levels of subroutines may be invoked without exhausting the stack buffers. Koopman has collected some program execution statistics that provide a measure of how large a stack buffer is "large enough."

The memory bandwidth issue is simply that, with a hardware stack buffer, memory access cycles are not consumed in accessing operands. Stack size of course always has a practical upper limit, and there may be some application program that uses the stack so as to exceed the maximum. Therefore some provision needs to be made to detect and react to an overflow condition, that is, more complicated stack management hardware. The problem is exacerbated in a multitasking system, where context switches can be very expensive, since the entire stack buffer may need to be saved and then restored later.

The stack machine design space has been fully explored by machine designers and manufacturers, and most processors today have at least some hardware support for stack manipulation. The next section looks at some particular examples, with emphasis on machines with greater stack support than exist in conventional processors. These generally have the better performance and are thus more attractive to the embedded systems designer who has run up against the performance limits of conventional machines.

Examples of Stack Machines

The design space outlined in Figure 5.1 can be referenced by a three character notation for stack machine classification, representing respectively the stack number (S or M), the stack size (S or L), and the operand number (0,1, or 2). This classification scheme has been populated with examples by Koopman (Table 5.1). One of his observations is that all categories of the design space are represented by actual machines, with the major design variable being operand number.

Table 5.1. Stack Machine Taxonomy

Category   Sample Machines

SS0   **INMOS Transputer** - single chip microprocessor designed for parallel pro-
            cessing.
            Burroughs family - a line of stack computers originating with the ALGOL
            B5000 machine.
SS1   **Hewlett Packard HP3000** - commercial minicomputer line based on 1-oper-
            and stack/accumulator architecture.
SS2   **Intel 80x86** - commercial microcomputer family with a general-purpose regis-
            ter architecture.

SL0   **G Machine** - special-purpose machine built to perform graph reduction in
            support of functional programming languages (research prototype).
SL1   **Raytheon AADC** - designed for direct execution of APL in military environ-
            ments. Execution unit uses 1-operand stack notation.
SL2   **Advanced Micro Devices AM29000** - a RISC processor with 192 registers
            128 of which are a stack cache.
            RISC I - among the first RISC machines.
            SOAR - Smalltalk On A RISC. Smalltalk is a bytecode stack machine.

MS0   **IBM APL Machine** - IBM360/25 with writable control store used to emulate
            APL.
            Rockwell Microcontrollers - general-purpose microcontrollers that come
            with preprogrammed FORTH.
MS1   **Digital Equipment Corp. PDP-11** - early general-purpose machine that inte-
            grated support for stack usage into a register architecure.
MS2   **Motorola 680x0** - a family of microprocessors with a general-purpose regis-
            ter architecture.

ML0   **Pascal Machine** - experimental system for direct execution of Pascal
            (research prototype).
            Harris Semiconductor RTX2000 - a macrocell in the Harris standard cell
            library, so it can be built as a standalone processor or integrated with other
            devices.
ML1   **LISP Machine** - a class of machines that tend to have 1-operand addressing
            formats. May have extensive hardware stacks.
ML2   **PSP** - parallel stack machine. A register machine with hardware for saving
            context.
            SF1 - a stack frame computer designed for efficient high-level language
            execution.

Generally, the single stack machines are more academic designs, reflecting a desire for
simplicity, though more often driven by severe resource constraints. The 2-operand
designs tend to be more mainstream processors, represented in particular by RISC
machines, with their substantial hardware support for large numbers of on-chip registers.
The 1-operand designs are clearly intermediate between the other two, attempting to take

advantage of the simplicity of the basic stack machine design while using registers to overcome some of the limitations of either small stack buffers or limited stack addressing that might make the stack access a bottleneck in some application programs.

We will focus here less on the operand number of the machine and more on machines with nonzero stack number and substantial stack buffer size. These multiple stack machines are the machines that run counter to the mainstream and are on the extremes in terms of hardware stack support.

Multiple Stack Machines

The commercial stack machines are largely two-stack machines with 0-operand addressing and small stack buffers. Their design lineage is firmly rooted in the FORTH language, and they are very efficient FORTH machines. For the same reason that FORTH is a good language for implementing virtual machines, these stack machines are very efficient platforms for virtual machine implementations. A designer has the benefits of FORTH with far fewer performance limitations. Moreover, the stack machine has many of the strengths that might lead the embedded system designer to go outside the hardware mainstream for a processor to build a design around.

The major strengths of the two-stack machine can be traced to two factors. First, the 0-operand addressing leads to compact code because the instruction size is reduced (fewer bits required to encode an instruction). Second, the multiple stacks permit exploitation of parallelism to make subroutine calls and other context switches very inexpensive. This may also decrease the code density as well. Moreover, the machines are simple. These features have several auxilliary benefits for the embedded system designer.

1. Code size is reduced due to the short instructions and to the fact that inexpensive subroutine calls encourage program factoring into large numbers of short subroutines. Short programs reduce memory cost and component count, which in turn reduce power requirements. Moreover, system performance may be improved since the smaller memory requirements means that faster though more expensive memory could be used.

2. Decreased complexity means faster development time and increased adaptability.

Looking at the stack machine hardware design and the instruction set architecture in more detail will lead to more insight as to how these benefits are actually realized.

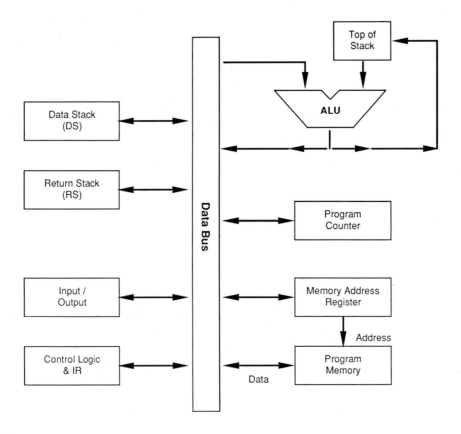

Figure 5.2. Stack Machine Generic Design

The generic stack machine has several hardware resources, including registers for the program counter and stack pointer, an ALU, and multiple stacks.

Multiple Stack Machine Design and Instructions

The generic hardware design for the the multiple stack 0-operand machine is illustrated in Figure 5.2.

The elements of the design are as follows:

Data and Return Stacks   Internal memories in combination with the mechanisms necessary to implement a LIFO stack. Only push and pop operations are permitted on the stack. The single difference between the data and return stacks is that the return stack is used to store return addresses, whereas the data stack stores operands. This distinction is not a physical distinction though.

ALU and Top of Stack Register   Performs logical and arithmetic operation on pairs of stack elements. The top of stack register holds the top element of the data stack, for use by the ALU.

Program Counter   Register Holds the address of the next instruction to be executed. It can be loaded from the bus to implement branches or be incremented to fetch the next instruction in sequence from the memory.

Program Memory   Uses a memory address register and random access memory.

A minimum set of machine instructions for the generic machine is described in Table 5.2. A generic stack machine instruction set includes memory access instructions, basic arithmetic and logic operations (whose operands are passed on the data stack), conditional branch instructions to implement iteration, and procedure call and return instructions. Given the 0-operand classification of the machine, the syntax for the instructions is most naturally expressed like FORTH in Reverse Polish notation. In this notation, reading from left to right, the operands appear before the operator, meaning that the operands are pushed on the stack and the operator is then applied to the operands. Any result of the operation is left on the data stack.

Given the basic machine resources organized in Figure 5.2, the greatest opportunity to improve performance in a hardware implementation of the stack machine comes when the machine designer can take advantage of the parallelism between control and ALU instructions to reduce the cost of performing a subroutine call. For example, in the

Table 5.2 Stack Machine Instruction Set

In this table, the instruction symbol is the equivalent FORTH instruction, wherever there is a direct correspondence.

Instruction	Data Stack input -> output	Description
!	N1 ADDR ->	Store N1 at location ADDR in program memory.
+	N1 N2 -> N3	Add N1 to N2 to give N3.
-	N1 N2 -> N3	Subtract N2 from N1 to give N3.
>R	N1 ->	Push N1 on the Return Stack.
@	ADDR -> N1	Fetch the contents of ADDR returning N1.
AND	N1 N2 -> N3	Bitwise AND N1 with N2 to give N3.
DROP	N1 ->	Drop N1 from the Stack.
DUP	N1 -> N1 N1	Duplicate N1.
OR	N1 N2 -> N3	Bitwise OR N1 with N2 to give N3.
OVER	N1 N2 -> N1 N2 N1	Copy N1 to the top of the Data Stack.
R>	-> N1	Pop the Return Stack N1 and push on Data Stack.
SWAP	N1 N2 -> N2 N1	Swap the top two elements of the Data Stack.
XOR	N1 N2 -> N3	Bitwise XOR N1 with N2 to give N3.
[IF]	N1 ->	If N1 is FALSE branch to address in next cell, otherwise, continue.
[CALL]	->	Perform subroutine call to address in next cell.
[EXIT]	->	Perform subroutine return.
[LIT]	-> N1	Treat value in next cell as a constant and push on stack as N1.

two-stack generic machine, when a call is made to a subroutine, the return address can be pushed onto the return stack at the same time as the program counter is loaded with the new address. This assumes an instruction format in which the address is encoded together with the CALL opcode within a single instruction word. Details of this encoding scheme are discussed later in the context of actual implementations.

Subroutine returns are accomplished by popping the return stack and placing the contents in the program counter register. This can take place at the same time as an ALU instruction, for example, *add*.

Because the opcode format for a stack machine is very simple (that is, no combinations of different operand types to encode in the instruction), the hardware design for decoding instructions can be quite straightforward. Moreover, if the word size of the machine is large compared to the number of instructions, pre-decoded instructions can be used to simplify the control hardware, and specific bit fields can be used to control classes of operations. The opportunity thus exists to combine several classes of operation in the one set of instruction bits.

For example, ALU operations and control operations might be combined in a single instruction. Where this is allowed by the machine design a common optimization is to have the compiler recognize when an ALU operation and return-from-subroutine operation occur together, and then pack the operations in a single instruction. When this can be done, the code is more compact and the cost of a subroutine return becomes zero.

A byte-encoded design culture may consider fixed-size 16-bit instructions to be wasteful, but as the preceding discussion indicates, there are opportunities for the compiler to combine operations that lead to the dual benefits of code compaction and better performance. Using larger instruction sizes enables the subroutine call to be encoded in the same length as all other instructions, at the expense of some address space limitations. For example, a simple and common scheme uses the first instruction bit to denote a subroutine call, in which case the remaining 15 bits can be used to encode the subroutine address. This gives the machine a linear program address space that is not huge, but it is large enough for many embedded applications. This unencoded hardwired design for instruction decoding saw early use in the Novix NC4016 machine.

Since the unencoded hardwired instruction format has many bit combinations that are unused, there have been design proposals for microcoded stack machines, the idea being to use fewer bits to encode the same instructions, while at the same time providing more flexibility, including the opportunity for the user to design instructions. With some or all microcode in RAM, instruction sets could be customized to the level of individual applications.

The disadvantage of the microcode approach is some increase in hardware complexity and time to decode instructions. Koopman has published empirical studies on the various stack machine approaches, with statistics on instruction usage in benchmark application suites, and the results indicate that the microcoded designs make a very practical tradeoff between more complicated instructions (and thus to some extent more powerful and expressive instructions) and the cycles required to complete the instruction.

Context Switching

The generic stack machine carries a potential liability with its separate stack memory since context switches in response to interrupts or task changes in a multitasking environment may be expensive. However, certain hardware design techniques can reduce this liability.

Generally, interrupt handling is much less expensive on the stack machines than it is on conventional designs since there are no registers to be saved, nor are there condition codes that need to be archived, since condition flags (like most other arguments) are stored on the data stack. Moreover, without a data or instruction pipeline, there is no additional penalty for saving the pipeline state on a context switch.

I/O service interrupts, a potentially frequent event that must be serviced quickly, are a special case in that they generally require little processing or temporary storage. For this reason, the stack machine can treat I/O interrupts as hardware-generated subroutine calls.

Interrupts resulting from stack overflow/underflow conditions are more significant because these are the most frequent exceptional conditions for a stack machine with reasonably sized stack buffers, and it is not a condition whose handling can be postponed. Of course there are tradeoffs between the buffer size, the frequency of the overflow interrupts, and the time taken to process the interrupt. Stack overflow is conventionally processed with a subroutine call that copies all or a portion of the stack to main memory.

Task switching is another significant operation that could involve a large overhead for flushing the stack buffers as well as maintaining multiple stack pointers. Alternatives for stack machines are to build multiple stack buffers in hardware or to divide a single stack into multiple stack segments for the different topics.

The commercial stack machines have evolved from the FORTH language architecture and are sometimes called FORTH engines. Their development and commercialization has been driven by the need for more powerful processors that could address some of the special requirements of embedded applications. Other stack machine architectures, based on languages like LISP and Prolog, have been designed and implemented. The commercial emphasis in these cases was the value that could be delivered by using these processors as part of tools like engineering workstations or as the basis of applications like expert systems. The stack machine designs for LISP and Prolog run well on the FORTH engines, and so it is worthwhile to take a closer look at these designs as a basis for embedded expert systems.

LISP and Stack Machines

As we have argued, many language designs take advantage of a virtual machine for the language in order to make the compilation task easier. The virtual machine occupies the middle ground between the underlying hardware and the machine that could execute the source code of the language directly. It is therefore often easier to have the compiler compile to the virtual machine instructions than to the lower level machine code. This makes the compilation step more efficient and less prone to error, as well as increasing the ease with which the language can be ported to different machines.

Often an additional advantage of this approach is that the virtual machine code can be unambiguously decompiled into the source code, which is possible if the source and the virtual machine code resemble each other. If the economic advantages of higher performance are significant enough, the virtual machine may be implemented in hardware. This line of development is what has led to the LISP machines–machines designed specifically to execute LISP.

Although there have been register-oriented LISP machine architectures, which fit conventional processors, the more general stack machine architectures have also been very popular. One of the more commercially significant is the stack architecture employed by the Xerox LISP machines, one of the many technology achievements of Xerox PARC.

The instruction set of a basic LISP stack machine is very simple and is composed of only 15 opcodes. Each opcode has some effect on the state of the value stack. The opcodes are listed in Table 5.3.

There has been considerable exploration of the possible implementation architectures for the LISP machines. Deutsch is perhaps the best-known advocate of 0-operand architectures for these kinds of high-level languages. He has been an articulate proponent of the view that an alternative to bigger and faster machines as a way to deal with increased information processing requirements might be found in less traditional machine and program organizations. Moreover, time spent in this pursuit would ultimately provide, at a fraction of the cost, the kind of capabilities now found only in the large and expensive workstations. The goal is embedded intelligence.

It is interesting to compare the instructions of Tables 5.2 and 5.3, noting that instructions for the primitive LISP machine are very similar to the instructions for the canonical stack machine.

Prolog is like LISP, both in being a popular implementation language for expert systems and in having spawned considerable research into machine architectures for its efficient execution. The Prolog machines are stack machines, and this language, too, exhibits quite substantial performance on the FORTH engines relative to implementations on high-performance CISC machines.

Prolog and Stack Machines

The virtual machines for Prolog, as developed by David Warren, by Bowen, Byrd, and Clocksin and by others, are stack machines. The Bowen, Byrd, and Clocksin design is 0-operand, whereas the Warren Abstract Machine is 1-operand. Warren has also worked on Prolog machine hardware designs with Evan Tick.

Table 5.3. LISP Machine Instruction Set

LISP machine instruction set for 0-operand class machines. The instructions are expressed in LISP syntax: (function arg_1 arg_2 . . .).

Instruction	Description
(VAR var)	Push the value of the variable **var** on the stack.
(SETQ var)	Store the top of the stack in the variable **var**.
(POP)	Pop the top of the stack.
(COPY)	Duplicate the top of the stack.
(CONST val)	Push the constant **val** on the stack.
(JUMP tag)	Jump to the location **tag**.
(FJUMP tag)	Jump to the location **tag** if the top of stack is NIL.
(TJUMP tag)	Jump to the location **tag** if the top of stack is non-NIL.
(NTJUMP tag)	Jump to the location **tag** if the top of stack is non-NIL. Do not pop stack.
(NFJUMP tag)	Jump to the location **tag** if the top of stack is NIL. Do not pop stack.
(FN n fn)	Call function **fn** with **n** arguments.
(BIND (v1... vn) **(n1... nk))**	Bind the variables **(v1... vn)** to the **n** values on the top of stack.
(UNBIND)	Save top of stack, unwind stack to last **BIND**, and undo. Push saved value.
(DUNBIND)	Like **BIND** but do not restore saved value.
(RETURN)	Return top of stack.

Hardware implementations of Prolog machines have been developed by several firms. In the United States, for example, the Xenologic machine, evolved from the research done at the University of California at Berkeley by Ted Dobry, Al Despain, and others. Mitsubishi has marketed the PSI machine, a Prolog engine that is a product of the Japanese fifth-generation project.

The Berkeley machine is based on the Warren Machine instruction set. The prototype, referred to as PLM-1 (Programmable Logic Machine-1), is designed to be a coprocessor for executing compiled Prolog. The host processor provides the memory and I/O services, implementation for external built-in Prolog functions, and a development environment for the embedded processor.

Three major modules compose the PLM-1: The Prolog machine interface (PMI), Prolog engine, and MicroEngine. The PMI handles the host bus protocol and memory requests by the Prolog engine. This includes provision for stack buffering. The Prolog engine itself consists of the machine registers and data path, as illustrated in Figure 5.3.

The Tick-Warren Prolog machine is a design exercise undertaken to estimate the Prolog language performance that might be achieved by exploiting advanced circuit technology, of the sort used for high-performance LISP machines. The design is centered on the microcontroller, a performance bottleneck given the complex nature of the instruction set.

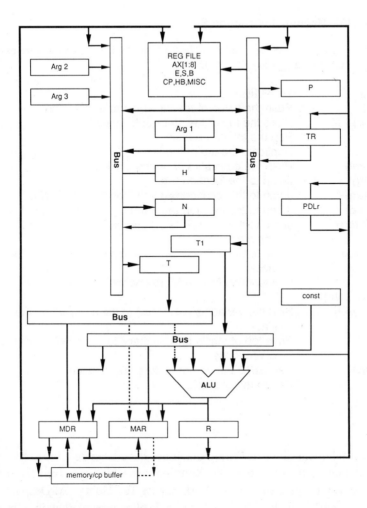

Figure 5.3. Prolog Machine Design

The major machine resources of the PLM-1 are the following:

Resource	Description
P	Program pointer. Points to the next instruction to be executed.
CP	Continuation pointer. Analogous to a return pointer.
E	Environment register. Points to the current environment stack frame.
N	Environment Size.
B	Backtrack register. Points to last choice point stack frame.
H	Heap pointer. Points to the top of the global stack.
HB	Heap backtrack pointer. Points to the top of the global stack at last backtrack point.
S	Structure pointer. Points into the global stack.
TR	Trail pointer. Points to the top of the trail stack.
AX1 . . . 8	Argument registers.
PDL	Pointer to a scratch pad stack
T,T1,R	Pipeline stage registers.
MAR,MDR	Memory interface registers.

The hardware is organized into four units: memory, instruction, execution, and micro-controller. The instruction unit (I-unit) primarily supplies instructions to the execution unit (E-unit), although some instructions having to do with procedure calls are processed directly. For example, one of the main tasks of the I-unit is computing clause addresses. The compiler expands *jump* or *call* instructions into *prefetch* or *prefetch_continuation* instructions, which causes the I-unit to attempt to prefetch the next clause to be executed into the I-unit. However, only the tag-indexed control instructions (for example, *switch_on_term*) are compiled this way. The *switch_on_term* arguments are cached, and this cache is accessed through the argument of the *prefetch* instructions. If the *switch_on_term* instruction is found in the cache, selection of the appropriate procedure is then made based on the tag of the register holding the first argument of the procedure call.

The I-unit actually maintains two instruction buffers, marked *current* and *future*. The address of the eventual clause computed by the *prefetch* instruction is latched into the future buffer program counter, which then contends for machine cycles in an attempt to fill up the future program instruction buffer. When the jump instruction is encountered, the buffers are switched.

The E-unit is organized as a three-stage pipeline:

- *C-stage:* Accesses the stack buffers and state registers.

- *E-stage:* Executes the ALU instructions and latches the results into the output registers.

- *P-stage:* puts away the results into the stack buffers and state registers.

High-level Prolog machine instructions may make an arbitrary number of passes through the pipeline.

The I-unit delivers the initial microinstruction address of the sequence of microinstructions corresponding to each machine instruction. The data path for the E-unit contains buffers for the stacks, including the trail and a temporary stack used during unification, as well as a register file.

The control stack holds two types of object, environments (which contain parameters and procedure variables) and choice points (which store control information). Neither of these are reliably local. Thus the buffer management is designed to ensure that the current environment is in the stack buffer, so all stack references can be forced to map into the buffer. Stack references are made through a base register and an offset, the base register being either the E or B register. The basic data paths of the E-unit are illustrated in Figure 5.4.

Timing estimates based on the Tick-Warren design suggest that a machine based on this design would significantly outperform current Prolog implementations.

Implementations of Prolog virtual machines on FORTH hardware have very good performance. We look at Prolog on the FORTH engines later in this chapter, but first we consider some particular examples of commercial FORTH-based stack machines.

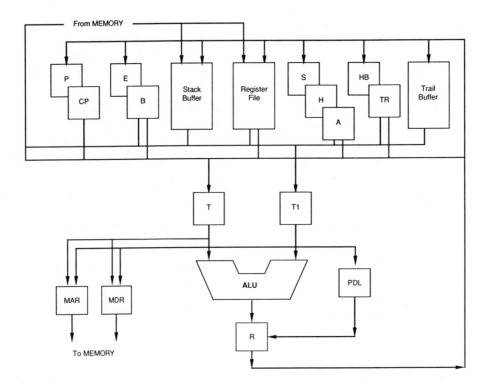

Figure 5.4. Data Paths of E-unit in Tick-Warren Prolog Machine

Examples of Hardware Stack Machines

This section looks at representative 16-bit stack computer designs. Three examples span the range available. The MISC M17 processor is a low-end, inexpensive machine with no hardware stacks. The Novix NC4016, is intermediate in price and performance and distinguished by dedicated off-chip stack buffers. Finally, we describe the Harris RTX 2000, a high-performance microcontroller with on-chip stack buffers.

The stack machines described here are all commercial offerings targeted at embedded applications. Many of these applications require a small processor with a small amount of program memory and must meet demanding constraints in terms of power, chip count, size, and performance. The 16-bit designs reflect the compromise between the minimal 8-bit machine, with its small instruction set, narrow data path, but inadequate arithmetic capabilities, and the power of the 32-bit architecture, with its corresponding huge appetite for memory and power.

The biggest disadvantage of the 16-bit stack machines for embedding intelligent applications is the small address space that can be addressed directly. Although some of these machines do provide support for extended addressing, there is always a price to pay, in performance, code size, or compiler complexity. Nevertheless, inference mechanisms implemented through virtual machines and then ported to the stack machines perform quite well, and in some cases they are superior in performance to implementations on conventional machines. So, for small- to medium-sized embedded intelligent applications, a stack machine can be a good choice.

MISC M17

The MISC M17 (Minimum Instruction Set Computer Inc.) is designed as a low-cost stack machine for embedded design. One of the design tradeoffs in its design involves the use of only a few top-of-stack registers and no on-chip stack buffers. The stacks are maintained in program memory instead of buffers. The architecture of the M17 is illustrated in Figure 5.5.

The M17 instructions are designed to execute in two clock cycles, that is, for each instruction cycle there are two clock cycles, one for instruction fetch and the other for the operation and stack memory access. The chip does incorporate a six-element instruction cache that can execute at the rate of one instruction per clock cycle. The cache is useful mainly for efficiently executing certain types of loops.

To encode subroutine calls, the lowest order bit of the instruction is set to 0, and the remaining higher order bits contain the address of the subroutine. This encoding strategy is a common one for the stack machines, buying code compactness and speed at the expense of some flexibility in addressing. One restriction, for example, is that subroutines in the M17 must start on even byte addresses.

In comparison to the canonical stack machine, the M17 provides a rich interconnect structure between the registers, allowing moderately complex stack operations to be performed within a single instruction cycle. The biggest difference between the two machines, however, is the use of program memory for the stacks. One advantage of this approach is that context switches between tasks can be fast since only the top three data stack elements and the top of the return stack are buffered in registers on the chip.

The M17 is implemented using 6600 gates on 2.0-micron HCMOS gate array technology. The main off-chip components required for operation are the 16-bit wide memory required for program and stacks. Maximum clock speed is 15 MHz.

The M17 is the stack machine that looks the most like a conventional processor and is mentioned here primarily as a stepping off point to the discussion of the pure stack designs. It serves to illustrate that the stack machine need not be considered such a radical design departure from the mainstream.

Novix NC4016

The Novix NC4016 is a 16-bit stack machine designed principally to execute FORTH language primitives, and it has the distinction of being the first single-chip FORTH machine. Its intended application areas include real-time control and high-speed execution of the FORTH language for general-purpose programming.

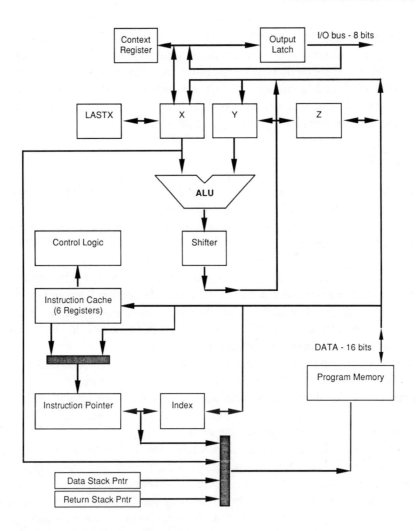

Figure 5.5. MISC M17 Machine Architecture

The NC4016 improves on the design of the M17 by having dedicated stack memories, though these memories are located off-chip. The disadvantage of this approach is the increased number of pins on the chip, as required to address the stack memory. The architecture of the NC4016 is illustrated in Figure 5.6.

Both the data stack and the return stack are dedicated 256-byte memories, with an on-chip stack pointer referencing the current stack address for each stack. The top two data stack elements are buffered by registers on-chip, whereas only the top of the return stack is buffered. A separate index register on-chip is used to implement countdown loops efficiently.

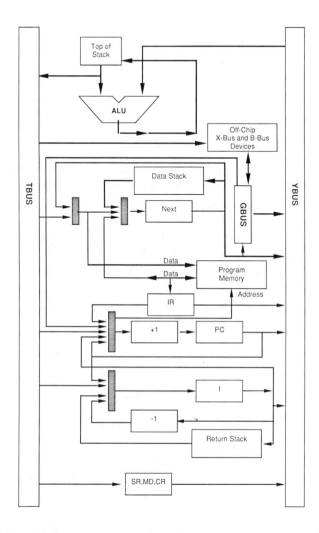

Figure 5.6. Novix NC4016 Machine Architecture

One feature of the off-chip stacks is that separate stack memories can be used in a multi-tasking application, with an off-chip page register used to control switching between the stacks, reducing the overhead of context switching. There is no on-chip underflow or overflow protection for the stacks.

In addition to the program and stack buses, the NC4016 has a separate I/O bus leading off-chip. This bus is organized as a single 16-bit bus with an additional 5-bit bus. These buses give the processor access to I/O devices without stealing cycles from the main memory. Some of these I/O bits are used to extend the memory address space, that is, they are encoded as the high-order bits on the address bus.

The instruction format of the NC4016 provides a good example of unencoded instruction formats for stack machines. For example, the bits of the ALU instructions are formatted into independent fields that simultaneously control different parts of the machine. Like the M17, the subroutine call of the NC4016 uses a single bit of the instruction to encode a subroutine call, the difference being that the NC4016 uses the highest order bit of the instruction. The effect of this choice is a limit on program size to 32K words in a single page.

The structure of the NC4016 is designed for single clock cycle execution of instructions. All instructions, with the exception of memory reference instructions, will execute in one cycle. Another feature is the ability to combine nonconflicting sequential operations into the same instruction, the best example being the combination of an instruction with subroutine return. Thus most subroutine returns are for free.

As an aid to coding applications or porting compilers intended for register machines, the first 32 memory locations on the NC4016 can be accessed as global user variables without the usual penalty for memory access. Thus these memory locations can be used to simulate a register set.

The NC4016 is implemented in 4000 gates on 3.0-micron HCMOS gate array technology. The maximum clock rate is 8 MHz.

Harris RTX2000

The Harris RTX2000 is a 16-bit stack machine design descended from the NC4016. It differs from the NC4016 in having a very high level of integration, including on-chip stack memories, hardware multiplier, and counter-timers. The architecture of the RTX2000 is illustrated in Figure 5.7.

The data and return stacks on the RTX200 are 256 elements deep, and an interrupt is generated on stack underflow/overflow as an aid to stack management. The data stack is 16 bits wide, and the return stack width is 21 bits. The additional bits on the return stack can be used with on-chip page controller logic to expand the effective program memory limit beyond the 32K bytes addressable within the subroutine call encoding scheme. A special far-call instruction is used to save the full return address in this case.

With respect to instruction set architecture, the RTX2000 is very similar to the NC4016. Both machines were designed to execute the FORTH language primitives; that is, they are "FORTH machines" and are designed specifically to permit some sequences of instructions to be combined into a single instruction word.

The RTX2000 is implemented on 2.0-micron standard cell technology, with a maximum clock rate of 10 MHz. Much of the increased functionality of the RTX2000 in comparison to the NC4016 comes from the use of standard cell technology. The standard cell approach allows the designer to work with standard libraries of logic that can be arbitrarily arranged on the silicon. RTX2000 machines can therefore exist in a number of configurations, with the counter-timers replaced, say, by some other standard logic unit that may be useful in a particular application. This capability makes the RTX2000 particularly attractive for the embedded control application.

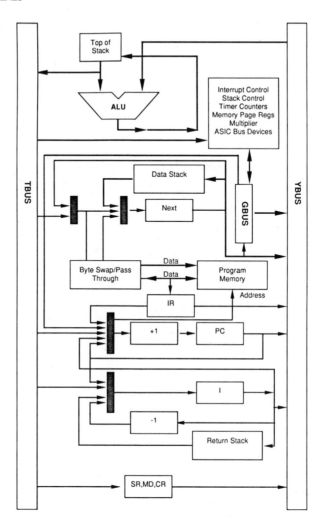

Figure 5.7. Harris RTX2000 Machine Architecture

32-Bit Stack Machines

Although the 16-bit stack machines are sufficiently powerful for many applications and meet the constraints of embedded application in facilitating the construction of small, efficient systems, some embedded applications require the power of a 32-bit machine, particularly when 32-bit integer arithmetic or floating-point calculation is required or where the application can make use of direct addressing of large memory spaces.

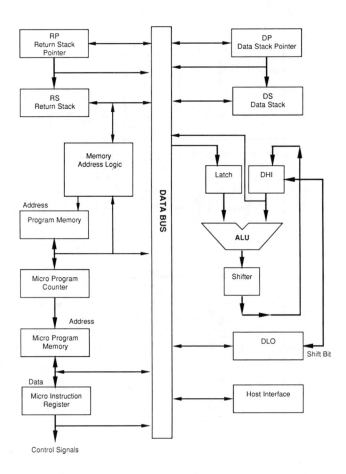

Figure 5.8. Harris RTX32P Machine Architecture

One of the immediate design problems with 32-bit stack machines is where to put the stacks. Separate off-chip stack memories such as are employed by the NC4016 will force the chip to have a pin-out of 64 for the stacks alone, so the off-chip approach is not appropriate for cost-sensitive applications. The remaining approaches to solving the problem are to have the stacks in program memory with small stack buffers on-chip, or to allocate silicon for on-chip stack memory.

Harris RTX32P

The Harris RTX32P is the 32-bit member of the Harris stack machine family. It differs significantly in design approach from the machine discussed earlier in that it uses on-chip microcode memory to achieve a significant flexibility in opcode architecture, as well as allowing for customization of the instruction set. The architecture of the RTX32P is illustrated in Figure 5.8.

Like the RTX2000, the RTX32P has both the data and return stacks on-chip. As an extension of the subroutine encoding used in other stack machines, the RTX32P packs the address of the next instruction in each opcode or refers to the address on the top of the return stack. A Next Address Register (NAR) assumes the function of the Program Counter (PC) in referring to memory locations subsequent to the current instruction as necessary. With the return stack and memory address logic isolated from the system data bus, subroutine calls, returns, and unconditional jumps can be executed in parallel with other operations.

The microcode memory is on-chip and is 2K by 30 bits wide, with each opcode allocated a page of eight 3-bit words. Instruction decoding is accomplished by loading the 9-bit opcode and using it as the page address into the microcode store (only the lowest 8 bits of the opcode are used).

The RTX32P is implemented on 2.5-micron CMOS standard cell technology in a 2-chip set. A data path chip contains the ALU, data stack, and ALU bits of the microcode memory. A control chip contains the rest of the system. The maximum clock rate is 8 MHz.

Other 32-bit stack machine designs are listed in Table 5.4.

Table 5.4. Other 32-Bit Stack Machine Designs

Machine	Developer	Description
SF1	Wright State University	Five stacks, designed for C and FORTH (Dixon 1987).
FRISC 3	Johns Hopkins University	On-chip stacks, stack management logic (Hayes et al. 1987).
WISC CPU/32	WISC Technologies	Ancestor of RTX32P (Koopman 1987).

Examples and Conclusion

One of the chief assertions of this book is that virtual machine design is a powerful and flexible approach to building a high-level application such as an expert system. A secondary but related assertion is that a virtual stack machine, as exemplified by the threaded code languages like FORTH, is a very practical architecture for virtual machines—supporting as they do highly factored software, much like a hardware design would be forced to, given the physical constraints that apply.

When a stack machine is implemented in hardware as opposed to simulated in software, the resulting performance improvement can enable entirely new classes of application. In particular, embedded applications that are more computationally intensive because they use expert system technology become practical.

The architectural approach to the software design that these assertions lead to is often overlooked or avoided as much because of the common wisdom about what it takes to build a knowledge-based system, as from a reluctance to consider alternatives. Still, the merits of building inference engines in an environment that supports efficient access to system hardware as well as high-performance virtual machine design should be clear. One measure of merit is the performance of expert system languages implemented in these environments.

The Prolog compiler described in Chapter 4 has been ported to a prototype version of the NC4016 chip and timed on the naive reverse benchmark program at 6000 LIPS with a 4 MHz clock. A compiler based on the Warren Abstract Machine has also been developed for the NC4016 (see Appendix A). This version runs twice as fast (12K LIPS at 4 MHz). The Harris RTX2000 runs at 10 MHz and a production version of the NC4016 is designed to run at 15 MHz, suggesting that 50,000 LIPS is possible with one of these processors. This is much faster than C language implementations of the Warren machine on the VAX, almost twice as fast as the best Prolog compiler code on the 80386 class machines, and approaches the speed of compiled Prolog code on Sun workstations.

In the case of an OPS implemented in FORTH, initial list-handling tests indicate that its performance is about 50 times that of the 8-MHz MC68000 (see Dress 1986). Extended-memory access necessary for practical programs slows performance by about a factor of two. Operation on a 32-bit stack machine is required before these languages can realize their performance potential.

Benchmarks are often difficult to interpret because they can confuse factors such as hardware architecture, implementation language, and compiler technology. One benchmark measure that does reasonably reflect on the set of assertions made here about virtual machines and stack machines is the execution rate of virtual machine instructions. The basis for measuring VM instruction rate is the assumption that the procedures that implement virtual machine instructions are of the same order of complexity, though virtual machine architectures themselves are then another factor that determine the ultimate performance.

As Table 5.5 illustrates, stack machines like the NC4016 support very efficient execution of virtual machine instructions, even when the virtual machine itself is not 0-operand. The implication of this result is that building virtual machines for other languages like Scheme, Smalltalk, or specific inference engines would lead to a comparable outcome, that is, equal or superior to performance on more conventional machines or to performance on even special-purpose hardware. Note that the Virtual Machine of the first Prolog in Table 5.5 listed is based on Bowen et al. (1983) and runs at 6000 LIPS on the NC4016 FORTH engine. The other Prologs are based on the Warren Abstract Machine (Warren, 1983). The Warren machine version runs at 12,000 LIPS on the NC4016.

The startling performance of the stack machines is due partly to the ability of these stack machine architectures to execute optimally one instruction per clock cycle. The machine's ability to execute a subroutine call in one clock cycle (the return is usually free) has important consequences for threaded code implementations of embedded application. Modularity is encouraged because it costs so little in performance.

Table 5.5 Comparison of Implementation Techniques

Language	Encoding Method	Interpreter Implementation Language	Hardware	Clock (MHz)	VM Instructions per Second	Reference
SmallTalk	Byte code	Microcode	Dorado	20	300,000	Deutsch (1982)
SmallTalk	Byte code	Microcode	68000	12.5	100,000	Deutsch and Schiffman (1984)
Scheme	Byte code	Macrocode	68000	5	30,000	Schooler and Stamos (1984)
Prolog	Threaded code	FORTH	NC4016	4	96,000	Odette and Wilkinson (1986)
Prolog	Threaded code	Macrocode	68000	5	33,000	Pichler (1987)
Prolog	Threaded code	FORTH	NC4016	4	132,000	Odette and Wilkinson (1987)
Prolog	Threaded code	C	Vax 11/780	-	66,000	Gabriel et al. (1985)

For real-time applications, context switching is a matter of 10 or so clocks, and interrupt latency is one clock. Thus a 10 MHz version of stack processor can dispatch an interrupt in 200 ns and switch contexts (for example, to another database or inference engine) in about 1 μs.

As an instance of comparing one promised system with another, the Towers of Hanoi benchmark on a FORTH engine-OPS machine will execute about ten times faster than it would on the 40-MHz, microcoded LISP engine. A system designed with a modest degree of parallelism, would provide the capability for executing an OPS-like, pattern-matching expert system at the rate of several thousand (OPS-like) rules per second on a small, embedded microprocessor-based system.

Successful embedded computing applications often test the engineering skills of their developers. Incorporating the basic advances in AI technology can pay off in a more effective application by enabling, for example, intelligent interpretation of sensor data, diagnosis of problems, and ways of coping better with complex control problems. The cost of increased functionality of this sort is often degraded performance and a more difficult integration task.

One danger in developing the knowledge-based component of an embedded system on high-powered commercial expert systems tools is overengineering. Advanced features of the tools tend to be used when available, limiting what can be done later on. One point of this book is that the danger of overengineering is particularly severe if the ultimate target is a dedicated or embedded system. Embedded hardware and software are as alien to the mainstream as are LISP machines and the early expert system tools.

We advocate a "when in Rome" approach; leverage the languages, tools, and techniques of embedded systems by building the representation and reasoning mechanisms on top. The experience is that threaded code languages offer a good platform on which to program for real-time control and inferencing. The bonus to this is the new hardware support for subroutine threading, which enables performance of OPS5 and Prolog rivaling or exceeding that of larger and more expensive machines on which many expert system applications are currently delivered.

Appendix A

The following Prolog program is a back-end code generator designed to generate instructions (object code) for the NC4016 or RTX2000 stack machines. The input to the program is the output of the Prolog compiler described in Chapter 4, which compiles the instructions of the Warren Abstract Machine to an intermediate form. This intermediate form generally has the syntax

```
instruction(first_argument, second argument, ...)
```

The code generator is largely table driven, with each instruction encoded into stack machine instructions by the Prolog procedure *encode/2*. The two arguments of *encode/2* are the WAM instruction and the corresponding hexadecimal code for the address of the procedure that implements the instruction (the instruction opcode for the NC4016 or RTX2000 Prolog Virtual Machine). The addresses are inserted in the table after the WAM source code is compiled on the target processor.

Clearly this WAM code generator could be used to generate code for any processor through a similar procedure—build an abstract machine on the target processor and then insert the opcodes of the abstract machine in the appropriate entries of the table.

After the Prolog compiler has compiled the source, but prior to invoking the code generator described here, the set of compiled procedures in the Prolog source program is collected into a list and asserted as *procedure_list(Procedures)*. The elements of this list are in the form

```
procedure(Name/Arity,Address)
```

and are used by the code generator to generate the appropriate addresses for procedure calls. There is a similar list (*string_list*) that is used to store the location of atoms in an atom table. This list is searched when a reference to an atom is made so that the correct address for the reference can be encoded.

The top-level predicate for the code generator is *encode/3*, which takes a starting address and the output of the Prolog compiler as input (third and first arguments, respectively) and returns a list of lists. Each member element of the output list contains the WAM instruction, the list of hex numbers, and the starting address for the code on the target machine. This format is useful for printing the resulting object code. The *encode/3* predicate is as follows:

```
encode([X|List],[[X,Code,Start_address]|List1],Start_address) :-
    code_block(X,Code,Start_address,End_address),
    encode(List,List1,End_address),!.
encode([],[],_).
```

The *code_block/4* predicate is responsible for generating the individual blocks of hexadecimal codes corresponding to each WAM instruction. The blocks are of variable length, with the minimum being 2 bytes and the maximum being 8 bytes for the *switch_on_term* instruction. The arguments to *code_block/4* are the WAM instruction, Hex code, starting address, and ending address, respectively. The code for *code_block/4* is as follows:

```
% ***************************************************************
% Generate blocks of code
% (addresses need to be derived from prior compilation of the virtual machine)
code_block(X,[Code],A,B) :-
    atomic(X),B is A + 2,
    encode(X,Code).
code_block(fail/0,[Code],A,B) :-
    encode(fail/0,Code),
    B is A + 2.
code_block(pair(X,1(Num)),[Code,Addr],A,B) :-
    encode_string(X,Code),encode_num(Num,Addr),
    B is A + 4.
code_block(Instr,[C1|Code],A,B) :-
    Instr =.. [switch_on_term|Args],
    encode(switch_on_term,C1),
    encode_switch_args(Args,Code),
    B is A + 8.
code_block(switch(Kind,_,_),[Code],A,B) :-
    encode(switch(Kind,_,_),Code),
    B is A + 2.
code_block(unify(void,N),[Num,Code],A,B) :-
    encode_short(N,Num),
    encode(unify(void,N),Code),
    B is A + 4.
code_block(Instr,Code,A,B) :-
    Instr =.. [Name,Type|Args],
    (Name = unify; Name = get; Name = put),
    encode(Instr,C),
    encode_args(Args,[C],Code),
    length(Args,Length),
    B is A + 2 + (Length * 2).
code_block(Instr,[C|Code],A,B) :-
    Instr =.. [Name,Arg1|Args],
    (Name = try; Name = retry; Name = trust),
    encode(Instr,C),
```

```
        encode_args(Args,[],Code),
        B is A + 4.
code_block(Instr,[C2,C1],A,B) :-
        Instr =.. [Name,Arg],
        (Name = get_nil; Name = put_nil; Name = get_list; Name =
            put_list),
        encode(Name,C1),
        encode(Arg,C2),
        B is A + 4.
code_block(execute(NameAr),[Code],A,B) :-
        encode(execute(NameAr,A),Code),
        B is A + 2.
code_block(Instr,[C1,C2],A,B) :-
        Instr =.. [Name,Arg],
        encode(Name,C1),
        encode(Arg,C2),
        B is A + 4.
code_block(call(Name,N),[Num,Code],A,B) :-
        encode_short(N,Num),
        encode(call(Name,_),Code),
        B is A + 4.
code_block(Name/Arity,[Code],A,B) :-
        encode(Name/Arity,Code),
        B is A + 4.
```

Individual instructions are encoded via the table described by *encode/2*. Each table entry has the WAM instruction, followed by the corresponding hexadecimal address, denoted by a lowercase *h* as the first character. The hexadecimal addresses refer to memory locations in the address space of the target machine. The memory addresses are computed after the Prolog virtual machine is compiled on the target processor. The code for *encode/2* is as follows:

```
% ***************************************************************
% Encode individual instructions

encode(x(1),h8312).
encode(x(2),h8316).
encode(x(3),h831A).
encode(x(4),h831E).
encode(y(1),hBE42).
encode(y(2),hBE4A).
encode(y(3),hBE4C).
encode(y(4),hBE4E).

encode(switch_on_term,h439F).
encode(switch(constant,_,_),h0122).
encode(switch(structure,_,_),h013C).
```

```
encode(try(_,_),h43A5).
encode(retry(_,_),h0182).
encode(trust(_,_),h43E0).

encode(get(constant,_,_),h01B4).
encode(get(value,_,_),h01D0).
encode(get(variable,_,_),h441C).
encode(get(constant,_),h0212).
encode(get(value,_),h0236).
encode(get(variable,_),h441C).
encode(get_nil,h432F).
encode(get_list,h4441).

encode(unify(constant,_,_),h02A8).
encode(unify(value,_,_),h44b9).
encode(unify(variable,_,_),h02E8).
encode(unify(constant,_),h0304).
encode(unify(value,_),h0322).
encode(unify(variable,_),h0346).
encode(unify(cdr,_),h036A).
encode(unify_nil,h4419).

encode(put(constant,_,_),h03B6).
encode(put(value,_,_),h03D2).
encode(put(variable,_,_),h03FE).
encode(put(unsafe_value,_,_),h44E0).
encode(put(constant,_),h040C).
encode(put(value,_),h44CF).
encode(put(variable,_),h442D).
encode(put(unsafe_value,_),h0472).
encode(put_nil,h049A).
encode(put_list,h43EB).

encode(call(NameAr,_),Code) :-
    procedure_list(Procedures),
    memberchk(procedure(NameAr,Addr),Procedures),
    A is Addr // 2,
    convert(A,Code).
% Code should be a branch
encode(execute(NameAr,Addr),Code) :-
    procedure_list(Procedures),
    memberchk(procedure(NameAr,JumpAddr),Procedures),
    A is JumpAddr // 2,
    convert(A,Code).
```

```prolog
encode(allocate,h446C).
encode(deallocate,h447F).
encode(proceed,hA020).
encode(escape,h0554).
encode(fail/0,h057A).
encode(fail,h0598).

encode(X,h0000).

% ***************************************************************
% The following are utilities that are used to encode substructures

encode_switch_args([X|Rest],[C|List]) :-
    (X = fail, encode(fail,C);
     encode_arg(X,C)),
    encode_switch_args(Rest,List).
encode_switch_args([],[]).

encode_args([X|Rest],List,Code) :-
    encode_arg(X,C),
    encode_args(Rest,[C|List],Code).
encode_args([],Code,Code).

encode_arg(A,C) :-
    (number(A),encode_num(A,C);
     atomic(A),encode_string(A,C);
     nonvar(A),
        (A = 1(Num),encode_jump(Num,C);
         encode(A,C) );
     var(A),C = A).

encode_string(S,Code) :-
    string_list(Strings),
    memberchk(string(S,_,Addr),Strings),
    encode_num(Addr,Code).

encode_short(N,Code) :-
    dec_hex(11,[B]),
    dec_hex(15,[F]),
    dec_hex(N,[Num]),
    name('4',[N1]),
    name('h',[H]),
    name(Code,[H,B,F,N1,Num]).

encode_num(N,Code) :- convert(N,Code).
```

```
% assumes byte addresses - converts to word addresses
encode_jump(Jump,Code) :-
    current_procedure(procedure(_,Addr)),
    Dest is (Addr + Jump) // 2,
    convert(Dest,Code).
```

```
% *************************************************************
```

```
extract_atoms([X|Rest],List) :-
    extract_atom(X,List),
    extract_atoms(Rest,List).
extract_atoms([],List).
```

```
extract_atom(A,L) :-
    atomic(A),not(number(A)),memberchk(A,L).
extract_atom(_,L).
```

```
% *************************************************************
```

```
% Decimal to Hex idecimal number conversion.
% Very Primitive
```

```
dec_hex(Num,N) :- Num < 10, name(Num,N).
dec_hex(10,N) :- name('A',N).
dec_hex(11,N) :- name('B',N).
dec_hex(12,N) :- name('C',N).
dec_hex(13,N) :- name('D',N).
dec_hex(14,N) :- name('E',N).
dec_hex(15,N) :- name('F',N).
```

```
convert(Dec,Hex) :-
    A is Dec//4096,
    B is (Dec - (A * 4096))//256,
    C is (Dec - (A * 4096) - (B * 256))//16,
    D is (Dec - (A * 4096) - (B * 256) - (C * 16)),
    dec_hex(A,[A1]),
    dec_hex(B,[B1]),
    dec_hex(C,[C1]),
    dec_hex(D,[D1]),
    name('h',[H]),
    name(Hex,[H,A1,B1,C1,D1]).
```

As an example of the output of the code generator, the code generated from the procedures of the naive reverse program is as follows:

```
% REVERSE

main :-
        list3(L),
        nreverse(L,X),
        write(X),nl.

nreverse([X|L0],L) :-
        nreverse(L0,L1), concatenate(L1,[X],L).
nreverse([],[]).


concatenate([X|L1],L2,[X|L3]) :-
        concatenate(L1,L2,L3).
concatenate([],X,X).


list3([temperature,pressure,velocity]).
```

The next section shows the intermediate structures that are output from the compiler and passed to the code generator. There are three types of structures. The first is a list of the procedures in the program, each element in the list having the structure

```
procedure(Name/Arity,Length)
```

The second structure is a list of the atoms in the program. These are used to construct a table that is placed at the end of the assembled code and contains the strings referenced by the code. The third structure type contains the procedure code, in the format

```
procedure(Name/Arity,[WAM Instructions])
```

The WAM instructions are encoded in a structure. The correspondence between the structures of the encoded instructions and the WAM syntax for source code should be apparent from inspection of the code.

```
[procedure(main / 0,46),
    procedure(nreverse / 2,84),
    procedure(concatenate / 3,62),
    procedure(list3 / 1,20)].
[temperature,pressure,velocity|_DA68].

procedure(main / 0,
    [allocate,
    put(variable,y(2),x(1)),
```

```
        call(list30 / 1,2),
        put(unsafe_value,y(2),x(1)),
        put(variable,y(1),x(2)),
        call(nreverse / 2,1),
        put(unsafe_value,y(1),x(1)),
        write / 1,nl / 0,
        deallocate,
        proceed]).


procedure(nreverse / 2,
    [switch_on_term(1(74),1(12),fail),
    try(else,1(70)),
    allocate,
    get(variable,y(1),x(2)),
    get_list(x(1)),
    unify(variable,y(2)),
    unify(cdr,x(1)),
    put(variable,y(3),x(2)),
    call(nreverse / 2,3),
    put_list(x(2)),
    unify(value,y(2)),
    unify_nil,
    put(unsafe_value,y(3),x(1)),
    put(value,y(1),x(3)),
    deallocate,
    execute(concatenate / 3),
    trust(else,fail),
    get_nil(x(1)),
    get_nil(x(2)),
    proceed]).


procedure(concatenate / 3,
    [switch_on_term(1(50),1(12),fail),
    try(else,1(46)),
    get_list(x(1)),
    unify(variable,x(1)),
    unify(cdr,x(4)),
    get_list(x(3)),
    unify(value,x(1)),
    unify(cdr,x(3)),
    put(value,x(4),x(1)),
    execute(concatenate / 3),
    trust(else,fail),
    get_nil(x(1)),
```

```
    get(value,x(2),x(3)),
    proceed]).

procedure(list3 / 1,
    [get_list(x(1)),
    unify(constant,temperature),
    unify(constant,pressure),
    unify(constant,velocity),
    unify_nil,
    proceed]).
```

Finally, the code generator emits code for the stack machine. As indicated, the approach used here could be easily modified and applied to generating machine codes for any target hardware.

procedure main / 0

Address	Code	Instruction
206C	446C	allocate
206E	8312 BE4A	put_variable Y2,X1
2072	03FE	
2074	BF42 0000	call list30 / 1,2
2078	8312 BE4A	put_unsafe_value Y2,X1
207C	44E0	
207E	8316 BE42	put_variable Y1,X2
2082	03FE	
2084	BF41 104D	call nreverse / 2,1
2088	8312 BE42	put_unsafe_value Y1,X1
208C	44E0	
208E	0000	escape write / 1
2092	0000	escape nl / 0
2096	447F	deallocate
2098	A020	proceed

procedure nreverse / 2

Address	Code	Instruction
209A	439F 1072	switch_on_term 1(74),1(12),fail
209E	1053 0598	
20A2	43A5 1070	try_me_else 1(70)
20A6	446C	allocate
20A8	8316 BE42	get_variable Y1,X2
20AC	441C	
20AE	8312 4441	get_list X1

20B2	BE4A 0346	unify_variable Y2
20B6	8312 036A	unify_cdr X1
20BA	8316 BE4C	put_variable Y3,X2
20BE	03FE	
20C0	BF43 104D	call nreverse / 2,3
20C4	8316 43EB	put_list X2
20C8	BE4A 0322	unify_value Y2
20CC	4419	unify_nil
20CE	8312 BE4C	put_unsafe_value Y3,X1
20D2	44E0	
20D4	831A BE42	put_value Y1,X3
20D8	03D2	
20DA	447F	deallocate
20DC	1077	execute concatenate / 3
20DE	43E0 0598	trust_me_else fail
20E2	8312 432F	get_nil X1
20E6	8316 432F	get_nil X2
20EA	A020	proceed

procedure concatenate / 3

Address	Code	Instruction
20EE	439F 1090	switch_on_term 1(50),1(12),fail
20F2	107D 0598	
20F6	43A5 108E	try_me_else 1(46)
20FA	8312 4441	get_list X1
20FE	8312 0346	unify_variable X1
2102	831E 036A	unify_cdr X4
2106	831A 4441	get_list X3
210A	8312 0322	unify_value X1
210E	831A 036A	unify_cdr X3
2112	8312 831E	put_value X4,X1
2116	03D2	
2118	1077	execute concatenate / 3
211A	43E0 0598	trust_me_else fail
211E	8312 432F	get_nil X1
2122	831A 8316	get_value X2,X3
2126	01D0	
2128	A020	proceed

procedure list3 / 1

Address	Code	Instruction
212C	8312 4441	get_list X1
2130	2140 0304	unify_constant temperature

```
2134        214C 0304        unify_constant pressure
2138        2155 0304        unify_constant velocity
213C        4419             unify_nil
213E        A020             proceed
```

Atom Table (null terminated ASCII codes)

Address	ASCII Code	Atom
2140	7465 6D70	temperature
2144	6572 6174	
2148	7572 6500	
214C	7072 6573	pressure
2150	7375 7265	
2154	0000	
2155	7665 6C6F	velocity
2159	6369 7479	
215D	0000	

Chapter 6 Examples and Future Directions

Introduction

It was necessary and desirable for this book to have a strong focus on the implementation details for the two primary expert system reasoning technologies. As a consequence, there are some topics beyond the technology that are not discussed in depth here but are clearly important to consider when building a complex embedded system. Similarly, there are clearly some newer technologies that might be very useful for some specialized applications, but they have not been addressed here. This chapter is meant as a survey-level treatment of these two areas.

In a sense, these subject areas address the future of embedded intelligence. One topic that is beyond the technology per se is knowledge engineering. Using the term "knowledge engineering" to refer to the current methods for codifying knowledge and mechanizing expertise is largely wishful thinking. With some exceptions, and these are in quite limited areas, current practice could hardly be deemed engineering. But, more than any other expert system application, embedding expertise within existing systems will require engineering discipline applied to the software to have any expectation of delivering the specified system within the inevitable constraints.

On the second topic, to state that newer technologies are in the future is not going too far out on a limb. Neural nets and programs that learn are but two examples of newer technologies that may have the most short-term impact on the development and application of embedded systems with substantial problem-solving expertise. Neural nets in particular may have an important role in embedded systems since they are best deployed, in current practice at least, as pattern recognizers. It won't be long before there are important applications where neural nets are integrated with front-end sensor systems and back-end expert systems. A likely applications area is process control.

Before introducing the future, let's look at some example embedded applications that have been developed using the approaches described here. These are included at the end of the book for completeness. The examples include an experiment control system based on Prolog and FORTH and a diagnostic system for a troubleshooting application. There is also an example of a very large expert system built for use on a mainframe. This mainframe embedded system illustrates the applicability of the ideas in this book far beyond the realm of embedded hardware and software combined in a single small and dedicated package. An embedded system may well be part of a much larger business operation, embedded in numerous interacting systems, both computer and human based. On the one extreme are small expert systems using single-board computers and designed, for example, as a component of a dedicated controller. On the other extreme are systems that embed expertise in business systems that span a continent and are the lifeblood of major business enterprises.

Examples of Embedded Applications

Prolog Controls a Spacelab Experiment

A full Clocksin and Mellish Prolog interpreter, implemented in FORTH (see the 1987 paper by Odette and Paloski for a complete description of the project), is currently in use as the basis of the astronaut interface for a series of Spacelab experiments. The Prolog interpreter, exclusive of stacks, is designed to reside in less than 10 Kbytes of memory on a microcomputer. The speed of the language on a microcomputer is more than adequate for the application.

The Prolog is being used as part of a real-time knowledge-based system to aid crew members in performing a series of experiments aboard the First International Microgravity Laboratory (IML-1) Spacelab mission. The series of experiments are known collectively as the Microgravity Vestibular Investigation (MVI) and are designed to study the role of the inner ear in space motion sickness. The astronaut interface serves to assist the operator in configuring the on-board physiological data acquisition and control system. The knowledge-based component of the system is designed to reduce the impact of task complexity on the quality of data collection. It also helps meet the need to maintain flexibility in meeting the objectives of the experiment. Further, the likelihood of the operator making a mistake during the experiment is increased due to motion sickness and the disorientation commonly experienced by spacecraft crew members (indeed, the study is designed to increase the understanding of space sickness). This can be compensated for somewhat by making the data collection system smarter.

The MVI experiments comprise six separate scientific functional objectives, each of which is addressed by performing 3 to 24 related experiments. These experiments will be performed during the IML-1 mission by teams of two astronauts. One astronaut serves as the experiment subject. He is strapped into a rotating chair mounted in the Spacelab

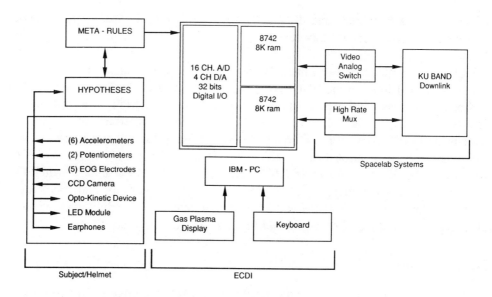

Figure 6.1. Experiment Control and Data Interface

The experiments are controlled through an equipment interface implemented on a personal computer. Communications and control equipment are mounted on an equipment rack in the shuttle.

center aisle and dons a helmet supporting various physical and physiological sensors. Throughout the experiments, he is presented with inertial, auditory, and/or visual stimuli, and his physiological responses to those stimuli are monitored, graphically displayed, and transmitted to Earth.

The other astronaut serves as the experiment operator. He is responsible for setting up and calibrating each of the sensors and for performing each step of the 65 experiments. During each experiment, he also monitors the response, safety, and well-being of the subject and communicates with ground-based scientific investigators.

The experiments will be controlled by the astronaut/operator using a rack-mounted console known as the Experiment Control and Data Interface (ECDI; Figure 6.1). The heart of this console is an IBM PC-compatible, 8086-based, laptop microcomputer. Within the ECDI, the PC bus is extended to a 9-slot expansion chassis, which houses all the data acquisition, control, and Spacelab system interface hardware. Data acquisition and control capabilities are provided by two analog interface boards containing a total of sixteen 12-bit differential channels of analog-to-digital (A/D) conversion, four 12-bit channels of digital-to-analog (D/A) conversion, and 32 bits of digital input/output (I/O) lines.

Analog data from electro-oculogram (EOG), head acceleration, and head position sensors attached to the subject and helmet will be sampled at either 128 Hz (5 channels) or 32 Hz (10 channels) and digitized using the A/D converters. Command signals, issued through the D/A converters and digital I/O ports, will control an optokinetic device, a light-emitting diode (LED) array, earphones, and other experiment stimulus-producing devices.

Following digitization, two channels of experiment sensor data will be graphically displayed in real time on the ECDI computer screen. In addition, all acquired data as well as all command and experiment condition data will be serially transmitted at 25.6 Kbits/sec to Spacelab downlink systems. Spacelab system interfaces are provided by two custom boards containing I/O mapped, 8742 Universal Peripheral Interface processors. These boards control data transfer between the experiment computer and either the Spacelab high-rate multiplexer (HRM) or the Spacelab video analog switch (VAS) using pairs of memory-mapped RAM ping-pong buffers and Universal Asynchronous Receiver/Transmitters. The HRM and VAS provide interfaces for digital and video data telemetry to ground-based scientific and mission control observers.

Expert System

Although Spacelab provides a unique facility for studying the effects of microgravity on various physical and physiological processes, its environment is less than optimal for performing complex scientific experiments. Crew time and training are limited, communication between astronaut/operators and ground-based scientific investigators is limited, and crew members are likely to experience some degree of motion sickness during the first few days of a mission.

The MVI expert system is designed to reduce the impact of these factors on the quality of the MVI data collection. This expert system should enhance the ability of the astronaut/operator to collect high-quality data in the Spacelab environment by managing the complexity of the experimental procedures and by offering guidance through the experiment operations.

The heart of the expert system is its knowledgebase, which is made up of a database containing facts about experiment procedures and protocols, a rulebase containing general rules for carrying out the experiments under normal and abnormal conditions, and a procedure base containing real-time routines coded in FORTH.

The rulebase is used to step the operator through each experimental protocol, as specified in the database, while simultaneously activating appropriate FORTH tasks stored in the procedure base. The knowledgebase is primarily declarative, relying on the Prolog inference engine for control; however, a special Prolog *builtin* predicate, peculiar to this implementation, is used to incorporate FORTH routines into the knowledgebase. The *builtin* procedure allows Forth procedures to be invoked from Prolog.

A knowledgebase structure was selected for representing the experiment procedure data rules in order to provide a flexible system that could be easily modified. This format allows separation of the data from the inference rules and real-time routines and thereby permits restructuring of rules without changing the data organization or real-time behavior. The knowledgebase stores both data and rules in blocks of text that can be read by the programmer and the expert principal investigators. The text feature aids in the development of user-friendly I/O routines and explanation facilities.

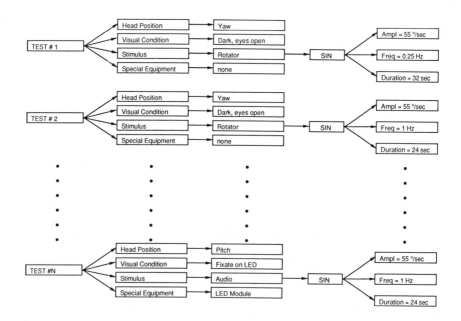

Figure 6.2. Database Structure

The Prolog database is used to record information about the experiment and the equipment used in it. The information may be accessed directly by the operator or may be used by the controller to direct the course of the experiment.

There is a top-level query language through which the experiment operator has access to the rulebase. Upon being queried, the rulebase extracts appropriate data from the database and provides that data as input to real-time algorithms in the procedure base. The real-time algorithms then use this data in the setup and execution of machine control tasks.

Database The MVI expert system database consists of six records, each of which encodes all of the operational requirements for a single functional objective. Each record can be represented as a tree structure (Figure 6.2). The primary node in each record is the functional objective identifier. Each of the n secondary nodes branching from the primary node identifies the location of all the information required to perform a single experimental protocol (test) within the functional objective. Four tertiary nodes branching from each secondary node identify the location of the head position, visual condition, experimental stimulus, and special equipment information required by the particular protocol. The set of nodes branching from the tertiary nodes contains the actual data pointed to by identifiers. All nodes further to the right add clarification and refinement to this data.

As an example, Figure 6-2 shows that the experimental protocol Test 1 of Functional Objective 1 requires that an inertial stimulus be provided by the rotating chair and that this stimulus have a sinusoidal velocity profile with an amplitude of 55 degree/sec, a frequency of 0.25Hz, and a duration of 32 seconds.

Prolog clauses of the following form are
used as database records describing an
experiment.

```
functional objective(1,vor_suppression,
    [test(1,head_position(yaw),
        visual_condition(d,[dark,eyes_open,straight_ahead]),
        stimulus(rotator(sin(ampl(55),freq(25),dur(32)))),
        special_equipment(none),
    test(2,head_position(yaw),
        visual_condition(d,[dark,eyes_open,straight_ahead]),
        stimulus(rotator(sin(ampl(55),freq(1),dur(24)))),
        special_equipment(none),
    test(3,head_position(pitch),
        visual_condition(f1,[fixate_on_LED_module_target]),
        stimulus(audio(sin(ampl(55),freq(1),dur(24)))),
        special_equipment(LED_module))]).
```

Figure 6.3. Example Knowledgebase Entry

Clauses in the Prolog database are used to record information about the experiment and the
equipment used in it.

The Prolog clause required to encode a data tree similar to that diagrammed in Figure
6.2 is presented in Figure 6.3. Each branch node is represented by a predicate having an
arity equal to the number of parenthetical objects following it and separated by commas.
For example, the arity of the *functional_objective* predicate is 3: the object *1* (the
functional objective number), the object *vor_suppression* (the functional objective
name), and a list (list elements are delimited by square brackets), which contains
objects, predicates, and other lists that identify the remainder of the data required for
Functional Objective 1.

Rulebase   The rulebase contains approximately 50 Prolog clauses, a small set of
which the operator accesses through the user query language. The operator can execute
a functional objective using the query $fo(X)$. The predicate fo is an acronym for functional objective. If $fo(X)$ is called with X instantiated to a functional objective number
for which a data record exists within the expert system database, that particular functional objective will be executed. If X is instantiated to a functional objective number for
which no data record exists, a second $fo(X)$ clause will be invoked to report the error. If
X is not instantiated when $fo(X)$ is called, the first functional objective record in the
database will be found and used for execution. Thereafter, successive functional objectives could be executed by forcing Prolog backtracking at the conclusion of each functional objective execution. This could be accomplished by requesting more solutions to
the top-level query.

With Prolog in FORTH, the FORTH-Prolog interface is simple. Prolog code is compiled with the Forth word CONSULTING. Within the Prolog, FORTH words can be called using the procedure builtin. FORTH words used by Prolog must have the following form R> DROP ... $TRUE. (this serves as the interface with this particular Prolog implementation.

```
/forth SCREEN 9
VARIABLE EVENTS
: SEE  SIMUL ACTIVATE BEGIN 1 EVENTS +! 500 MS AGAIN ;
: DONE  SIMUL ACTIVATE STOP ;

: $DATA_ON   R> DROP ." Start" CT SEE   $TRUE ;
: $DATA_OFF  R> DROP ." Start" CT DONE $TRUE ;

10 10 CONSULTING


/prolog SCREEN 10
member(X,[X,_]).
member(X,[_,Y]) :- member(X,Y).

data_on :- builtin($DATA_ON).
data_on :- builtin($DATA_OFF).

fo(X) :- functional_objective(X,Y,L),!,execute_fo(L).
fo(X) :- nl,nl,write(invalid_fo_number),nl.

execute_fo(L) :- member(test(N,HP,VC,ST,SE),L),
        perform_test(N,HP,VC,ST,SE).
execute_fo(L) :- nl,nl,write(fo_complete),nl.

perform_test(N,head_position(Pos),visual_condition(Eyes,_),
            stimulus(Input_Device),special_equipment(Device)) :-
        set_up(Device),
        restrain_head(Pos),
        command_subject(Eyes),
        data_on,
        start(Input_Device),
        stop(Input_Device),
        data_off,
        command_subject(relax).
```

Figure 6.4. Interface to the Procedurebase

The FORTH language procedures are compiled in standard fashion. Prolog procedures are compiled using extensions to the standard FORTH compiler.

Procedurebase

The procedurebase is a set of FORTH secondary and primary (code) definitions used to control all the MVI experiment hardware and to execute real-time data acquisition, display, and transmission tasks. Sample code demonstrating the mechanism used for building the procedure base is presented in Figure 6.4. The first code segment is contained in a file and is compiled using the FORTH *LOAD* command. The second code segment is compiled using a FORTH definition *CONSULTING*, which has an action similar to that of the Prolog predicate *consult* (Clocksin and Mellish 1981).

Logic Driven Real-Time Procedures

The main advantage of this real-time expert system is its ability to perform real-time data acquisition and control tasks on a goal-driven basis. To perform Functional Objective 1 of the MVI experiments, for example, the operator could type in *fo(1)* at the ECDI keyboard. This would cause Prolog to locate the first *fo(X)* rule, instantiate the *X* to 1, and attempt to prove the rule true by satisfying all the goals on its right-hand side. To satisfy the final *execute_fo(L)*, as a subgoal of *fo(X)*, Prolog would locate the first *execute_fo(L)* rule and attempt to satisfy each of the goals on its right-hand side.

The first of these goals, *member(test(N, HP, VC, ST, SE),L)* identifies the parameters of the first test in the database record associated with Functional Objective 1 (Figure 6.3) using the member rules given in Figure 6.4. The second of these goals, *perform test(N, HP, VC, ST, SE)*, causes Prolog to perform that test using the *perform_test* rule. Prolog performs the test as a side effect of trying to prove the *perform_test* goal true.

The goals in the body of *perform_test* clause sequentially perform a generic vestibular experiment. For example, using the Prolog execution logic and the database record presented in Figure 6.3, the variable *Device* would be instantiated to *none* in the *perform_test* rule. The first goal in the body of that rule would then become *set_up(none)*, indicating that no special equipment is required to perform this particular test. The operator would be informed of this fact when Prolog attempted to satisfy the goal (code not shown). As the Prolog execution continued, the operator would next be instructed to restrain the subject's head in the yaw position, then to be sure that the subject's eyes are in the dark, and finally to command the subject to keep his eyes open and look straight ahead (code not shown).

Next, having completed the setup phase of the test, the expert system would begin performing the test. To do this, Prolog would attempt to satisfy the *data_on* goal, which is a Prolog procedure interfaced to the FORTH language through the procedure built-in. The FORTH definition *$DATA_ON* would be executed as Prolog attempted to determine whether the *data_on* goal is true (the last FORTH word in the *$DATA_ON* definition is *$TRUE*, which indicates to Prolog that the goal has succeeded). Thus, in satisfying the *data_on* goal, Prolog indirectly executes the FORTH definition *SEE*.

In the current example, *SEE* activates a background task called *SIMUL*. In the MVI expert system, however, the *data_on* goal activates a FORTH background task that acquires analog data from the subject, graphically displays selected data channels on the computer screen, and transmits the acquired data into the Spacelab downlink systems. Once the data acquisition, display, and transmission systems had been activated, the expert system would initiate the experiment stimulus, by calling the procedure *start(Input_Device)*. In the MVI expert system, this procedure indirectly activates another FORTH background task, which controls *Input_Device* in accordance with parameters passed to the task from the database.

Once the stimulus provided by the input device was complete, the *start(Input_Device)* goal would succeed. The expert system would then turn off the device control background task as Prolog satisfied the *stop(Input_Device)* goal and the data acquisition task as Prolog satisfied the *data_off* goal. Finally, the operator would be notified that the test was complete and would be instructed to allow the subject to relax as Prolog satisfied the *command_subject(relax)* goal.

At this point, the expert system would have completed performing the experiment. Prolog would have satisfied *perform_test,* which, in turn, would satisfy *execute_fo,* which is the last goal of *fo(1)*. The system would therefore notify the operator that *fo(1)* was complete and would await further instruction. The operator would then have the option of accepting this solution (thereby concluding the experiment) or of asking Prolog to find a new solution, should one exist. The latter option would cause Prolog to backtrack to attempt to resatisfy the initial goal. The Figure 6.4 rule base is set up so that backtracking would result in an attempted resatisfaction of the *execute_fo(L)* goal. Prolog would successfully resatisfy this goal if it found another test (one not previously found) on the list of tests associated with Functional Objective 1. If such a test were found, it would be executed using the logic just presented (only the parameter values would change).

Thus, following each test in the functional objective, the operator would be given the option of proceeding with the next test or aborting the study. By this mechanism, a small set of Prolog procedures (Figure 6.4) can be used to carry out every test under all functional objectives. If the operator chooses to backtrack to the next test after all tests for a particular functional objective have been performed, the *execute_fo(L)* goal would fail. This failure would cause the *fo(1)* goal to fail and Prolog to await a new input goal from the operator.

Real-Time Operation

The MVI expert system provides real-time experiment control by activating and deactivating the FORTH background and terminal tasks on a goal-driven basis. A portion of the MVI round-robin multitasking loop is presented in Figure 6.5. Prolog (and the expert system) reside in the *OPERATOR* task, which is the primary terminal task in the round-robin loop; all keyboard entries are handled through this task. When the MVI computer is turned on, the only active task is *OPERATOR*. The expert system controls the graphics display terminal task and the device driver background tasks as side effects of responding to operator queries. Only those tasks that need to be active at any point in the experiment protocol are activated. Once a task has completed its required action, it is deactivated.

To maintain accurate, high-rate (128-Hz) data sampling intervals, data acquisition is controlled by an interrupt service routing (ISR) triggered by a Spacelab clock signal. The data transmission background task is controlled by the ISR to ensure synchronization between the MVI data stream and the Spacelab downlink system. The expert system can control data acquisition and transmission by masking and unmasking the Spacelab clock interrupt signal and by changing the ISR in use by altering its vector address. Either of these techniques can be employed on a goal-driven basis. By using this multitasking technique, various real-time processes can be executed concurrently with the expert system. This reduces the required logical inference processing rate of the Prolog database.

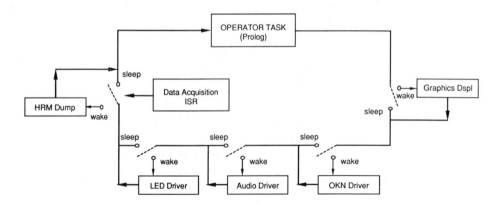

Figure 6.5. Round-Robin Task Switching

The MVI system switches tasks on a round-robin basis.

The knowledgebase used for experiment control contains high-level knowledge of the functional objectives of the investigation and how these objectives may be met by sets of different experimental procedures. Objectives may be met by as few as 3 and as many as 28 experiments. The knowledgebase knows about possible alternatives at each step of the experimental procedure and can assist the experimentor as required. Other types of knowledge of use to the operator include detailed representations of the set-up and calibration and of the operation of each device and experiment.

Prolog was chosen as the knowledgebase implementation language because of its database component and its goal-directed inference mechanism. The ability of Prolog to backtrack facilitates recovery from error or equipment failure. Backtracking also helps to ensure that the objectives of the experiment are met by managing alternative strategies. These aspects of the language are good fits to the needs of the application.

In addition, issues of software reliability and design verification must be addressed by any expert system that is to fly in space. Hardware and software must both be tested prior to flight certification. Prolog was chosen as the implementation language because it was felt that it would be easier to verify the design and test the program in Prolog than in either a conventional language or some other AI language.

FORTH was chosen both to implement the Prolog interpreter and for the real-time procedures in the procedurebase because of its speed, compactness, and ability to support rapid prototyping. With an interface for executing FORTH programs from Prolog, both knowledgebase and real-time components are interactive. This is a significant advantage during development, compared with alternatives that involve compiling C programs, linking with a Prolog module, loading the result, and only then running the program.

The IML-1 mission was originally scheduled to fly in May 1987, but due to the Space Shuttle *Challenger* accident, IML-1 has been postponed until April 1991. The hardware is complete and is currently being certified and flight qualified. The software development is 80% complete, with the available memory (64 Kbytes) currently divided about equally between the procedurebase and the Prolog code. The Prolog itself is divided nearly equally between clauses that are used for experiment description (that is, as a database) and clauses used to describe testing protocols.

Diesel Electric Locomotive Repair

One of the earliest examples of a significant and practical expert system application was an embedded system developed at the General Electric research labs in Schenectady, N.Y. The system was delivered to the field for testing in July 1983. Referred to as DELTA (Diesel Electric Locomotive Troubleshooting Aid) or CATS-1 (Computer Aided Troubleshooting System), its design goal was to help service engineers troubleshoot problems and formulate solutions in the repair of diesel engines. This particular task was a good one for an expert system since GE had acknowledged experts and the knowledge could be codified directly into rules.

The project began with a survey of existing locomotive diagnostic systems in the fall of 1980. The survey concluded that the bases of existing systems were simple analytical models that provided a good deal of information but did not have much diagnostic ability. By the spring of 1981, the expertise of expert field technicians was being modeled using expert system methods, and by the fall of 1981, there was a prototype of a diagnostic unit that could handle problems with the fuel unit. This prototype used about 45 rules. The system was prototyped in LISP, but then redesigned in FORTH so that it could be embedded an a package that could be located on the shop floor. The package included a Digital Equipment Corporation PDP-11/23 with 1 megabyte of memory and a hard disk. The processor was encased in a steel box with a high-impact plastic face.

Railroad personnel must detect and repair a large variety of faults that have partially disabled a diesel electric locomotive. The information available to them is a list of symptoms reported by the engine crew. More information can be gathered in the shop by taking measurements and performing tests, but these activities may consume excessive shop time if performed by inexperienced personnel. The DELTA system was designed to guide the field engineers in performing the tests and isolating the fault.

The system uses a little over 500 rules, with about 300 of these rules used to represent the knowledge of a senior field engineer. The remaining 200 rules form the help system. The help system uses both CAD drawings and video stored on the laser disk.

An outline of the way that control is transferred during the reasoning processes is given in Figure 6.6. Initial facts are gathered using a fixed sequence of questions, for example, the unit number, model year, and reported symptoms. An associative information table provides such additional facts as standard features for the unit, history of failures, failure propensity for this model, and so on. All these facts are available at the start of the reasoning process.

The rules that are used are collected into related sets by functional area; for example, there are rules related to the electrical system, mechanical systems, and so on. Rules within each area are further subdivided according to hypotheses about the fault areas. Examples of this sort of organization include operator error, power failure, and so on.

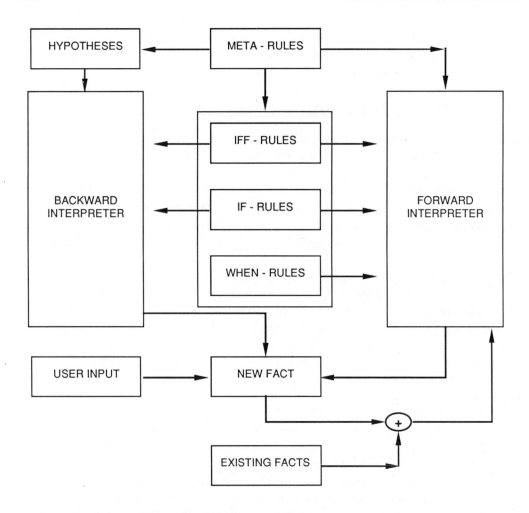

Figure 6.6. Inference Mechanism Configuration

A set of rules that function as indices into the rule set are used to retrieve subsets of the rules that could apply to the hypotheses suggested by the initial observations. The rules that are brought in are used in a backward fashion to prove or disprove the hypotheses in turn. The result is a collection of successful hypotheses indicating the faults, and a set of corresponding corrective actions.

Inference Engine

Because the inferencing process can work in either a forward or a backward fashion, there are two control strategies that are mixed by the system to arrive at the successful hypotheses and corrective actions.

The process begins after the initial facts are loaded by the user, as indexing rules (meta rules) are used to load sets of rules of various types.

The first control strategy is goal-directed reasoning. A backward rule interpreter tries to evaluate each hypothesis using the current set of rules and facts. Evaluation begins by first scanning the list of facts to determine whether the hypothesis is already known to be either true or false. If neither is the case, the rule sets are scanned to determine if the hypothesis could be proved true or false by the application of one or more rules. If it can, then the subgoals of the rule are added to the list of hypotheses and are recursively evaluated in turn. When no hypothesis can be directly inferred by a rule, the system will request information from an external source such as a sensor or the system operator.

During this goal-directed control strategy, the system will shift gears into data-directed reasoning whenever a new fact is either inferred from a rule or input from a sensor. The forward interpreter will try to execute any rule that has the new fact in its premises. This includes the meta rules.

The meta rules determine whether any new rule knowledge is required or if the existing sets of rules need to be reorganized. Meta rules may also reorganize the existing set of hypotheses.

The meta rules are one of four rule types used by the system. The other types are called *iff* rules, *if* rules and *when* rules. The *iff* and *if* rules will direct the inference process to infer new facts directly from existing facts. The two types of rules are accessed by both the backward and forward interpreters.

The *when* rules are used to activate procedures associated with a new fact. These rules are only used by the forward interpreter.

While the forward interpreter has control, if any of the rules has a satisfied premise the rule is executed and the forward interpreter iterates through the rules again. If no rule can be executed by the forward interpreter, control is returned to the backward interpreter.

The backward interpreter continues executing until a hypothesis is proved or until the entire set of hypotheses has been exhausted.

Representation Language

The language that is used to build rules consists of a small set of functions. Like most FORTH-based rule languages, the function set is extensible. The language contains a set of predicate functions used in the conditions of each rule premise, a set of verbs describing actions and inferences in the conclusions of each rule, and several utility functions for interacting with the user and display equipment. The functions are described in the following table.

The rule syntax is the common *IF* (premise) *THEN* (conclusion) form, where the results of the evaluation of the separate clauses in the premise are *AND* ed together to determine if the premise is satisfied. The arguments of the predicate functions in the premise are a triple of the form <object attribute value>. The utility functions can be present in either the premise or the conclusion of a rule.

Table 6.1 Function Set for Building Rules

Predicate

Function	Description
EQ	Equal: Evaluates its argument and returns a flag.
EVAL−ALL	Evaluate All: Exhaustively evaluates its argument and returns a flag.
NE	Not Equal: Evaluates its argument and returns a flag.
NC	Not Confirmed: Evaluates its argument and returns a flag.
ND	Not Disconfirmed: Evaluates its argument and returns a flag.
ASK−Y	Ask Yes: Prompts user with a question, writes a new fact, returns a flag.
ASK−N	Ask No: Prompts user with a question, writes a new fact, returns a flag.
UDO	Do: Requests action of user, writes a new fact, returns a flag.
MENU	Menu: Displays menu selections, writes a new fact, returns a flag.

Verb

Function	Description
WRITE	Write: Writes its argument on list of facts.
CLR	Clear: Removes its argument from list of facts.
EVAL	Eval: Activate Backward Interpreter to verify its argument.
EVAL−ALL	Eval All: Activate Backward Interpreter to verify its arguments.
ASK	Ask: Prompts user with a question, writes a new fact.
UDO	Do: Requests action of user, writes a new fact.
STOP	Stop: Displays termination message and terminates session.
MENU	Menu: Displays menu selections, writes a new fact.

Utility

Function	Description
DISPLAY	Display: Display message to user.
PAUSE	Pause: Pause and wait for acknowledgement from user.
SHOW	Show: Show file on user screen (may be CAD or alphanumeric).
SCREEN	Screen: Clear graphics.
VDSHOW	Video Show: Display video image on auxiliary monitor.

An example of a rule is given below. This rule is used in determining the status of the fuel pressure gauge.

```
IF:
  UDO    [ FUEL−PRESSURE−TEST−GAUGE STATUS ATTACHED ]
  ASK−Y  [ FUEL−PRESSURE−TEST−GAUGE READING SAME−AS FUEL−GAUGE ]
THEN:
  DISPLAY [ FUEL−PRESSURE−GAUGE STATUS OK ]
  WRITE   [ FUEL−PRESSURE−GAUGE STATUS OK ]
  WRITE   [ FUEL−PRESSURE−GAUGE STATUS ALREADY−TESTED ]
```

During testing in the field, the rule set was expected to expand to roughly double its initial size.

Expert Systems for Sales and Marketing

From the one extreme of the smaller stand-alone system in which the intelligence is embedded under constraints of memory resources and speed, we go to the other extreme of very large and complex systems that are embedded in even larger systems. The larger system includes computer networks of mainframe scale connected over and between continents, communicating with thousands of terminals. On this scale the demands are still performance and resources, as well as integratability and compatibility with human corporate business units. The following application area comes from financial services. Example systems in this area have been built by Applied Expert Systems, Inc. (APEX) and Chase Lincoln First Bank.

As the rules of business have changed for information-intensive industries like the financial services, as they constantly do either by competition or legislation, there have been many opportunities to build strategic information-based applications. Recently, Expert system technology has been a large part of many of these applications. The limit of the technology's applicability is to a large degree a measure of its ability to be embedded in the systems that already exist.

Among the most important application area has been support for sales and marketing of financial services products. Expert sales support brings knowledge of both personal finance and technology to bear on the problem of how to cost-effectively sell financial products to the middle-income market. The task is to help ordinary people sell complex products to ordinary people.

The high end of the market for personal financial advice is relatively small but profitable, and is already served adequately by the personal financial planning subsidiaries of life insurance companies or private banking services. The needs of this upscale market are different, more geared towards diversification of assets, minimization of financial risk and tax consequences. The higher net worth and income of this market segment justifies a more personalized client relationship.

From the experience financial services firms have had with this market, they believe that understanding client needs and building and managing the client relationship is an effective sales approach. However, in anything but the upper end of the market, it's just been too expensive to deliver a sales approach that understands clients' needs because the expert labor component is high.

In the new business environment of the 1990s it becomes strategic to try to move this approach downmarket to retail financial services: the sale of financial products like bank accounts, money market funds, annuities, life insurance, and mutual funds. The target market for these products is often termed the *middle market,* that is, people with modest net worth and income whose financial needs (educating children, purchasing a home, providing for retirement) often outstrip their financial resources and whose financial resources cannot support the current delivery mechanisms for needs analysis and advice. For example, advice from a financial planner may cost $1000 to $2000 to deliver; PC-manufactured advice, usually based on spreadsheets and boilerplate text producing a one-size-fits-all report, may still cost over $250 to deliver.

But analyzing needs and delivering advice is just one part of the equation if the application is to be strategic. Servicing the middle market demands integration across the corporate functions of marketing, product development, information systems, and sales. The expert system application must be embedded in existing and future systems that support these functions.

The sales and marketing application area is strategic because changes in the attitude, behavior, and lifestyle of the middle market will force a financial services institution to deploy its resources differently in order to capture and maintain a large share of what is a cost-conscious and value-oriented group.

Marketing and product development functions of the institution need to be more informed about consumer needs and more targeted toward their chosen market segments as product development and proliferation is very costly. Yet, distribution channels, like bank branches and life insurance agents, are very costly and provide little value to the consumer. A typical insurance agent costs $200,000 to train over five years, with about 85% attrition over that period. Because of competition by the automatic tellers and effective direct mail campaigns like those waged by the mutual fund companies, there is increasing pressure to improve the effectiveness of a branch operation of a bank, securities firm, or insurance company in selling an expanding array of products—to somehow bring expertise in order to find the right cluster of products for the particular consumer and to establish and maintain an intimate and trusted client relationship while making the sale in as few calls as possible.

Customer data files and transaction accounting systems for products already exist and represent decades of development. Therefore, large scale deployment of expertise within these organizations implies embedding intelligence to take advantage of the data that is already there.

The expert sales support systems are built around a core expert system, which performs financial needs analysis given basic financial data provided by the client. Financial needs analysis encompasses the creation of a systematic set of monetary objectives and action plans for an individual or a family. Analysis of goals is tempered by the family's income and net worth. The analysis includes many considerations:

- tax planning
- education planning
- estate planning
- investment advice
- retirement planning
- risk (insurance) planning

For many people, a well-executed financial plan can make a significant difference in whether they achieve their investment goals and increase their long-term net worth by lowering taxes, marshalling expenses and, in some cases, just being better informed on financial alternatives.

The client data and the expert's recommendations are stored together in a second major piece of the application, a marketing information system. In many cases, particularly where the information/transaction systems have been product-oriented and not customer-oriented, this is the first time that the home office has access to detailed consumer information. Extracts of the base information can be exported into conventional database systems for query and reporting, or these extracts may be configured as a platform for a marketing/product-development expert system.

The kind of marketing information that can be obtained in this way is unique because, for the first time, it permits the marketer to understand the market needs in depth based on expert-level financial analysis of thousands of cases, and the marketer need not rely solely on crude lifecycle models that only consider a few demographic variables like age, salary, marital status, and number of dependents.

The final piece of such a system is a sales-scripting module that is connected to an on-line product catalog, and it provides a capability for matching specific products to customer needs. In addition to the value added to the sales process, the sales script acts as a training mechanism for the sales person. New products added to the product catalog will appear in the sales script the next day, supplying appropriate sales points and other information for the agent (like commissions to be made on the sale, where to get additional information about the products, and how many points the sale will contribute towards the Hawaiian Vacation Sales Contest).

The output of the application is a series of reports generated via a natural-language production module that tailors the text to the individual client's situation. The organization, tone, and content of the client report are specific to the individual client. The agent's report suggests particular products and corresponding sales points that are tailored to the client, given the attitudinal information supplied by the client on the questionnaire.

Implementation

The key to success in the implementation stage of a large embedded system is to be able to work in a more conventional style with large development teams working from written specifications, facing periodic code review and rigorous testing. At the same time, the development teams should be able to take advantage of the body of AI development technology—rapid prototyping, domain-level programming, and the ability to work on incompletely specified problems at a high level of abstraction.

The reason a conventional approach is key is that there is a good body of knowledge about managing projects that employ twenty and even more knowledge/software engineers. With that number of people, chains of technical communication are long, and procedures and interactions involved in organizing and performing the work are complex. Integration of separately produced modules and components is difficult at best, and can become totally impossible if careful design and control are not followed at every stage of the work.

This style of development might seem the antithesis of the rapid prototyping approach that has become the model for expert system development. However, the AI development tools are workable (even essential, as claimed) for these projects. The advantages of working in a prototyping style accrue largely to its speed, rather than the absence of structure. Not understanding a problem completely at a particular stage of development is a deficiency for which AI technology provides a temporary solution; it is not a style of development.

The AI style also pays dividends if changes in the knowledge are not totally in the control of the client or development team. Rules and regulations are able to change at the whim of a government; the success of the development project and the ability to provide for ongoing product maintenance can depend on the ability to react quickly to such changes.

To implement a large commercial expert system, particularly one that is to be embedded in the business systems of a large enterprise and given the current state of the art in the commercial expert-system-development environment, this requires significant invention of new technology and development of new project-management procedures and methodologies. Application vendors generally have their own development technology, and they do not rely on the commercial technology suppliers largely for this reason.

Furthermore, embedding the same sort of intelligence in different computing and business environments requires engineering access to the reasoning and representation components for flexibility in packaging.

Development Phase   The major goals for the development phase are to implement the required expertise, including the calculations and rules that generate the specified observations and recommendations, and build the system interfaces.

One major collaborative effort that takes place in the beginning is the design of the class structure in the representation system. Due to the large number of knowledge engineers (KEs) on a project this size, it is essential that they all agree on the same reference terms. Class names, attributes and values may be used throughout the system, while the rules and the procedures for each area of expertise may be relatively self-contained. The major result of these design sessions is a style document used by the KEs throughout the project in order to coordinate their efforts.

The knowledge representation system is relatively conventional in features and functionality with the exception of the capabilities for handling individual cases (data sets) required by high-volume batch processes. One noteworthy aspect of the APEX design approach is the explicit representation of observations and recommendations. Instances of observations and recommendations are created by the expert program during processing, and are then used by the text generation system to craft the output reports.

To develop the reasoning in the system, the APEX KEs use a proprietary Program Description Language (PDL) to go from the specification to the program. The language was developed from the pseudo English that the KEs use in their structured interview notes to capture the expert logic. The fundamental technical strategy behind the APEX development environment is support for the KEs in their work patterns in contrast with approaches that require a KE to be more programmer than analyst.

Pilot Phase   The pilot phase is the beginning of the full-scale deployment. Deployment is generally the longest phase of application development and, in many respects, the most difficult. Solving the organizational problems that arise during the installation and early use of any large-scale automation project constitutes at least 80% of the work required to ensure the success of the overall program.

The pilot is designed to test the process, identify the major organizational, logistical, and cultural problems, and forge solutions before scaling up to deploy to the entire salesforce. The pilot program itself may be phased so that the elapsed time from first use to full use is often months and sometimes years.

From the developers' point of view, the start of deployment means helping the client firm devise training programs covering the concept and the operation of the system and mechanisms for reinforcing what the program is meant to accomplish along with providing procedures (sales tracks) to facilitate success. In addition to training programs for the end users, there must be technical training for system operators in such tasks as system backup, assignment of user I.D.s and passwords and installation of updated versions of software.

The major issues at the start of deployment involve logistics and culture. Logistics typically bog down the start of any large-scale deployment: the need for all sorts of support materials, such as advertising, brochures, and training materials.

Cultural issues in this case include moving the salesforce from the culture of the one-call close toward needs-oriented selling that is supported by the expert system. Needs-oriented selling usually entails two to three customer meetings before any sale. The longer sales process is due to the extra steps involved in understanding the client needs, devising a solution to those needs, and then presenting the recommendations to the client. The one-call close is part and parcel of the single-need or product-push approach. Changing the culture from one-call to needs-oriented selling is no easy task because it means changing the way salespeople work as well as how sales management manages their staff. For example, in the one-call close environment many sales managers manage by the numbers—make one hundred phone calls a week, schedule ten meetings, and close two sales.

The process of changing the culture in the banks doesn't have the obstacle of the entrenched sales process but only because a sales culture and a sales process often don't exist at all in a bank.

Cultural issues may also be just inertial. People have an image of themselves that is resistant to change. (Can you change a banker to a salesperson, in their own mind?) People also structure their workday and workweek in a particular way, and once in the groove, particularly a groove that is successful, they are unwilling to change. (How do you explain having to schedule fifteen minutes per client for data entry in the new system?) Finally, people are going to ask what's in it for them.

Technical innovation of any sort rarely happens without affecting people. The pilot phase is designed to both introduce the technology and shake out program bugs and gaps in functionality as well as tune the solutions to identified innovation-management problems, i.e., embed the system in the human part of the enterprise.

Futures

Methods

The topics that are most important to consider here involve the engineering approaches and disciplines required to build a knowlege-based system. These include the most basic design choices surrounding the use of one particular reasoning model over another. They also include the more process-oriented aspects of building a system, that is, the knowledge acquisition and engineering per se.

Any sort of knowledge used in support of a problem-solving task can be extracted in two ways. The first involves extensive and formalized interviewing of experts. The second requires the developer/knowledge engineer to acquire the expertise and then introspectively articulate the problem-solving knowledge in the program. Both methods are useful and valid. The latter is often a natural side effect of the former.

The structures used by the designer to encode the knowledge for use by and within the computer can take many forms, and the collection of data structures actually used is determined by the engineering considerations. As for most embedded systems, scarcity of resources is the most general engineering consideration.

Example data structures as a basis of knowledge representation include

- Lists

- Tables

- Decision trees

- Hierarchies

- Networks

In earlier chapters, knowledge was represented in CLIPS using lists (for WMEs) and networks (for rules). FORPS uses tables for representation, as does Prolog.

Methods for knowledge extraction have two forms. The knowledge can be extracted directly from the expert by asking the expert to articulate facts, decision rules, experience, observations, and so on. This method uses face-to-face interviews or some form of questionnaire. The representation scheme for the knowledge is determined during the course of the interviewing or questioning process.

Knowledge can also be extracted indirectly. This is done by asking the expert to perform some task that indirectly reveals the sort of knowledge that the expert is using to solve the problem. This method can also suggest an organization for the knowledge or can be used in support of an a priori organization that may have been chosen for engineering purposes. Examples of these methods include hierarchical clustering techniques, which can suggest a structure relating the objects/things referred to in the problem solving, and multidimensional scaling, which can be used to attach numerical values to attributes used in the problem solving.

Direct Methods

Direct methods include interviews, questionnaires, and observation of expert problem solving.

Interviewing requires a set of skills that in many cases can be acquired only with training and experience. Among the people skills required is the ability to enlist the expert's cooperation in the process, which often means allaying the experts' fears that they might be replaced by the computer. The interview itself often begins with general questions that only gradually become more specific. The experts should do most of the talking, with ample opportunity to develop their own vocabulary to describe the problem. Interviewers need to be on guard against imposing their own biases.

While not imposing a structure, it is always good practice to have specific goals set for the interview. It is also a good idea to keep in mind that the experts may tire or become bored easily, so interview sessions should be short and relatively infrequent. It is also important for the knowledge engineers to write up their interview notes immediately after the interview, so that everything is captured while the memory of the interview is still fresh. A good schedule would therefore be to have an interview in the morning and note sessions in the afternoon. Sample interview forms are given in Figure 6.7.

Another direct knowledge acquisition technique is the questionnaire. One advantage of the questionnaire is that it facilitates very focused acquisition, which is also very efficient. Another advantage from the expert's point of view is that the questionnaire allows the expert to answer questions at times that fit their busy schedules. Questionnaires are generally the preferred way to acquire many sorts of scaling information. Examples of these include weightings and uncertainty measures.

Direct knowledge acquisition can also be done by observation. In this approach the expert is observed while performing the problem-solving task. While being observed, the expert is asked to think aloud and articulate any assumptions that are made in support of each decision.

One particular knowledge acquisition technique is known as Protocol Analysis (see Ericsson and Simon, 1984). The underlying model underlying Protocol Analysis is supported very strongly by the mechanization of the OPS languages. Protocol analysis is better for tasks in which thinking aloud might be natural than for tasks that are perceptual or where verbalization might interfere with task performance. The gist of the approach is to follow the expert's focus of attention as the expert works through the recognize-act cycle.

KE Notes Outline

The KE notes that are written following each session should be in a reasonably uniform overall format. Individual styles can vary within the uniform outline. The following is a suggested outline for the notes. Any section not relevant to a particular KE'ing session can be skipped.

Each KE session for a topic after the first should be a discussion of the notes from the previous session on that topic. If the attendees have not had a chance to read the notes prior to the session, they should do so at the session.

Date: _____

Attendees: _____   **Topic:** _____

Corrections to Previous Notes: _____

Reference Topic and date. Use the same identifying subheading or label as the item corrected.

Resolutions to Issues from Previous Notes: _____

Reference Topic and date. Use the same identifying subheading or label as the item corrected.

Results of Session: _____

Decisions, reasons, or significant information on session topics. Give individual subtopics a meaningful label that can be referenced in corrections in later sessions.

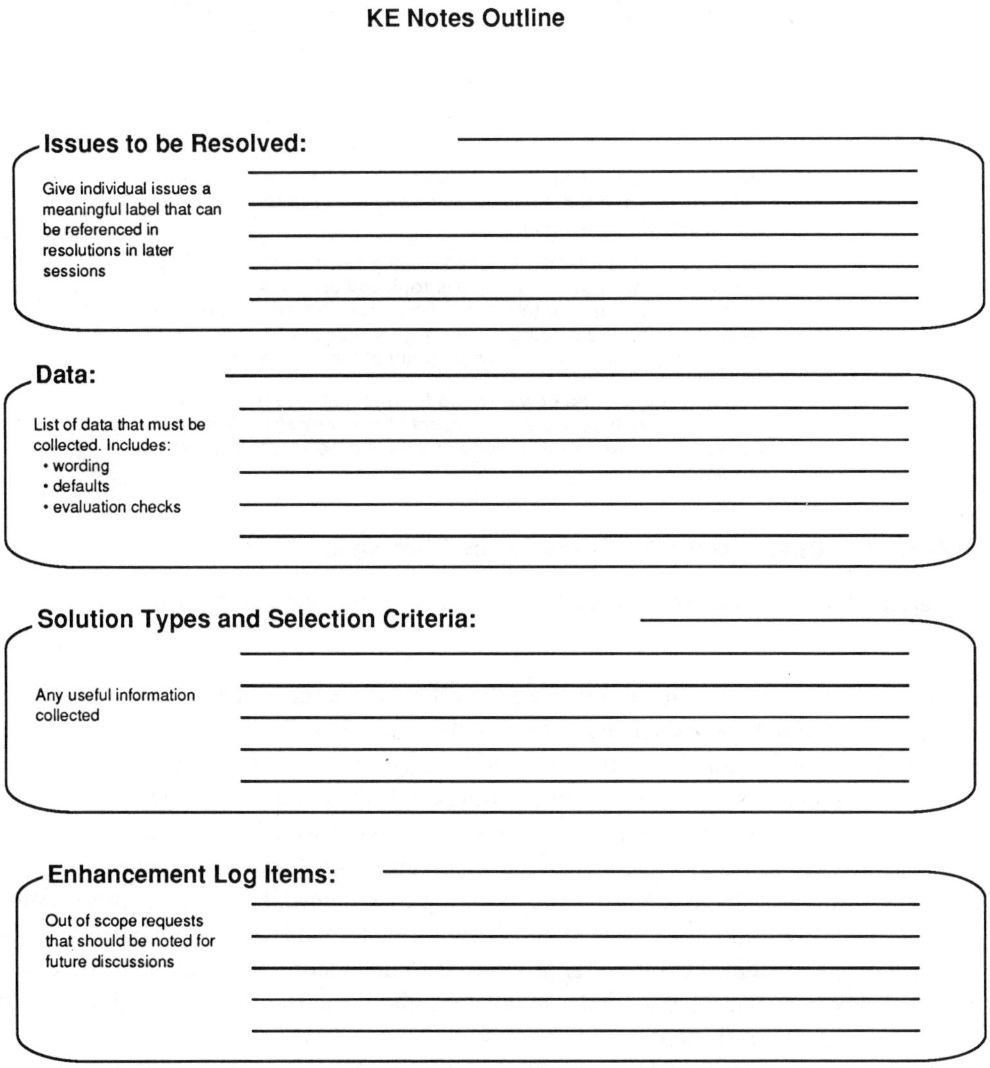

KE Notes Outline

Issues to be Resolved:

Give individual issues a
meaningful label that can
be referenced in
resolutions in later
sessions

Data:

List of data that must be
collected. Includes:
• wording
• defaults
• evaluation checks

Solution Types and Selection Criteria:

Any useful information
collected

Enhancement Log Items:

Out of scope requests
that should be noted for
future discussions

Figure 6.7. Sample Knowledge Engineering Documentation

It is good practice to keep extensive records of knowledge engineering session, with forward and
backward references to other sessions in the process.

Selection from a transcript with a test engineer

OK so here's the problem report... I'm checking the operating
history... no reports of other problems... there haven't been any
major repairs and there haven't been any major parts replaced as
part of scheduled maintenance.

Now let's look at the maintenance history for last year... no big
problems -- that's good. The parts replaced are about what you'd
expect for an engine of this age... no major work needed on the
windings or on the bearings... that's good because in rotating
machinery that's where there's a potential for a big problem.

Wait a minute... if the power rating for this machine is correct
there are more losses than I'd expect. Let's look at the loading on
the test. OK now overall it doesn't look like we've got an electrical
problem.

Figure 6.8. Direct Knowledge Aquisition by Observation

Fragment of a very long transcript of a knowledge engineering session (fictional).

The analysis may be more complicated than the simple recognize-act cycle of CLIPS
or OPS. For example, consider the transcript that might have come from a session with
the diesel electric locomotive expert that the DELTA system was based on (Figure 6.8)

In the first and second paragraph of the transcript, the expert is apparently reasoning
in a data-directed fashion, checking the data and looking for anything that can be used
to make any immediate conclusions. The first paragraph suggests that a metarule is being
used to initialize and focus the process by looking first at certain sources of information.
In the second paragraph, the information is being used to make certain conclusions about
the state of the machine. During this process, the conclusion is reached that there is an
inconsistency between the data and a hypothesis about the state of the machine, so the
mode of reasoning is shifted.

The third paragraph illustrates the initial stages of a backward, goal-directed mode of
reasoning. A hypothesis has been formulated and the problem-solving process turns into
a search for evidence that either supports or refutes the hypothesis.

Direct knowledge acquisition methods have limitations as a means for acquiring
expertise from an expert. For example, critical assumptions used by the expert may be
implicit and very difficult for an expert to articulate (see Hawkins 1983). Methods like
protocol analysis assume that the verbal reports and the mental problem-solving activity
are correlated. Such correlation may be difficult to confirm (see Bainbridge 1986). There
are a number of studies that suggest that much of human problem-solving activity cannot
be directly elicited (Dixon 1981). Other studies suggest that there is expertise that cannot
be elicited from experts because they are not aware of its significance in the problem-
solving activity (Collins 1985).

Because of these limitations, indirect methods for knowledge acquisition are becoming increasingly important in knowledge engineering. These indirect methods were originally developed by psychologists as a means to overcome the cognitive defenses that impede communication (see Kelly 1955).

Indirect Methods

Indirect methods require the expert to perform a series of tasks that may not be directly part of the problem-solving task, but which may reveal important aspects of the knowledge that the expert is using to solve the problem.

In one such indirect method, the expert is asked to make similarity judgments on pairs of objects. The assumption is that the attributes on which the similarity judgments are based come from a multidimensional space. The result of the procedure is that the attribute is assigned a numerical value as a function of the various objects. Thus this approach is best used where the attribute is reasonably represented by a number.

As an example, an expert might be asked: For each possible pair of the following objects, in what percent of all possible situations in your experience is the first object likely to be more dangerous than the second?

- Circular Saw

- Paint Brush

- Hammer

- Screw Driver

- Power Drill

The result of this exercise might be a table representing the judgment of the expert (the table is necessarily symmetric).

	(1)	(2)	(3)	(4)	(5)
1) Circular Saw	–	.85	.65	.75	.60
2) Paint Brush	.15	–	.30	.40	.35
3) Hammer	.35	.70	–	.70	.40
4) Screw Driver	.25	.60	.30	–	.35
5) Power Drill	.40	.65	.60	.65	–

The entries represent percentages; for example, row 1 column 2 represents the judgment that 85% of the time a circular saw is more dangerous than a paint brush. If the percentages are interpreted as probabilities the table can be restated in terms of standard deviations under the assumption that the distribution of probabilities is Gaussian. Using a Gaussian PDF (Probability Distribution Function), the new table is

	(1)	(2)	(3)	(4)	(5)	AVG
1) Circular Saw	0	1.05	.40	.68	.25	2.35
2) Paint Brush	−1.05	−	−.54	−.75	−.40	−2.20
3) Hammer	−.40	.54	−	.54	−.25	0.40
4) Screw Driver	−.32	.25	−.54	−	−.40	−1.33
5) Power Drill	−.75	.40	.25	.40	−	0.78

The standard deviations are averaged and displayed in the last column of the table to give a measure of relative danger as a reflection of the expert's experience. They would be normalized to zero in use (that is, the lowest danger measure is zero).

The sort of information requested from the expert in this case is data about dominance, repeated judgments of choices that one object is ranked above another object. When the attribute is continuous, a numerical representation can be used to structure the knowledge about the relationships between the attributes for different objects.

Information about similarity, which includes any measure that can be intrepeted as distances between objects, can be used to structure and relate attributes through a heirarchy. With this approach, the goal is to discover clusters rather than a scale.

One example of this is the Johnson Hierarchical Clustering method. In this technique, the expert is asked to make judgments about the similarity of objects, and the resulting heirarchy can be used as a tool to guide discussions that are to elicit the attributes that the expert is using to make the distinctions on which the similarity measures are based.

In this sample seven different types of medical problems are organized into clusters. The procedure works as follows. Start with the following similarity matrix:

	(1)	(2)	(3)	(4)	(5)	(6)	(7)
(1) Abrasion	−	1	1	3	4	10	11
(2) Cuts		−	1	3	3	9	12
(3) Punctures			−	2	4	6	10
(4) Burns				−	8	8	9
(5) Fractures					−	6	6
(6) Cancer						−	2
(7) Occupational Disease					−		−

The three closest are combined into aggregate group (1a) where the distance from the aggregate to the nonaggregate is the minimum of the distances from the members of the aggregate. The matrix is reformed as follows:

	(1a)	(2)	(4)	(6)	(7)
(1a) Abrasion-Cut-Puncture	−	2	3	6	10
(2) Burns		−	8	8	9
(4) Fracture			−	6	6
(6) Cancer				−	2
(7) Occupational Disease					−

The same procedure is used to reduce the matrix again as follows:

	(1b)	(4b)	(6b)
(1b) (Abrasion-Cut-Puncture)-Burn	–	3	6
(4b) Fracture		–	6
(6b) Cancer-Occupational Disease			–

After a final reduction, the clusters are put together as a hierarchy, in another representation of the matrix reduction process (Figure 6.9). The hierarchy can now be used as a basis for questioning the expert about the attributes used as the means of classifying the entities. Indirect methods like the Johnson Hierarchical Cluster are good for eliciting structures and attributes. Structures and attribute information of this kind are ideal for expert systems that do selection or classification. Example tasks are diagnosis and situation assessment.

The main disadvantage of all the indirect methods just described is that the number of choices or judgments required from the expert grows rapidly with the number of objects to be judged. However, the use of these approaches is growing and they are incorporated into a number of computer programs for automated knowledge engineering. Gaines (1986) and Shaw (1982) studied the use of Kelly's repertory grids in knowledge engineering and developed some experimental knowledge acquisition programs. The Expertise Transfer System (ETS) developed by John Boose (1985) also uses repertory grids, while later systems incorporate induction subsystems to generate rules directly. Parsaye (1988) reviews several tools for acquiring and verifying knowledge.

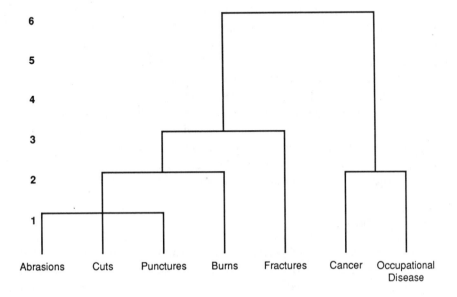

Figure 6.9. Cluster Hierarchy

The final cluster hierarchy for the underwriting risk example.

Neural Nets

The newer technologies that are important to consider are related both to the issues of designing knowledge-based systems as well as the basic technology underlying the operation of the system. Technologies associated with design and architecture include approaches that support machine learning and automated knowledge acquisition. These were touched upon in the last section of this chapter. A very promising technology that has not been discussed in this book is the neural net. The day is not far away when neural net components can be specified, engineered, and built like any other hardware/software hybrid.

The neural net is a technology whose day has come, and gone, and now has come again. The high-level goal is to try to achieve some of the functionality of the vertebrate brain through networks of computing units whose behavior is similar to that of the basic elements of the brain. These brain elements are called neurons—thus the term neural nets. Neural nets make good pattern recognizers. For some animals, pattern recognition may be the sum total of their cognitive capability (see Lettvin et al. 1959).

The electrophysiology of the neuron is quite complex. For our computing purposes, we abstract from this complexity the fact that the neuron is electrically excitable. When the excitation surpasses a certain threshold, a propagating electrical signal is generated. When this happens, the neuron is said to "fire." This signal travels to the terminals of the neural cell where a transmitter is released that will electrically excite the following cell. The neurons in the network are usually connected in close physical contact at a specialized region called the *synapse*.

Given that the size of the synaptic connection and the amount of transmitter released can vary, there can be quite a bit of variation in the effect that a cell can have on the cells to which it is connected. Another factor that moderates the effect of simulation is that the excitable region of the cell may be varying distances away from the point of synaptic contact, and any intervening leaky electrical cable, like the cell membrane, can attenuate the excitation. For at least these two reasons, the activity of neurons that connect to a particular cell is weighted differently in determining whether or not the cell will fire.

The artificial neuron is designed to mimic the first-order characteristics of the biological neuron. The output of an artificial neuron is determined by the weighted sum of its inputs applied to a threshold function. The architecture of a neural net is then a matter of the topology of the network connections, the weights assigned to the individual connections in the network, and the threshold function.

Network Training

A network of artificial neurons (hereafter called simply neurons) is trained so that an application of a particular set of inputs produces the desired set of outputs. Both inputs and outputs can be represented in a vector notation and are therefore referred to as *vectors*. Training is a matter of applying an input vector, adjusting the weights on the connections according to a predetermined procedure until the desired output vector results. This is done until all input vectors produce consistent output vectors.

In supervised training, an input vector is paired with an output vector as a *training pair*. During the training, the output vector is compared to the desired output vector and the error is fed back through the network to adjust the weights so as to reduce the error. This continues until the error over the entire training set is acceptable.

In unsupervised training, the network is trained in terms of input vectors alone, with the goal of the training to produce consistent sets of output vectors for consistent sets of input vectors. Interpretation of the input/output mapping is only done after the training process.

The basic training algorithms are related to the early learning algorithms of Hebb, which in turn are based on some observed behaviors of biological neurons. Simple Hebbian learning is unsupervised training designed to adjust the weights in the network so that oft used paths of activity are strengthened. Thus the net learns by repetition. Network weights are increased in proportion to the product of the excitation levels of the source and destination neurons.

Although Hebbian learning has been used to construct a number of neural nets, there are more effective training algorithms that allow learning of a broader array of patterns at higher learning rates. One of these, the backpropagation algorithm is detailed in the next section. Wasserman (1989) gives a good overview of the range of neural net training algorithms.

Backpropagation

Backpropagation is a systematic method for training multilayer artificial neural networks. As in other neural nets, the neurons in a backpropagation network sum their inputs according to the weights and then apply the result to a threshold function to determine their output. For backpropagation networks, the threshold function is usually the sigmoid-shaped function described by

$$\texttt{OUT} = 1/(1+e^{-\texttt{IN}})$$

where *IN* is the weighted sum of the inputs to the neuron and *OUT* is the neuron output. One good reason this function is used is that it is simple to differentiate with respect to the net input signal.

A multilayer network architecture for a neural net that might be trained with backpropagation is given in Figure 6.10.

As in all supervised training schemes, each input vector is paired with a target output vector in a training pair. During the training, the input vector is applied and the output vector is compared to the target. The error between the output and the target vectors is used to adjust the weights in the network. Training is usually done with a number of repetitions over a set of training pairs. After enough iterations, the error signal should be reduced to an acceptable level. The weights are adjusted during the backpropagation of the error in proportion to the current gain of the connecting neuron.

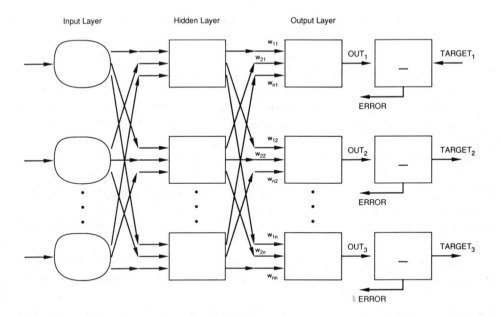

Figure 6.10. Two-Layer Backpropagation Network

Layer i connects with layer j with the weights w_{ij}. The output is compared to the target and the error signal is used in the backpropagation algorithm to adjust the weights.

Some of the drawbacks of the backpropagation method include the duration and the uncertainty of the training process. Complex problems can require days or weeks to train a network, and the network may not train at all. Failure to train can be caused by neuron populations that are driven to operate in regimes where the gain is very small, so that the per trail change in the weight is very small. Another problem is the possible existence of local minima in the error function, so that the network will train to a set of weights that appear to provide the best fit of input to output, but are not in fact as good as could be achieved.

Chapter 1 Readings / References

Embedded Applications

Anderson, K. R., Coleman, D. E., Hill, C. R., Jaworski, A. P., Love, P. L., Spindler, D. A. and Simaan, M. 1989. Knowledge-based statistical process control. In *Innovative Applications of Artificial Intelligence,* Schorr, H. and Rappaport, A. eds. Cambridge, Mass.: MIT Press.

Bajpai, A., and Marczewski, R. 1989. Charley: An expert system for diagnostics of manufacturing equipment. In *Innovative Applications of Artificial Intelligence,* Schorr, H. and Rappaport, A., eds. Cambridge, Mass.: MIT Press.

Brand, H. R., and Wong, C. M. 1986. Application of knowledge based system technology to triple quadropole mass spectrophotometry. *Proc A.A.A.I. Conf,* 812–819.

Burns, N. A., Ashford, T. J., Iwaskin, C. T., Starbird, R. P., and Flagg, R. L. 1986. The portable inference engine: Fitting significant expertise into small systems. *IBM Systems Journal,* 25 (2):236–243.

Embedded Systems Programming. San Francisco, Calif.: Miller Freeman Publications.

Fox, M. S., Lowenfeld, S., and Kleinosky, P. 1983. Techniques for sensor-based diagnosis, *Proc. IJCAI.*

Cognitive Science

Ericsson, K. A., and H. A. Simon. 1984. *Protocol Analysis.* Cambridge, Mass.: MIT Press.

Forgy, C. L. 1982. RETE: A fast algorithm for the many pattern/many object pattern matching problem. *Artificial Intelligence* 19:17–37.

Forgy, C. L. 1984. *The OPS83 Report System,* version 2. Production Systems Technologies, Inc.

Forgy, C. L. 1981. *OPS5 User's Manual,* CMU-CS-81-135. Pittsburgh: Carnegie Mellon University.

Newell, A., and H. Simon. 1972. *Human Problem Solving.* Englewood Cliffs, N.J.: Prentice-Hall.

Knowledge Representation

Genesereth, M. R., and Ginsberg, M. L. 1985. Logic programming. *CACM* 28(9):933–9941.

Hayes-Roth, F. 1985. Rule based systems. *CACM* 28(9):921–932.

Mylopoulos, J., and H. J. Levesque. 1984. An overview of knowledge representation. In *On Conceptual Modelling,* Brodie, M. L., Mylopoulos, J., and Schmidt, J. W. 1984. New York: Springer-Verlag.

Logic Theorist

Newell, A., Shaw, J. C., and Simon, H. A. 1956. The logic theory machine: A complex information processing system. *IRE Trans. on Information Theory* 2:61–79.

Logic

Kowalski, R. 1979. *Logic for Problem Solving.* New York: Elsevier Science Publishing Co.

Turner, R. 1984. *Logics for Artificial Intelligence.* Chichester, England: Ellis Horwood Limited.

AI and Expert Systems

Barr, A., and Feigenbaum, E. A. 1982. *The Handbook of Artificial Intelligence.* Pitman.

Frames, Scripts

Katz, J. J., and Fodor, J. A. 1963. The structure of a semantic theory. *Language* 39:170–210.

Minsky, M. 1981. A framework for representing knowledge. In *Mind Design,* John Hauge-land, ed., Cambridge, Mass.: MIT Press, pp. 95–128.

Schank, R. 1972. Conceptual dependency: A theory of natural language understanding. *Cognitive Psychology* 3:552–631.

Schank, R., and Abelson, R. 1977. *Scripts, Plans, Goals and Understanding.* Hillsdale, N.J.: Lawrence Erlbaum.

Chapter 2 Readings / References

Instruction Set Architectures:

Fernandez, E. B., and Lang, T. 1986. Instruction-set architectures and high-level languages. In *Software-Oriented Computer Architecture,* E. B. Fernandez, and T. Lang (eds.). New York: IEEE Computer Science Press.

Klint, P. 1981. Interpretation techniques. *Software—Practice and Experience,* 11:963–973.

FORTH:

Bradley, M. 1986. *C Forth-83 Glossary.* Mountain View, Calif.: Bradley Forthware.

Brodie, L. 1982. *Starting Forth.* Englewood Cliffs, N.J.: Prentice-Hall.

Brodie, L. *Thinking Forth.* Englewood Cliffs, N.J.: Prentice-Hall.

Haydon, G. 1983. *All About FORTH.* Mountain View, Calif.: Mountain View Press.

Moore, C. 1974. FORTH: A new way to program a minicomputer. *Astronomical Astrophysics Supplement,* 15:497–511.

Trelease, R. B. 1987. The Forth wave in AI. *AI Expert* 2(10):58–66.

Threaded Code:

Bell, J. R. 1973. Threaded code. *Comm. ACM,* 16(6):370–372.

Duff, C. B. 1986. ACTOR, A threaded object-oriented language. In *Proceedings of the 1986 Rochester Conference on Real-Time Applications of Artificial Intelligence,* L. Forsley (ed.) Rochester, N.Y.: Institute of Applied Forth Research, Inc., p. 13.

Epstein, A., and Gilliatt, C. 1985. The Magic/L programming language. *Proceedings, 1985 Rochester Forth Conference,* pp. 9–22.

Kogge, P. 1982. An architectural trail to threaded-code systems. *IEEE COMPUTER,* 22–32.

Loeliger, R. G. 1981. *Threaded Interpretive Languages.* Peterborough, N.H.: Byte Books.

Meinzer, K. 1979. IPS—An unorthodox high level language. *Byte* 4(1):146–159.

Philips, J. B., Burk, M. F., and Wilson, G. S. 1978. Threaded code for laboratory computers. *Software—Practice and Experience,* 8:257–263.

Schleisiek, K. 1983. Multiple code field data types and prefix operators. *JFAR* 1(2):55–64.

Byte Code:

Deutsch, L. P. 1973. A Lisp machine with very compact programs. *Proc. IJCAI,* 697–703.

Deutsch, L. P. 1982. The Dorado Smalltalk-80 implementation: Hardware architecture's impact on software architecture. In *Smalltalk-80. Bits of History, Words of Advice,* Glenn Krasner, ed. Reading, Mass.: Addison-Wesley.

Deutsch, L. P., and Schiffman, A.M. 1984. Efficient implementation of the Smalltalk-80 System. *Conference Record of the Eleventh Annual ACM Symposium on the Principles of Programming Languages,* pp. 297–302.

Goldberg, A., and Robson, D. 1983. *Smalltalk-80. The Language and Its Implementation.* Reading, Mass.: Addison-Wesley.

Schooler, R., and Stamos, J. W. 1984. Proposal for a small scheme implementation. *Technical Report,* MIT/LCS/TM-267. Cambridge, Mass.: Massachusetts Institute of Technology.

Warren, D. H. D. 1983. An abstract Prolog instruction set. *Technical Note 309,* SRI Computer Science and Technology Division.

Chapter 3 Readings / References

Brownston, L., Farrell, R., Kant, E., and Martin, N. 1985. *Programming Expert Systems in OPS5: An Introduction to Rule-Based Programming*. Reading, Mass.: Addison-Wesley.

Buchanan, B. G., and Shortliffe, E. H., eds. 1984. *Rule-Based Expert Systems: The MYCIN Experiments of the Stanford Heuristic Programming Project*. Reading, Mass.: Addison-Wesley.

Dress, W. B. 1986a. Communicating Asynchronous External Data to an Expert System. *Proceedings of the Eighteenth Southeastern Symposium on System Theory*. IEEE Computer Society. pp. 294–296.

Dress, W. B. 1986b. REAL-OPS: A real-time engineering applications language for writing expert systems. *JFAR* 4(2):113–123.

Forgy, C. L. 1982. Rete: A fast algorithm for the many pattern/many object pattern match problem. *Artificial Intelligence* 19(1):17–37.

Forgy, C. L., and Shepard, J. J. 1987. Rete: a fast match algorithm. *AI Expert* 2(1):34–40.

Keravnou, E. T., and Johnson, L. 1986. *Competent Expert Systems: A Case Study in Fault Diagnosis*. London: Kegan Paul.

Skapura, D. M. 1989. A faster embedded inference engine. *AI Expert* 4(11):42–49.

Waterman, D. A. 1986. *A Guide to Expert Systems*. Reading Mass.: Addison-Wesley.

CLIPS

Giarratano, J. C. 1988. *CLIPS User's Guide*. Athens, GA: COSMIC, University of Georgia.

Giarratano, J. C., and Riley, G. 1989. *Expert Systems: Principles and Programming*. Boston Mass.: PWS-Kent.

Muratore, J. F., Heindel, T. A., Murphy T. B., Rasmussan, A. N. and McFarland R. Z. 1989. Space shuttle telemetry monitoring by expert systems in mission control. In *Innovative Applications of Artificial Intelligence*, H. Schorr, and A. Rappaport, eds., Cambridge, Mass.: MIT Press.

Chapter 4 Readings / References

Bowen, L. M., Byrd, D. L., and Clocksin, W. F. 1983. A portable Prolog compiler. *Logic Programming Workshop '83*, pp. 74–83.

Clocksin, W. F. 1985. Design and simulation of a sequential Prolog machine. *New Generation Computing* 3:101–120.

Clocksin, W. F., and Mellish, C. S. 1981. *Programming in Prolog*. Berlin: Springer-Verlag.

Conery, J. S., and Kibler, D. F. 1981. *Proceedings of the Conference on Functional Programming Languages and Computer Architecture*, pp. 163–170.

Dress, W. B. 1985. A FORTH implementation of the heap data structure for memory management. *JFAR* 3(3):39–50.

Fagin, B. and Dobry, T. 1985 The Berkeley PLM instruction set: An instruction set for Prolog. *UCB Technical Report* 86/257, University of California at Berkeley.

Kahn, K. M. 1986. Uniform. A language based upon unifications which unifies (much of) LISP, Prolog and ACT 1. In *Logic Programming. Functions, Relations, and Equations,* D. DeGroot and G. Lindstrom, eds., pp. 411–438.

Kornfeld, W. A. 1983. Equality for Prolog. *Proceedings IJCAI*, pp. 514–519.

Kumar, V., and Lin, Y. 1986. An intelligent backtracking scheme for Prolog. *Technical Report AI,* TR86-41, University of Texas at Austin.

Odette, L. 1987. How to compile Prolog. *AI Expert* 2(8):48–57.

Odette, L., and Paloski, W. 1987. Use of a Forth-based Prolog for real time expert systems. II. A full Prolog interpreter embedded in FORTH. *JFAR,* pp. 477–486.

Odette, L., and Wilkinson, W. 1986. Prolog at 20K LIPS on the Novix? *FORML Conference Proceedings.*

Paloski, W., Odette, L., and Krever, A. 1986. A Prolog in Forth for real-time expert systems. *Proceedings 1986 Rochester Forth Conference.*

Park, J. 1984. *MVP-FORTH Expert System Toolkit*. Mountain View, Calif.: Mountain View Press.

Ray, P. V. 1984. A Prolog compiler for the PLM. *UCB Technical Report,* 84/203, University of California at Berkeley.

Shapiro, E. Y. 1983. Logic programs with uncertainties: A tool for implementing rule-based systems. *Proc. IJCAI*, pp. 529–532.

van Emden M. H. 1984. An interpreting algorithm for Prolog programs. In *Implementations of Prolog,* J. A. Campbell, ed., Chichester, England: Ellis Horwood.

Van Roy, P. 1984. A Prolog Compiler for the PLM. *UCB Technical Report,* 84/203, University of California at Berkeley.

Walther, C. 1985. A mechanical solution of Schubert's Steamroller by many-sorted resolution. *Artificial Intelligence* 26(2):217–225.

Warren, D. H. D. 1983. *An Abstract Prolog Instruction Set. Technical Note 300.* Menlo Park, Calif.: SRI International.

Chapter 5 Readings / References

Stack Machines:

Dixon, R. 1987. A stack-frame architecture language processor. *J. Forth Application and Research* 5(1):11–25.

Harris Semiconductor. 1988. *RTX2000 Instruction Set*. Melbourne Fla.: Harris Semiconductor.

Hayes, J., Fraeman, M., Williams, R. and Zaremba, T. 1987. An architecture for the direct execution of the Forth programming language. In *Proceedings of the Second International Conference on Architectural Support for Programming Languages and Operating Systems,* pp. 42–49.

Hayes, J. and Lee, S. 1989. The architecture of the SC32 Forth Engine. *J. Forth Application and Research* 5(4):493–506.

Jennings, E., 1985. The Novix NC4000 Project. *Computer Language* 2(10):37–46.

Jones, T., Malinowski, C. and Zepp, S. 1987. Standard Cell CPU Toolkit Crafts Potent Processors. *Electronic Design* 35(12):93–101.

Koopman, P. 1987. Writable instruction set, stack oriented computers: The WISC concept. *J. Forth Application and Research* 5(1):49–71.

Koopman, P., Jr., 1989. *Stack Computers—The New Wave,* Chichester, England: Ellis Horwood.

Miller, D. 1987. Stack machines and compiler design. *Byte* 12(4):177–185.

Stacks:

Bobrow. D. G., and Wegbreit, B. 1973. A model and stack implementation of multiple environments. *Comm. of the ACM* 16(10)591–602.

LISP Instruction Sets for Stack Machines:

Deutsch, L. P. 1973. A LISP machine with very compact programs. *Proc. IJCAI,* pp. 697–703.

Deutsch, L. P. 1980. ByteLISP and its Alto implementation *Proc. LISP Conference,* pp. 231–242.

Masinter, L. M., and Deutsch, L. P. 1980. Local optimization in a compiler for stack-based LISP machines. *Proc. LISP Conference,* pp. 223–230.

Rowan, W. 1980. A LISP compiler producing compact code. *Proc. LISP Conference,* pp. 216–222.

Schooler, R. and Stamos, J. W. 1984. Proposal for a small scheme implementation. *Technical Report MIT/LCS/TM-267,* Massachusetts Institute of Technology, Cambridge, Mass.

Prolog Machines:

Bowen, D. L., Byrd, L. M., and Clocksin, W. F., 1983. A portable Prolog compiler *Logic Programming Workshop,* Universidade Nova de Lisboa, pp. 74–83.

Dobry, T. P., Patt, Y. N., and Despain, A. M. 1984. Design decisions influencing the microarchitecture for a Prolog machine. *Proc. Micro* 17:217–231.

Gabriel, J., Lindholm, T., Lusk, E.L., and Overbeek, R.A. 1985. A tutorial on the Warren Abstract Machine for computational logic. *Technical Note ANL-84-84,* Argonne National Laboratory.

Mills, J. W. 1989. A high performance low RISC machine for logic programming. *Journal of Logic Programming* 6(2):179–212.

Pichler, C. 1987. Personal communication.

Tick, E., and Warren, D. H. D. 1984. Towards a pipelined Prolog processor. *Proc. IEEE Symposium on Logic Programming,* pp. 29–40.

Tick, E. 1983. An overlapped Prolog processor. *SRI Technical Note 308.*

Warren, D. H. D. 1983. An abstract Prolog instruction set. *Technical Note 309,* SRI Computer Science and Technology Division.

FORTH and Prolog:

Odette, L. L. 1987. Compiling Prolog to Forth. *Journal of Forth Application and Research,* pp. 487–534.

Odette, L. L., and Wilkinson, W. 1986. Prolog at 20,000 LIPS on a Novix? *Proc FORML Conference,* pp. 112–118.

Odette, L. L., and Wilkinson, W. 1987. Implementation strategies for language oriented architectures. *Proc Rochester Forth Conference.*

Odette, L. L., and Paloski, W. H. 1987. Use of a Forth based Prolog for real-time expert systems II. A full Prolog interpreter embedded in Forth. *Journal of Forth Application and Research,* pp. 477–486.

Paloski, W., Odette, L. L., and Krever, A. 1986. Use of a Forth based Prolog for real-time expert systems. *Proceedings Rochester Forth Conference,* pp. 167–69.

Paloski, W. H., Odette, L. L., Krever, A. J., and West, A. K. 1987. Use of a Forth based Prolog for real-time expert systems I. Spacelab life sciences experiment application. *Journal of Forth Application and Research,* pp. 487–534.

Smalltalk:

Deutsch, L. P. 1982. The Dorado Smalltalk-80 implementation: Hardware architecture's impact on software architecture. In *Smalltalk-80: Bits of History, Words of Advice,* Glenn Krasner, ed., Reading, Mass.: Addison-Wesley.

Deutsch, L. P. and Schiffman, A. M. 1984. Efficient implementation of the Smalltalk-80 system. *Conference Record of the Eleventh Annual ACM Symposium on Principles of Programming Languages,* pp. 297–302.

OPS:

Dress, W. B. 1986. REAL-OPS—A real-time engineering applications language for writing expert systems. *J. Forth Application and Research* 4(2):113–123.

Chapter 6 Readings / References

Neural Nets

Burr, D. J. 1987. Experiments with a connectionist text reader. In *Proc. IEEE Conference on Neural Networks,* M. Caudill and C. Butler, eds., pp. 717–724.

Hebb, D. O. 1961. *Organization of Behavior*. New York: Science Editions.

Lettvin, J. Y., Maturana, H. R., McCulloch W. S., and Pitts, W. H., 1959. What the frog's eye tells the frog's brain. *Proceedings IRE* 47(11): 1940–1951.

Rosenblatt, F. 1962. *Principles of Neurodynamics*. New York: Spartan Books.

Rumelhart, D. E., Hinton, G. E., and Williams, R. J., 1986. Learning ineternal representations by error propagation. In *Parallel Distributed Processing,* vol. 1. Cambridge, Mass.: MIT Press, pp. 318–362.

Wasserman, P. D. 1989. *Neural Computing: Theory and Practice*. New York: Van Nostrand Reinhold.

Cognitive Science

Ericsson, K. A., and Simon, H. A. 1984. *Protocol Analysis*. Cambridge, Mass.: MIT Press.

Newell, A., and Simon, H. 1972. *Human Problem Solving*. Englewood Cliffs, N.J.: Prentice-Hall.

Knowledge Representation

Hayes-Roth, F. 1985. Rule based systems. *CACM* 28(9):921–932.

Mylopoulos, J., and Levesque, H. J. 1984. An overview of knowledge representation. In *On Conceptual Modelling,* M. L. Brodie, J. Mylopoulos, and J. W. Schmidt., eds., New York: Springer-Verlag.

Applications

Kindle, K. W., Cann, R. S., Craig, M. R., and Martin, T. J. 1989. PFPS: Personal financial planning system. In *Innovative Applications of Artificial Intelligence,* H. Schorr, and A. Rappaport, eds., Cambridge, Mass.: MIT Press.

Knowledge Engineering

Bainbridge, L. 1986. *Asking Questions and Accessing Knowledge: Future Computing Systems*. New York: Elsevier.

Boose, J. H. 1985. A knowledge acquisition program for expert systems based on personal construct psychology. *International Journal of Man-Machine Studies*. 23(5):495–525.

Dixon, N. 1981. *Preconscious Reasoning*. New York: John Wiley and Sons.

Gaines, B. R. 1986. An overview of knowledge acquisition and transfer. *Proceedings of the AAAI Knowledge Acquisition Workshop,* Banff, Canada.

Hawkins, D. 1983. An analysis of expert thinking. *Journal of Cybernetics*.

Kelly, G. A. 1955. *The Psychology of Personal Constructs*. New York: Norton.

Parsaye, K. 1988. Acquiring and verifying knowledge automatically. *AI Expert* 3(5):48–63.

Shaw, M. L. G. 1982. PLANET: Some experience in creating an integrated system for repertory grid applications on a microcomputer. *International Journal of Man-Machine Studies* 17(3):345–36.

Index